The Small and the Mighty

T

The Small and the Mighty

Twelve Unsung Americans
Who Changed the Course of
History, from the Founding to
the Civil Rights Movement

SHARON McMAHON

THESIS

THESIS

An imprint of Penguin Random House LLC
penguinrandomhouse.com

Most Thesis books are available at a discount when purchased in quantity for sales promotions or corporate use. Special editions, which include personalized covers, excerpts, and corporate imprints, can be created when purchased in large quantities. For more information, please call (212) 572-2232 or email specialmarkets@penguinrandomhouse.com. Your local bookstore can also assist with discounted bulk purchases using the Penguin Random House corporate Business-to-Business program. For assistance in locating a participating retailer, email B2B@penguinrandomhouse.com.

LIBRARY OF CONGRESS CONTROL NUMBER: 2024940366

ISBN 9780593541678 (hardcover)
ISBN 9780593541685 (ebook)

Printed in the United States of America
1 3 5 7 9 10 8 6 4 2

BOOK DESIGN BY CHRIS WELCH

For Chris, who has always believed that anything is possible,
and that I am capable of achieving it.

CONTENTS

INTRODUCTION **New York, 1804**   1

Angel of the Rockies

ONE **Clara Brown, Kentucky, 1830s**   17

TWO **Bleeding Kansas, 1850s**   23

THREE **Clara Brown, Colorado, 1870s**   34

The Next Needed Thing

FOUR **Virginia Randolph, Virginia, 1890**   45

FIVE **Henrico County, Virginia, 1907**   54

America the Beautiful

SIX **Katharine Lee Bates, Cape Cod, 1859**   69

SEVEN **Katharine Lee Bates, England, 1880s**   78

EIGHT **Katharine Lee Bates, Chicago, 1890s**   81

Forward Out of Darkness

NINE **Inez Milholland, New York, 1910**   95

TEN **Maria de Lopez, California, 1911**   104

ELEVEN   Rebecca Brown Mitchell, Idaho, 1856   112

TWELVE   Inez Milholland, the West, 1916   123

THIRTEEN France, 1916   134

An Orientation of the Spirit

FOURTEEN   Anna Thomas Jeanes, Philadelphia, 1822   145

FIFTEEN   William James Edwards, Alabama, 1869   154

SIXTEEN   Julius Rosenwald, Illinois, 1862   165

SEVENTEEN Booker T. Washington, Virginia, 1856   172

Go for Broke

EIGHTEEN   The Inouyes, Hawaii, 1924   187

NINETEEN   The Minetas, California, 1942   198

TWENTY   Daniel Inouye, Europe, 1943   205

TWENTY-ONE   Norman Mineta, 1950s   214

Momentum

TWENTY-TWO   Claudette Colvin, Alabama, 1950s   225

TWENTY-THREE Septima Clark, Charleston,
              South Carolina, 1898   237

TWENTY-FOUR   America, 1950s   249

TWENTY-FIVE   Teenagers in the American South, 1950s   258

TWENTY-SIX   Montgomery, Alabama, 1955   268

CONCLUSION   279

Acknowledgments   283

Notes   285

The Small and the Mighty

NEW YORK

1804

Alexander Hamilton was going to die. And he knew it.

He was stoic, though his pain was great. His brow was feverish, his body now partially paralyzed from the bullet lodged in his spine. Dose after dose of wine and laudanum were poured down his throat to take the edge off. The tang of coagulating blood hung so heavy in the July air that the people tending to his injuries could nearly taste it on their tongues. As his wounds oozed, his body grew ever more gray and still.

It was late morning, and while the sun was high in the sky, the shadowy specters of a man meeting his untimely end collected in the corners of the room. Perhaps sensing his time was near, Hamilton asked for the minister of the church to which his family belonged to bring him Communion. But Reverend Bishop Moore refused. He didn't approve of dueling, and he didn't believe Hamilton to be a good enough Christian to deserve the Episcopal rites. It was Hamilton's wife, Eliza, who warmed the pew that Alexander paid for, but A. Ham, as he signed his letters, was rarely seen in Trinity Church.

"Please," Alex might have whispered, "call Reverend John Mason." Mason was a friend who pastored a Presbyterian church. Mason too refused, saying it gave him no pleasure, but he could not privately give Communion to anyone.

Hamilton became desperate in his last hour to receive the sacrament of the Last Supper. He turned back to Bishop Moore, his eyes pleading for help. "Dueling is barbaric," Moore told him, "and the church can't condone it." With the strength he had left, Hamilton assured Bishop Moore that he regretted his actions, and offered his forgiveness to Aaron Burr for shooting him. If he lived, he promised to spend his days demonstrating just how sorry he was.

Moore relented, and Hamilton, with great difficulty, swallowed the sip of wine and the morsel of bread.

The Hamiltons' seven living children assembled around him as his blood slowly soaked into the floor of his friend's home, a stain that would remain there in memoriam for years. Hamilton opened his eyes, drank in the tearstained faces of the children he delighted in, and slowly closed them again, his lids now feeling quite heavy. For the last time, he kissed the sweaty forehead of his toddler son, Philip, named after the son who had himself died in a duel just a few years earlier.

Eliza felt grief's icy fingers tighten its grip around her chest. Her breath grew rapid, shallow, each unconscious contraction of her diaphragm pushing air painfully through her lungs.

It can't end like this, she might have thought. *These babies need you.*
Please God, no.
No.

Eliza didn't know it yet, but Alex had already penned her a goodbye letter, just in case things ended poorly during his duel with the vice president of the United States. It read:

> *This letter, my very dear Eliza, will not be delivered to you unless I shall*
> *first have terminated my earthly career. The consolations of Religion, my*

beloved, can alone support you. . . . Fly to the bosom of your God and be
comforted.

With my last idea, I shall cherish the sweet hope of meeting you in a
better world.

Adieu, best of wives and best of women. Embrace all my darling chil-
dren for me.

Ever yours,

A H[1]

You, my friend, may have heard a version of this story before. But
there is one character in this scene who you may not have met. A man
who, if we shift our focus just slightly, to the edge of Hamilton's death-
bed, opens a portal to a new and fascinating drama. A man whose constant presence in the lives of the Hamiltons gave him access to the inner
sanctum on this, the most somber of occasions. A man so overcome with
his own emotion at losing his friend that tears openly streamed down his
face and he had to excuse himself to regain control.

His name was Gouverneur Morris.

When Hamilton died at the young age of forty-seven (or forty-nine,
depending on which record of his birth is to be believed), it was Morris
who bore witness to the rudimentary autopsy performed then and there.
The doctor fished through Hamilton's abdominal cavity for the bullet
that had hit a rib, pierced his liver, and tore through his diaphragm before stopping in his spinal column.

At the funeral service, Gouverneur Morris sat on the altar of Trinity
Church in Manhattan, facing the mourners who had assembled to send
Hamilton off into eternity. The size of the crowd was so large that when
Morris rose to speak, people strained to hear. The sea of bodies clad in

wigs and wool absorbed the sound of his voice, and in the back of the sanctuary, Morris seemed to be whispering.

He admitted to the audience that he was struggling to keep it together, and that, "I fear that instead of the language of a public speaker, you will hear only the lamentations of a bewailing friend."[2]

Morris spoke of the Constitutional Convention, the private meetings where he and Hamilton had played integral roles seventeen years before. Hamilton had been afraid that their efforts at the convention, in which a nation was birthed after the travail of a hot summer's labor, would not be enough. Would the union hold? Would the experiment in a new democracy ultimately prove successful? "In signing that compact he exprest his apprehension that it did not contain sufficient means of strength for its own preservation; and that in consequence we should share the fate of many other republics and pass through Anarchy to Despotism. We hoped better things."[3]

Perhaps more than any other pair of founders, Morris and Hamilton were intellectual equals. Morris matched Hamilton's wit and his skill in the law, and the two bonded over their loyalty to George Washington during the revolution. While Hamilton was a fatherless immigrant, Morris was raised at an estate that bore his family's name: Morrisania. Hamilton was five foot six and slight of build, while Morris was over six feet and portly. New York would be nothing without the both of them. While Hamilton wrote its financial systems into existence, Morris laid out the grid system that still governs its streets.

Gouverneur Morris, a friend so dear that he drew near to Hamilton in the hour of his death, didn't make it into the Broadway show. He was a scholar, a diplomat, a patriot—all terms that were chiseled onto his headstone when he died a dozen years after eulogizing Hamilton. But no one profits from his likeness. You probably wouldn't recognize him without a caption below his portrait.

And that's a shame. Because without Gouverneur Morris, America as we know it would not exist.

But before we get into that, a bit of background is in order.

Morris had a peg leg, a disfigured arm, and a way with the ladies. His right arm "had all the flesh taken off by a scald,"[4] boiling water painfully bubbling off his skin and forcing him to leave school for a year. He lost his leg as a young man after a carriage accident, his horses spooking, rearing up, and dashing away without him. Gouverneur was thrown, his leg tangling in the reins and the wheel. He was so badly mangled that doctors had no choice but to amputate below the knee and replace his leg with a wooden one.

Morris's disability didn't stop him from dancing the night away in pubs and at parties, and it certainly didn't stop him from making the romantic rounds in Europe. In fact, he was such a philanderer that John Jay wished Gouverneur had injured a certain other appendage instead of his leg.

Gouverneur Morris was a bachelor until his fifties, perhaps because he never had a shortage of interested girlfriends without the need for vows. Many of the women who found him appealing were married themselves, a fact that seemed to bother Morris little. When he did marry, it was to his housekeeper, Nancy, who had been accused of murdering her own baby. A baby fathered by her sister's husband.

Morris's physical maladies followed him until the end of his life. By then, his gout—a disease of those who could afford to eat a diet that promoted the growth of uric acid crystals in the joints—caused excruciating pain in his remaining foot.

Unlike Hamilton, Morris did not die in a duel for his honor. Instead, he perished after a painful—and almost entirely self-inflicted—death. Ultimately, an undiagnosed infirmity—a UTI? kidney stones?—caused him so much agony that he felt the only option available to him was to remove a piece of whalebone from his wife's corset and attempt to create a type of catheter that he hoped would clear the blockage and bring him relief. Instead, it probably brought an infection, and he was dead not long after.

Now you might be thinking: *Sharon, are you really surprised that we don't have a national holiday dedicated to this guy, this philanderer? This man who married his (allegedly) baby-murdering housekeeper?*

But here's what you might not know: Morris contributed to the early republic as much or more than people like Ben Franklin or John Adams. In fact, his impact is still among the most meaningful of any of the founding fathers. It was Gouverneur—jovial, disabled, and a bit of a rake—whose brilliant mind conceived America's great statement of purpose, the one still recited by schoolchildren. It was his hands that etched "We the people, in order to form a more perfect union . . ." onto animal skin with a goose feather.

He is the author of some of the most consequential words in world history: the Preamble of the new United States Constitution.

Americans often imagine that the Constitution was written by a bunch of white dudes wearing pants buttoned below the knee, wigs perfectly curled near their faces, because that's exactly what is depicted in the paintings we see in our textbooks. And to an extent, it's true: ideas were argued and hammered out by a conglomeration of men, old and young, wearing period-appropriate clothing.

But which man spoke more than any other at the Constitutional Convention, an event that fully 25 percent of participants abandoned before the job was completed? (This isn't an exaggeration. . . . one quarter of the attendees at the Constitutional Convention literally went home before the summer was over. They were like, "Listen, it's been real, but I've got to head home. Best of luck to you gentlemen.") It was Morris who clocked in at 173 speeches, despite being absent for a full month of the convention. He argued for things like aristocratic rule and against enslaving other human beings.

Historians often regard James Madison as the father of the Constitution, because his ideas and research on democracy helped shape it thematically, but Morris's role has perhaps even greater importance. The Preamble he authored established a national identity, described how this new governing document would uphold and protect the shared values men from the twelve states wished to convey. (I say twelve and not thirteen, because Rhode Island refused to send any delegates to the Constitutional Convention.) At age thirty-five, he was chosen to be part of the small committee of men who took all the ideas that had been debated at length and formed them into a document that was short enough to be reprinted in a newspaper and easy enough to read so that ordinary Americans could understand it.

The Constitution was a bold experiment, a practical yet visionary document that nurtured a new nation. It is an entirely human creation, complete with spelling errors (the scribe, Jacob Shallus, might have misspelled Pennsylvania because Alexander Hamilton dictated it incorrectly).[5] Each article, and later, amendment, reflects a balance between the big ideas of moral philosophers, Enlightenment-era thinkers, the pragmatic Yankees, the egalitarian Quakers, and the high-brow gentility of tidewater planters.

Though you may not have heard of him, Morris was known at the time to be an exceptionally talented writer and communicator. James Madison later said that there was no one who could have done a finer job writing the Preamble and forming the final Constitution. Madison wrote, "A better choice could not have been made, as the performance of the task proved."[6]

Morris's legacy benefited the United States even after his death. His family's land—fifteen hundred acres of it—had been purchased from a Dutch farmer whose last name was Broncks, and you can now walk down 138th Street in the Bronx, the spelling changed to end with a more Americanized *x*, knowing that in 1816, a man once lived there who stuck a whalebone up his private parts and died.

What's more, we have him to thank for the party of Lincoln. Gouverneur Morris and his wife, Nancy, had only one child, Gouverneur Morris

Jr., who grew up to be a railroad executive and one of the founders of the Republican Party. I like to think that Morris senior would have been secretly gleeful about this fact. Morris senior, along with Hamilton, was an avowed Federalist, and he hated what the Democratic Republicans became under Thomas Jefferson. Had he lived long enough, there's no question that Morris would have vehemently opposed the populism and chaos that the first Democratic president, Andrew Jackson, brought to the table. Unlike Jackson, Morris was vocally against slavery, and perhaps he would have used his considerable means to financially support his son's quest to start a new political party.

Hamilton had been New York's most famous champion, and news of his sudden passing spread rapidly. On the morning of his funeral, shops were shuttered and flags flew at half-mast all across New York. The hooves of Hamilton's horse *clip-clop, clip-clopped* on the cobblestone streets, the gray steed carrying empty boots turned backward in the stirrups, a symbol of what had been lost.

But Gouverneur Morris, who contributed just as much to the founding of our nation, faded quickly from view.

How many more Americans who changed the course of history are waiting to be discovered?

In this book, I intend to find out.

———

Before this uniquely American journey we're embarking upon gets too far away from the station, I'm Sharon McMahon. It's pronounced like McWoman, except it's McMan. The *ho* in the middle is silent.

Like Hamilton and Morris, like you, I too hope for better things.

At age twelve, I had a paper route that required me to rise before dawn in the frigid winters of northern Minnesota. As I walked multiple miles each morning, placing the carefully folded daily inside the screen door of subscribers, I sneakily read the news. Making sure the paper was perfectly refolded so the customers couldn't tell their paper had been pre-read, I would pick up on page two as I passed over the bridge spanning the river, turn to the back of Section A as I navigated the German Shepherd who guarded the house with the long gravel driveway, and make it to the comics by the time the apartment building loomed on the horizon.

One Christmas morning, I was out the door before my younger siblings were awake, racing through my route so I could return as quickly as possible for our gift opening. No cars buzzed past. No delivery trucks lumbered into the loading dock of the grocery store. It was dark and still, and the air felt unseasonably warm.

I finished the last of my deliveries, shedding my jacket because I'd practically run three miles with a heavy load of papers flopping at my hip. As I crossed the bridge over the river, the kind of river whose waters carved gorges and canyons into rock before tumbling into the churning foam of waterfalls, I noticed movement out of the corner of my eye.

In the distance, I saw them: auroras. The northern lights. Not the more common faint glow of green that we sometimes glimpsed from our second-floor bathroom window, but the kind that choreographed a ballet set to the unheard symphony of the universe. Great columns of pink and purple shot up above treetops, mint green and deep blue sashayed above my head in a private show, for me and only me, it seemed.

It ended almost as quickly as it began, as the auroras gave way to the first streaks of daylight over the vast expanse of an inland sea: Lake Superior. I suddenly felt very small, a child on a bridge on a round rock that orbited a medium-size star in one of nearly an infinite number of galaxies.

And yet, when the sun crested the horizon and light filled the sky, the auroras didn't disappear. I just couldn't see them anymore. The rising of the sun didn't erase the excitations of light particles in the earth's electromagnetic field. The colors were still there, it's just that daylight made them hard to see.

So too is much of history: the overshadowing suns—the men with the best military strategy, the people with the most ships, those with vast fortunes and political power—they eclipse the beauty that is there, waiting for us in the quiet predawn hours. The people outside the dominant caste, those whose impact has been missed by people who either don't know where to look or who have intentionally decided not to, the auroras of history: it is their stories I have come to find the most interesting.

When I went to high school and began to truly study history, it was the names I didn't recognize that were often the most intriguing. *Who* spoke at Alexander Hamilton's funeral? Why have I never heard of him before? In the days before the internet put the entirety of human knowledge at our fingertips, the library was my friend. The library, still the most democratic institution on earth, perched but a block away from my childhood home.

Mary, the slight librarian with wire-framed glasses whose face reminded me of an inquisitive bird, would greet me with a small smile and a pleasant hello when she saw me at each visit. The library was where you could read about the 1835 Halley's Comet sighting, then go immediately to the card catalog (It was electronic, okay? I am not *that* old.) and find more information about all the things that fascinated you.

When I became a classroom teacher, it was the auroras of history I loved to share with my students the most. "And did you know . . . DID. YOU. KNOW," I would say, building suspense for the sixteen-year-olds whose eyes stared back at me, "did you know that women made the best spies in World War II?"

It is from many years in the high school classroom, and now the much larger classroom of the internet, where millions of people pepper me with their questions in real time, that I learned to anticipate what people will say and wonder about. Some people call me America's Government Teacher. Trevor Noah said I was *not* a thirst trap. George W. Bush smirked, with a twinkle in his eye, when he learned that people in my community call themselves Governerds.

I wrote this book because I have long suspected that the best Americans are not always famous. More than twenty years of research has confirmed my intuition. The best Americans are not the critics, they are the doers. They are the people who went for broke when everyone else yelled to turn back. They are those who know that one becomes great because of who they lift up, not who they put down. I have learned that no one reaches their final moments of mortal existence and whispers to their loved ones, "I wish I had gotten in some more sick burns in the comments section on Facebook."

And like Morris, like Hamilton, like you and me, these great Americans are flawed and complicated. Centuries later, we're still raising eyebrows at some of Morris's choices. Many of his qualities are not what we'd write down in a list of traits we'd like our children to emulate. And the whalebone thing was really unfortunate.

Morris wrote in the Preamble:

> We the People of the United States, in Order to form a more perfect Union, establish Justice, insure domestic Tranquility, provide for the common defense, promote the general Welfare, and secure the Blessings of Liberty to ourselves and our Posterity, do ordain and establish this Constitution for the United States of America.

But perhaps when our fifth grade teachers asked us to memorize these lines, we weren't able to fully internalize their meaning. We were eleven years old; let's cut ourselves some slack. What does the Preamble mean? Put more simply:

We, the citizens of this new country that is wholly independent from Britain, want you to know that we intend to:

Establish justice. This phrase gives us a sense of moral rightness, of equality, and of fairness.

Ensure domestic tranquility and provide for the common defense. This demonstrates a government's duty to maintain a sense of peace within its own borders, and establishes its commitment to protect its people from foreign threats.

Promote the general welfare. This means to work for the common good. Over the centuries, what constitutes the "common good" has changed significantly. What was viewed as the common good in 1787 can only be projected onto the present in the vaguest of terms, especially since many of the rights we now enjoy were only extended to a minority of people when the words were originally written. What common good means today is still being refined.

Secure the blessings of liberty to ourselves and our posterity. This promise is now a hallmark of any democracy—the protections of civil liberties under the law, and a limiting of the power of the government so people are shielded from an overreaching and authoritarian regime—something Gouverneur Morris said Hamilton feared until the very end.

The text of the Preamble imagined America at its finest:

Just.

Peaceful.

Good.

And free.

With astonishing regularity, Americans have held fast to these ideals, despite the clickbait stories that portend calamity. And America has too often fallen short of these standards. Both of these things are true at the same time.

America has been just, and it has perpetuated injustice. We have been peaceful, and we have perpetrated acts of violence. We have been—and are—good. And we have done terrible things to people who didn't deserve them. It has been the land of the free while simultaneously sanctioning oppression.

Such is often the experience of any government run by fallible human beings. Sometimes we surprise ourselves in our capacity for greatness, and sometimes the weight of regret wraps around us like a chain.

The ideals outlined in the Constitution represent our national purpose, the raft we must cling to in the storm, the breath in our lungs, the beat in our chest: Just. Peaceful. Good. Free.

Ordinary people conjured this mission. Ordinary men like Gouverneur Morris.

What you're about to read are the stories of the small and the mighty. The stories of people you may not have heard of, but who changed the course of American history anyway. Not the presidents, but the telephone operators. Not the aristocrats, but the schoolteachers. You'll meet a woman astride a white horse riding down Pennsylvania Avenue; a young boy detained in a Japanese incarceration camp; a formerly enslaved woman on a mission to reunite with her daughter; a poet on a train; and a teacher who learns to work with her enemies. More than one thing is bombed, and multiple people surprisingly become rich. Some rich with money, and some wealthy with things that matter more.

It is my hope that by the time you turn the last page of this book, these small and mighty people will become like familiar friends, part of a community of ancestors, a great cloud of witnesses who surround us, those who light the path we journey in our quest to make the world more just, more peaceful, more good, and more free.

I'll be your guide along the way. Welcome.

And buckle up.

☆

Angel of the Rockies

———————

ONE

CLARA BROWN

Kentucky, 1830s

The marketplace buzzed with activity on a sizzling Kentucky day. And just up ahead, to the right, near the wooden platform in the center of town, a heartrending scene was unfolding.

Clara Brown clutched her youngest child close, Eliza Jane's tear-sodden face disappearing into the fabric of Clara's dress. Eliza was prone to "fits" of behavior she had difficulty controlling, and she was now sobbing.

"Shhhhhh," Clara whispered to her. "You have to be a brave girl now."[1]

She tried to dry Eliza's face. To wipe her nose. To imbue her with her motherly strength so Eliza could take her turn on the auction block and be sold to a "decent" family, one that would not punish her too harshly. A family that would give her somewhere warm to sleep, and enough food to sustain her and help her grow tall and strong. If Eliza stood there looking like a blubbering mess, she might fetch a bad price and go to a family that couldn't—or wouldn't—care for her.

When Clara was born around 1800,[2] she was born enslaved to enslaved parents. As a child, she was sold to a man in another state, a fate that would soon befall her own offspring.[3] Kentucky wasn't home to the vast plantations of Virginia, where she came from; the land here was more mountainous, the farms were more compact. It's likely that Clara had many jobs as she grew up, learning to cook, clean, garden, wash, and iron alongside the other enslaved women she lived with.

Unusually for a woman in her circumstances, Clara married for love. Because so little has been recorded about the lives of enslaved people, and what was recorded was often from the perspective of the people who owned them, diaries and letters from the time tell us that Clara's owners were very happy that she married Richard, and that they threw the new couple a wedding feast to celebrate the union.[4]

It's difficult today not to be cynical about these accounts—if the enslavers felt genuine affection for Clara and Richard, why didn't they free them? What were they actually happy about? Was it that they had a family of strong workers living on their farm now, a family that would soon bear children they could sell or enslave as well? Was the marriage for love anything more than dollar signs in the eyes of the people who owned Clara and Richard?

Clara and Richard welcomed a son, Richard Jr., daughter Margaret, and twin baby girls, Paulina Ann and Eliza Jane.[5] Unlike many enslaved people, the family was allowed to live together and to tend to their own garden plot. In the evenings, the children could play in the creek that ran through the property.

Clara's life changed forever one summer day. In the distance, she heard the unmistakable sound of her eight-year-old daughter screaming, "MAMAAAAAAAAA!" Clara felt a punch in her gut and a weight on her chest that made it hard to breathe. She took off in the direction of her daughter's voice, her legs moving her six-foot frame at a speed they had never carried her before. She found Eliza creekside, pointing downstream.

"What! What happened? What is it?" Clara cried, the panic rising in her throat.

"PAULINA!" Eliza cried. "PAULINA!"[6]

Eliza had tried in vain to reach her twin, Paulina, who was tangled in the branches that swirled at the edge of the creek. Eliza had watched as her wombmate disappeared under the surface.

Paulina's body was recovered a short time later. But Eliza's mind was not. Clara worried desperately about her, worried how she would be treated the rest of her life if she couldn't snap out of her episodes of staring blankly off into the distance and the crying jags that lasted for hours unabated. Eliza barely slept, which meant Clara barely had a chance to close her eyes.

Today we would recognize the PTSD that Eliza was experiencing, the flashbacks of trying to rescue her entangled sister that seized her at night. The crippling feelings of guilt that it was her fault, the regret she felt because they shouldn't have been in the creek to begin with.

When the family's current owner, Ambrose Smith—the one who had thrown them the wedding feast—died in 1835,[7] the family had to be separated and sold, one by one, to settle his estate. Each member of Clara's family, her husband and four beloved children, took turns stepping up onto the auction block, hoping against hope for some kind of miracle that might allow them to stay together. But none came.

The sight of fragile little Eliza with her tearstained face, eyes swollen from crying, being wrenched from her arms and hoisted atop the platform, caused a pain unlike any Clara had known. When Paulina died, Clara grieved. But delivering her dead baby girl into the arms of the Lord—Clara was a woman of great faith—was far different than delivering her sobbing, living daughter into the arms of an unknown enslaver. She knew there was a good chance they would never meet again outside of heaven. It was a grief she shared with many thousands of mothers whose babies were taken and who never again had the chance to kiss the tops of their heads, to remark on how much they were growing, or to marvel in pride at who they were becoming.

"SOLD!" the auctioneer yelled, pointing at the man who had just purchased her flesh and blood. Eliza was carted away, nestled in the back of a wagon among sacks of feed and bolts of fabric. Clara watched her disappear, praying that Eliza would not be afraid, that she would find the strength to be a good girl, and that she would always know that she was loved.[8]

She vowed to find her again someday, even if it took the rest of her life.

When it was Clara's turn to step on the auction block, she was sober, her eyes fixed on the horizon. She couldn't allow herself to look into the faces of the people who stared her up and down. She didn't allow herself to cry for Eliza, or for her husband, or her two older children, all sold to different enslavers. She held her head high, turning on command so the auction attendees could see her from all angles, silent in her rage and despair.

Clara was sturdy. Experienced enough to take to most jobs quickly, but young enough to still have many decades of work left in her. Her buyer was a man named George Brown. He motioned to a spot for Clara to sit in his wagon. The auction block, and Clara's life as she knew it, slowly disappeared from view as she rolled toward a new, unknown life.

George Brown was a merchant—a hatter—and instead of working outdoors, Clara now had a job inside the Brown home. Over the years, as she helped raise the Browns' three daughters, she thought endlessly of her own three girls. Her Margaret, was she happy? Did she marry? Her Eliza, did she grow out of the crying spells? How tall was she now? Her Paulina, was she watching from above? Could she hear how often Clara talked to her as she folded laundry and stirred the supper bubbling on the stove? She hoped her son and husband remembered her, as she did them.

Clara spent the next twenty years cooking, cleaning, and washing for the Browns.[9] She couldn't read or write, but with their help, she tried to keep track of what happened to her children and husband.

Margaret, she heard, had died of a respiratory condition. Clara's husband, Richard, sold down the river to one of the deadly plantations in the Deep South, was also gone. Her son, Richard Jr., was presumed dead, because the Browns had not been able to find a trace of him for many years. Eliza had initially been sold to an enslaver in Kentucky, but by 1852, she was twenty-six years old, and the only thing Clara had been able to turn up was a rumor that Eliza had headed west.[10]

When George Brown died and his relatives freed Clara, as stipulated in his will, Kentucky law gave her one year to leave the state. Stay any longer, and she risked re-enslavement. The Brown daughters found a job for her in St. Louis, working with a family as a housekeeper and cook.

For the first time in her life, at age fifty-six, Clara was working for pay. Her new employers, Mr. and Mrs. Jacob Brunner, were German immigrants, and they taught Clara how to make the foods they enjoyed, which were quite different from what Clara had learned to cook back in Kentucky.[11]

Out of curiosity, I became interested in what German immigrants to the Ozarks were eating in the 1850s. We know from the records that Clara learned to cook a variety of German dishes, and that her newfound skills would later come in handy. I found a historian at Deutschheim, a German heritage site in the Ozarks, who described the great lengths that German immigrants went to to have variety in their diets—it was not part of their food culture to eat the same five things in rotation, as was common in frontier communities.[12] German immigrants at the time believed strongly in the concept of kitchen gardens and orchards, and a German seed catalog from the 1850s boasted hundreds of kinds of apples, pears, and stone fruit seeds. German produce favorites were soon adapted to the warmer Ozark climate.

Dr. Erin McCawley Renn says that German immigrants scoffed at the typically American cash crop system of planting their fields with nothing but tobacco or corn to sell, believing that it ruined the soil fertility and made it difficult to feed your family. The rule of thumb was to grow a hundred heads of cabbage per person, and that should be enough, if they were stored in your underground cellar properly, to last the year.[13]

(And before you gasp at a root cellar holding five hundred heads of cabbage, it was mostly stored as sauerkraut.) One German immigrant from the 1840s described the fifty-six types of vegetables he grew in his kitchen garden, ranging from eggplant to radishes to six different kinds of peas, all surrounded by a picket fence to keep the pigs and chickens out.

When November came and hogs across the state were butchered, Germans introduced many varieties of sausages that Anglo-Americans had never tried: mettwurst, sommerwurst, bratwurst, and more. All of these were likely new to Clara. German immigrants were also big on soup, often eating it for at least one meal a day. Soup was something you put on the stove in the morning, and when anyone was hungry, you just helped yourself, sopping up the broth with a hunk of rye bread. Clara learned not just how to keep her employers fed and happy but how to make efficient use of her time in the kitchen and how to store food for the cold winter months, making pickles and vinegars and other fermented foods that helped keep people healthy when fresh produce wasn't available.

While living in St. Louis, Clara asked every Black person she met if they had heard of her daughter Eliza. No, came the answer, over and over.

"Sorry, auntie," children said.

"No, ma'am, I don't know her," said the men at the train station.[14]

The Brunners wanted to move to Kansas, and Clara accepted their invitation to accompany them there.[15] She had exhausted her search for Eliza in St. Louis, and the change of scenery would give her access to new people who might have encountered her now grown baby girl.

Clara would have no way of knowing what kind of world she was headed to as she made her way to what would come to be called Bleeding Kansas.

TWO

BLEEDING KANSAS

1850s

M any, many bad things in America lead back to my least favorite president: Andrew Jackson. Chief among the bad things is the notorious Dred Scott Supreme Court decision of 1857, which is widely, and I do mean WIDELY, regarded as the most idiotic thing the high court has ever committed to paper.

Dred Scott was an enslaved man in Missouri, a slave state, whose enslavers brought him to Illinois and Wisconsin territory, which were considered free soil. When they returned to Missouri, Dred Scott claimed that he should be free, because crossing into free soil made him a free man.

No surprise, his enslavers disagreed. Dred Scott sued. And the final outcome of the case, decided on by the Supreme Court, was that Dred Scott didn't have any standing to bring a lawsuit. Why? Because, the court said, all African Americans, no matter if they were enslaved or free, were not citizens of the United States. The court, led by Chief Justice Roger Taney, said that "they were at that time considered as a subordinate and inferior class of beings who had been subjugated by the dominant race, and, whether emancipated or not, yet remained subject to their authority, and had no rights or privileges but such as those who held the power and the Government might choose to grant them."[1]

Taney (which is pronounced *Tawney*), was a close adviser to and served in the cabinet of Andrew Jackson. And it was Jackson, an enslaver himself, who appointed Taney to the Supreme Court.

Roger Taney was slim, with noteworthy jowls. He had a wavy, chin-length bob, much like what you see young celebrity women of the twenty-first century sporting every spring. Taney was from Maryland, a Catholic who married the sister of Francis Scott Key, the author of "The Star-Spangled Banner." Roger and Anne Taney supposedly had an agreement to raise any of their sons Catholic, like him, and any daughters Episcopalian, like Anne. As the fates would conspire, the couple had six daughters.

In recent years, a school in Maryland changed its name from Taney to Thurgood Marshall, after a champion of civil rights who was also from Maryland. Statues of Taney have been removed from various Maryland locations, and in February 2023, a Roger Taney statue was taken down inside the United States Capitol building—a movement led by several members of Congress.

The *Dred Scott* case was happening right around the same time that Clara was emancipated and went to St. Louis. Following the Supreme Court's decision, Clara, who for the first time in her life was free from bondage, was now formally regarded as "not a citizen" by her own government. There isn't a record of what Clara might have thought and felt about *Dred Scott*, but she likely didn't need the likes of Roger Taney to tell her what she had already experienced: that many people considered her less than based solely on the color of her skin.

Y'all already know that the United States was wrenched in two because of slavery—and only barely knitted back together. If anyone tries to tell you the Civil War was a war for "state's rights," calmly look them in the eye, and ask, politely and inquisitively, what exactly the states wanted the "right" to do?

You can follow up with, "Make their own rules about what?"

The answer is, of course, that they wanted to make their own rules about whether they had the right to enslave people. All the "way of life" and "self-determination" and "economic conditions" roads lead right back to slavery. You can also spare me the arguments of "other places in the world enslaved people," "the United States was one of the first countries to end slavery," and "Africans sold other Africans into enslavement."

First, there was no one in the world engaged in chattel slavery like the United States, where people were kidnapped and held permanently, with no hope of escaping the condition. That was not the cultural norm in other parts of the world. Nor was the idea that all subsequent generations of children "followed the mother," being born into permanent enslavement. The United States saw enslaved women as sources of value because of the enslaved workers they could in turn produce.

Secondly, the American South was one of the LAST places in the world to end enslavement. One of the last. Not the first.

And finally, it's absolutely true that Africans helped enslave other Africans. But why? Because of the economic incentive created by Europeans to kidnap and sell people. Without an economic incentive, what would be the point of ripping human beings away from their families, imprisoning them in the most squalid and horrifying conditions, and selling them to slave traders to be shipped across the Middle Passage, where hundreds of thousands of them, possibly even millions, would perish before ever reaching the New World?

Enslavement in the United States was widely accepted. While only a small percentage of the country as a whole actively enslaved people, the entire country's economy, not just the economy of the South, rested on the backs of enslaved Africans. Did you take sugar in your tea? It was probably grown on a plantation that used enslaved labor. Did you wear cotton clothes? Ditto. Did you produce cheap shoes in New England with no right or left foot? You sold them to enslavers to put on enslaved people's feet.

Northern merchants relied on taxes from the slave trade to make improvements to their cities. For example, Newport, Rhode Island, used the money brought in from taxation on the enslaved to pave its streets.[2] Northern shipbuilders, carpenters, rope makers, blacksmiths, bankers, auctioneers, insurers, sailors, textile mill owners and workers, and more all relied on contracts from companies engaged in the slave trade.

Denim was first created from the indigo dyeing and cultivating knowledge that came from enslaved Africans in South Carolina. Denim was originally classified under the umbrella of what was referred to in the United States as "negro cloth," and there are dozens of examples of "escaped slave" advertisements that said the people who fled to freedom were wearing jeans.

Eliza Pinckney, who is widely credited as being the botanist behind the establishment of indigo as a cash crop, relied on enslaved labor and the knowledge from enslaved Africans to help her extract the blue dye from the green plant, which is not a simple or straightforward process.[3]

Levi Strauss, founder of the famed denim brand, was hardly the inventor of denim. What he did was take an idea from a collaborator and add rivets to the pants, which made them more durable. And then he marketed the heck out of them. He was in San Francisco at exactly the right moment, the 1850s, when the California gold rush hit. And while he was there, he made sure to advertise that he did not hire Chinese or Black workers—that his denim blue jeans were made only by white people, even though the cotton and indigo were grown by enslaved labor.[4]

In 2022, one of the oldest pair of Levi's still in existence was sold at auction. They are believed to be from the 1880s, and were discovered in an abandoned mineshaft, incredibly well preserved. Printed inside on a pocket is the phrase "The only kind made by white labor," a slogan Levi's adopted later in the nineteenth century. The jeans sold for $76,000.[5]

This is but the merest taste of how the nation as a whole, not just the South, benefited from and approved of the practice of enslaving other human beings. Were some individuals morally opposed to it? Sure, I'll grant you that. Some people were actively working for abolition. Some people refused to buy goods that had been made by enslaved labor. But most did not. Most looked the other way, reaping the benefits of an economy built on the backs of the enslaved.

In 1803, the United States nearly doubled in size when Thomas Jefferson decided to move forward with the Louisiana Purchase, which, by the way, he wasn't even sure was constitutional. He considered asking Congress to amend the Constitution to give the president the right to grow the nation's territory, but ultimately he decided it was better to ask for forgiveness than for permission. The new territorial areas weren't automatically granted statehood, though—they still had to meet the criteria, which included having a critical mass of residents who were in favor of it.

In 1820, two new states wanted to join the union: Missouri and Maine. A fierce debate erupted when Missouri applied for statehood, because the territory permitted slavery. When I say fierce debate, what I actually mean is *violent* debate. In her book *The Field of Blood*, historian Joanne B. Freeman writes about the extreme violence within the U.S. Congress during the decades leading up to the Civil War. She writes, "There seemed to be *so* much violence in the House and Senate chambers. . . . Shoving. Punching. Pistols. Bowie knives. Congressmen brawling in bunches while colleagues stood on chairs to get a good look. At least once, a gun was fired on the House floor."[6]

Some people from the North did not want to admit Missouri, because it would tip the balance of slaveholding versus non-slaveholding states, and because the Constitution said that enslaved people were to be counted as three-fifths of a person. If they were admitted, it would give slaveholding states even more political power because of proportional representation in the House of Representatives.

The middle decades of the nineteenth century pulsed with energy about what should happen to the western territories. The acquisition of Texas and other parts of the Southwest from Mexico in 1848, the glimmering allure of the California gold rush beginning in 1849, the irresistible current of expansion that propelled a veritable cavalcade of farmers, ranchers, and gold prospectors across the country, streaming through the wilderness and the desert, over the Rockies and all the way to the Pacific. This cavalcade consisted not just of European settlers; many free African Americans were making their way west too.

The Mississippi had long functioned as a vital conduit for north-south transit. But the western states and territories yearned for something different. Not just for a river of water but for one of steel. A railroad, the artery that would connect the East with the West.

One tiny man, Stephen Douglas, who you might recognize as Abraham Lincoln's opponent in a future presidential election, really wanted that steel river to course through Chicago. Members of Congress disagreed about which route the railroad should take: through slave territory, or entirely within the designated free soil? To get the railway of his dreams, Douglas offered a compromise in 1850.

"Let's leave the matter of slavery to popular sovereignty," Douglas advocated. "Let states and territories decide what they want to do for themselves when it comes to slavery."

"Let states decide for themselves? I think not," Charles Sumner, leader of an antislavery coalition in Congress, said.

Sumner believed allowing for popular sovereignty was the recipe for allowing new states and territories to morph into "a dreary region of despotism, inhabited by masters and slaves."[7]

"You must," Stephen Douglas argued, "provide for continuous lines of settlement from the Mississippi Valley to the Pacific Ocean." He told the

Senate not to "fetter the limbs of [this] young giant,"[8] and to let the residents of the states decide for themselves if they will be a slave state or a free state. Ultimately, Congress agreed to Douglas's proposal. The Missouri Compromise, which restricted slavery in the Louisiana Purchase to south of the 36th parallel, and admitted Maine as a free state while Missouri retained the right to enslave people, was repealed. Popular sovereignty became the new law of the land, when the Kansas-Nebraska Act was signed in 1854 by President Franklin Pierce.

Pierce was perhaps the most tragic of our presidents. His wife, Jane, hated his political aspirations and begged him to resign his position as senator, which he did. The Pierces had a baby son who died after a few days of life. They then had two more sons, Frank and Benny. When Frank was four, he died of typhoid, leaving only two-year-old Benny.

Shortly after resigning from the Senate, and over Jane's strenuous objections, Pierce accepted his party's nomination for president. He won the election. His victory was Jane's worst nightmare, and a sense of dread about her impending fate enveloped her. Soon, she would be forced to move to Washington, D.C., pretending to support her husband's vanity project: the presidency. In January 1853, two months before his inauguration, Franklin, Jane, and Benny were traveling to New Hampshire via train. Benny was standing up to look out the window when the axle of the train broke, causing the train to tumble down an embankment. The sounds of Jane's screams as the train rolled off the tracks sounded like a whisper in comparison to what Franklin heard once the train had stopped and they discovered that their son Benny had been crushed and nearly decapitated.

Pierce said it was his life's greatest regret that he couldn't stop Jane from glimpsing the body of their son, their only remaining child. Jane fully believed Benny's horrific death was God punishing them for Franklin's vain political pursuits.[9]

When Pierce assumed the presidency, huge crowds gathered, the largest of any inauguration to date. As he ascended the Capitol steps, the audience commented on how handsome he was. But his countenance was bleak. Jane refused to attend.

Pierce declined to swear an oath on the Bible, choosing instead to affirm his duties as president. He memorized a solemn speech that said, in part: "My countrymen: it is a relief to feel that no heart but my own can know the personal regret and bitter sorrow over which I have been borne to a position so suitable for others rather than desirable for myself. . . . I ought to be, and am, truly grateful for this rare manifestation of the nation's confidence; but this, so far from lightening my obligations, only adds to their weight. You have summoned me in my weakness; you must sustain me by your strength."[10]

For years, Jane made no public appearances at all and remained cloaked in mourning clothes. She cloistered herself upstairs at the White House, writing letters and talking to her dead son, Benny. Her first official White House role didn't come until nearly two years after Pierce took office.

Pierce was getting little support from his wife, but also no support at all from his vice president, William Rufus King. King was so sick with tuberculosis in the weeks leading up to his scheduled inauguration that he traveled to Cuba for a change of air, hoping the warm climate and sunshine would help him recover.

Congress granted a special dispensation for King to be sworn in as vice president from Cuba, and he finally took the oath twenty days after Pierce became president.

After languishing in Cuba for weeks, King realized his health was not improving, and he needed to try to make it back to the United States. He pulled it together, boarded a boat, and arrived at his Alabama plantation. A few days after he arrived home, William Rufus King died. He never made it to Washington during his vice presidency.

At that time, the Constitution had no provision to replace the vice president. Franklin Pierce had three dead sons, a wife who was in such poor mental and physical health that she couldn't leave her room, an absent and (shortly thereafter) dead vice president, and the first bubbles of a civil war fast becoming a simmer.

So it was this sad sack, Franklin Pierce, a northern Democrat trying in vain to hold a fracturing nation together, who signed the Kansas-Nebraska Act in 1854. The bill birthed two new territories, but it also ignited a brutal uprising known as Bleeding Kansas, in which groups from other states that opposed enslavement and groups that demanded its legality flooded the territory in an attempt to gain the upper hand in the game of popular sovereignty.

Pierce turned to alcohol for solace, and soon, his drinking spiraled out of control. He lost control of his party, and at the end of his term in office, he failed to be renominated by the Democrats. Jane died from tuberculosis a few years after leaving the White House. Pierce died a few years after Jane, in 1869, from cirrhosis of the liver caused by his excessive drinking.

After Pierce left office, a new Democratic president moved into the White House in 1857. James Buchanan was the only bachelor president . . . or was he? Multiple historians believe Buchanan and William Rufus King, Pierce's dead vice president, were lovers. King and Buchanan lived together for thirteen years. They were frequently teased for their effeminate mannerisms. Andrew Jackson referred to them as "Miss Fancy and Aunt Nancy," which were nicknames that probably suggested exactly what you think they suggested.[11]

Buchanan and King openly dreamed of being president and vice president together. William Rufus King came from a remarkably wealthy family, enslavers of over five hundred people. In fact, King helped found a city you may have heard of because of the civil rights movement: Selma, Alabama.

The pithy National Park Service regards Bleeding Kansas like this: "During Bleeding Kansas, murder, mayhem, destruction, and psychological warfare became a code of conduct in Eastern Kansas and Western Missouri."[12]

Most of the inhabitants of Kansas were not slaveholders; they were poor, and slaves were expensive. Proslavery Missourians flooded across the border to vote illegally in elections. Abolition groups funded and sent settlers to the region to try to create a critical mass of people who would oppose enslavement. More than four dozen people died in political killings. Homes and businesses were looted, burned, and destroyed.[13]

Murder, mayhem, destruction, and psychological warfare hung thick in the air as Clara Brown arrived in Kansas. What was happening there was a microcosm of the nation as a whole: the anger wound itself ever more tightly inside the chests of men until it broke with an audible pop, and the country was soon thrust into civil war.

Back in Congress in May 1856, Representative Preston Brooks of South Carolina was enraged. As an enslaver himself, he abhorred antislavery sentiment, and said, "The fate of the South is to be decided with the Kansas issue. If Kansas becomes a hireling [free] state, slave property will decline to half its present value in Missouri . . . [and] abolitionism will become the prevailing sentiment. So with Arkansas; so with upper Texas."

Preston Brooks was provoked by antislavery Senator Charles Sumner when Sumner gave a speech denouncing Stephen Douglas and another senator named Andrew Butler. Sumner called Douglas a "noisesome, squat, nameless animal," and publicly accused Butler of having taken a mistress. Butler's mistress, Sumner asserted, was a "harlot," who was "ugly to others, but lovely to him."[14]

That mistress was the enslavement of Africans.

Andrew Butler was Preston Brooks's cousin. And even though Brooks was in the House and Sumner was in the Senate, Brooks heard about Sumner's "harlot" speech. Three days went by, until May 22, 1856, when Brooks waited for the Senate to conclude its business for the day. Brooks entered the chamber, walked up behind Charles Sumner, who was getting ready to mail out some copies of his speech, and started beating him with a cane.

Preston Brooks struck Charles Sumner again and again, blows raining down with sickening thuds, until Sumner was unconscious, bleeding profusely, and severely injured.

Considering his message delivered, Brooks left the Senate chamber. Charles Sumner was so gravely wounded that he was not able to resume his seat in Congress for three years. *Three years.*

Meanwhile, Congress investigated Preston Brooks for the assault, but they failed to censure him. As in, they couldn't even pass a resolution saying, "Yeah no, that was not cool, we shouldn't be beating people in Congress." They couldn't even do that.

Brooks resigned from Congress in July 1856. And was then immediately reelected one month later.

So no, America is not "the worst it's ever been" today, despite what some news anchors might be trying to convince you of, because if they can make you afraid, they can gain your attention and your money. Has anyone been beaten half to death on the floor of the Senate over the topic of whether it's cool to enslave people this week? No? Okay.

If it makes you feel any better at all, Preston Brooks died of croup, choking violently to death before he could take his seat after his reelection. He was only thirty-seven.[15] But the aftershocks of the beating lived on. The stage was set for the outbreak of the Civil War.

THREE

CLARA BROWN

Colorado, 1870s

Clara Brown was living in Missouri and Kansas while the bejowled Roger Taney said she and everyone who looked like her wasn't a citizen. Her missing daughter, Eliza, was still the first thought in her mind each morning and the last before bed. Hope, that thing with feathers, perched in her peripheral vision, just out of reach, as she cooked and cleaned, singing quietly to herself, as Bleeding Kansas exploded around her.

The talk of the town where Clara was living was of the West, of Colorado, where gold was rumored to have been discovered. Clara wondered if Eliza Jane might have joined the gold-seeking pioneers, and the more she thought about it, the better a change of scenery sounded to her. She was free to do as she pleased, so Clara decided she would head west, start a laundry business, and use her earnings to fuel her search for Eliza.

By the spring of 1859, the Colorado gold rush was in full swing. Mere rumors of the precious metal were enough to drive the '59ers, following the shimmering mirage of a prosperous future they glimpsed on the horizon. Clara, caught up in this tide of hope, joined forces with a respected wagon master, Colonel Benjamin Wadsworth.[1] His thirty-wagon caravan was headed west, and Clara, with her tenacity and unique features—her towering height, her deep complexion, her high cheekbones, and her piercing brown eyes—convinced him to let her be their cook.

She'd cook for twenty-five men in the caravan, fixing the Appalachian and German dishes she'd perfected over fifty years, walking beside the wagon train. In return, the Colonel would transport her laundry equipment.

For eight weeks, nearly sixty-year-old Clara walked, sometimes shushing through prairie grasses as tall as her cheeks, sometimes ascending steep, rocky hills with the vigor of a woman half her age. Not only did she walk the entire seven hundred miles to Colorado, she also prepared three full meals a day in between walks for two dozen ravenous people.

One woman, Margaret Frink, wrote in her memoir that she saw "A Negro woman . . . tramping along through the heat and carrying a cast iron bake stove on her head, with her provisions and a blanket on top, bravely pushing on."[2] Historians like Lawrence de Graaf believe Frink's description might match that of Clara Brown.

One Tennessee newspaper, reflecting in 1886 on the opening of the West thirty years earlier, described Clara as being the first woman to cross the "Great American desert," a term widely used in the nineteenth century for what we now commonly call the High Plains. The *Savannah Courier* said that the wagon train encountered "some 800 Indians along the way," but that Clara wasn't afraid of Indians, because she had Indian blood in her veins and "her grandparents [had] been savages."[3] There is no corroborating evidence for this statement, so it's likely that it was inserted for dramatic effect—how exactly would the public fact-check this in the nineteenth century?

On May 6, 1859, the Colorado gold fever escalated. A prospector named John Gregory struck gold near Central City, Colorado, fueling the hopes of those en route, though some remained skeptical of what they might find.[4] By summer's end, disillusionment led about fifty thousand Colorado settlers to turn back east in frustration, selling their equipment and supplies to westward travelers like Clara, who held on to their dreams.

When her wagon train finally arrived in Colorado, Clara was likely the first Black woman to cross into the territory, the first to breathe in the sunshine and the dry air of the mountains. Fortune seekers threw together barely habitable shacks in towns that sprang from the ground like weeds. Clara eventually settled in Central City and started a business cooking and washing for townspeople. Miners, often men with few legitimate job prospects back home, didn't know if they would strike it rich, so they generally arrived alone. If they were married, their wives stayed behind until they got word that there was somewhere worth coming to.

As Clara saw the abject poverty of many of the miners and laborers, her heart went out to them. She was much older than most, and her motherly instincts longed for someone to dote on. She tried to bring a semblance of civilization to what many regarded as the truly wild west, hosting prayer meetings and helping to start the Union Sunday School with two Methodist ministers she befriended.

Wherever she went, Clara became known for her kindness and her tenacity. If someone arrived in Colorado Territory, scrawny from hunger and with not a penny to their name, Clara would give him a place to sleep and food to eat until he could find employment. In exchange, she earned their loyalty. When the laborer could finally afford to send out his laundry, there was no question he would return to Clara.

Clara's laundry business thrived. A miner's shirt, be it blue or red flannel, could be laundered for fifty cents or two pinches of gold dust.[5] Clara worked tirelessly from her two-room cabin, boiling water for washing, gathering and chopping wood for fuel to boil the water, scrubbing clothes on her washboard, hanging them to dry in the sunshine, and ironing them into submission. Laundering was backbreaking work, but it proved to be a gold mine in its own right. By the end of the Civil War, Clara had amassed more than $10,000,[6] which is the modern equivalent of nearly $250,000.

We should just go ahead and put Clara's picture in the dictionary next to the term "self-made." Everything Clara had, she earned from her own hands, from the sweat of her brow and the steel in her resolve.

As the mining towns of Colorado grew, so too did the community's needs. Crowded conditions meant contagious illnesses spread at a rapid clip, one man's coughing in a mine shaft quickly infecting everyone around him. The arrival of womenfolk meant babies were born. More people and families meant a greater need for institutions like schools and churches to serve them. Clara opened her home to the sick as needed, nursing them to the best of her ability. She acted as midwife for laboring women, and said that her dwelling was a "hospital, a home, a general refuge for those who were sick or in poverty."[7] She gave generously to help fund the first Protestant and Catholic churches in town.

Clara developed a reputation that stretched far beyond the confines of her town and into the entirety of the American West. As new people arrived in Colorado, they soon heard tell of a woman who was always quick with a meal or a bandage, a cot for a nap, or a place to rent for the month. They called her the Angel of the Rockies.[8]

She became well-known to the governor of Colorado, who sent her on a mission back to Kansas to convince more people to move to Colorado.[9] She visited churches and schools, telling Black people that they had real opportunities in her adopted home state.

For the first time, Clara had a problem many prospectors would have given anything for: what to do with all her money? Real estate seemed like a sound choice, so Clara invested in properties—homes to rent out or sell, vacant lots to build on, mining claims she hoped would prove fruitful. Her mounting earnings gave her the margin she needed to breathe a little easier. Still, she never stopped thinking about Eliza. How she would have given up everything she had to feel the smoothness of her baby girl's cheek in her hand, to drink in her scent, to feel the rise and fall of her chest as she held her close.

When the Civil War ended, her friends told her about how Kentucky was now free, and a longing stirred inside her—somebody had to know something about Eliza. Although Clara was strong, she had grown old and she knew that if she was ever going to make the trip back south to look for news of Eliza, now was the time.

When she arrived in Kentucky, weeks of searching helped her find distant relations, but not her daughter. She told everyone she met about how much better life was in the West—how the sun was brighter and the mountains never left you without a view to gaze upon. How you could get along with all kinds of people in the brand-new little towns, and live wherever you liked, without apologizing to anybody. She told them about how she had become friends with the governor. She assured them that work would be plentiful once they got there, but her relatives couldn't afford to start the long journey.

So Clara paid for many of them to relocate—accounts range from sixteen to thirty relatives and friends—and she helped them get on their feet when they arrived. For the wagon train that was required to move her loved ones to Colorado, Clara was quoted double the price that a white man would have been expected to pay. She reached into the pouch that enclosed her money, feeling the weight of it in her hand, knowing that she might not have the chance to earn more. She closed her eyes and pictured what Eliza might look like as a grown woman of twenty, or of thirty or forty. Maybe someone had helped her daughter leave behind the weight of the past for something better. She gave the wagon master the sum he asked for, willing the tears not to fall.[10]

You might think that you're one step ahead of me, and that this is a story about how Clara becomes a millionaire, a mine owner tapping the veins of one of her claims in the Colorado mountains. I wish that were true, but it's not, unfortunately. By 1873, Clara lost most of her properties to flood and fire, and most of her savings had been embezzled by an unscrupulous attorney who had promised to help illiterate Clara manage her financial matters. After all her self-initiated success, all that she had done for others in her community, she was now a poor, elderly woman who was left with no choice but to move in with a friend at a lower altitude.

Colorado enacted a program that designated anyone who had arrived in the territory before 1865 an "official pioneer," bestowing upon them a pension and a nod to their indomitable spirit.[11] Clara was now in the position of needing the money, and believing herself eligible, applied for the pension program. She was denied.

Was it because she was a woman, or because she was Black? Perhaps both. But her friends were outraged on her behalf. People who knew and loved Clara mounted a letter-writing and speech-giving campaign to lobby for Clara's inclusion as an official pioneer. Their efforts worked, and Clara became the first woman to receive the designation. She had pioneered Colorado every bit as much as the miners and the speculators whose laundry she had done. She had helped shape the state in ways no one else could.

Still, hope perched just out of her now-failing sight. Clara never stopped asking everyone she met if they had ever heard of her daughter Eliza Jane. She offered anyone who might have a clue as to her whereabouts a $1,000 reward.[12] And then, when Clara was eighty-two years old, her heart leapt out of her chest when someone finally said: "I think I might know who you're talking about."

A letter was dashed off, and when the reply came back, Clara could barely breathe with anticipation. "Yes." A telegram came back. "I think we're talking about the same person. She lives in Council Bluffs, Iowa."[13] Clara was now subsisting on nothing but her pioneer pension, but within days, her beloved community raised sufficient funds to buy her a ticket for the multiday train trip to Iowa.

I like to imagine Clara at the train depot, surrounded by her chosen Colorado family. She hoists her tall frame up the train steps, and at the top, turns around to look at the assemblage of people who know and love her.

"Goodbye now," I hear her saying.

"Goodbye, Clara! Good luck!" the crowd calls back. Women dab at the corners of their eyes with handkerchiefs. Men hoist children onto their shoulders, their little hands waving wildly, as slowly, the train begins to chug away from the station. Clara waves her handkerchief out the window.

"Goodbye now!" her voice echoes, long after the train was out of view.

A newspaper reporter got wind of the possible connection that had been made between Clara and a woman named Mrs. Brewer. *The Leavenworth Times* reported on Clara's 1882 journey into the heart of Iowa:

> Yesterday morning on the Denver Short Line train, Mrs. Brown arrived in Council Bluffs. She came up on the streetcar and when at the corner of Broadway and 8th Street, her long-lost child was pointed out to her, standing on the crossing. With a scream, she jumped from her seat, rushed out of the car, and in an ecstasy of joy, mother and child were clasped in each other's arms.
>
> Unheeding the lookers on, unheeding the mud in the streets . . . they sat down. The sight was at once amusing and touching. In that embrace, the joys and sorrows of a lifetime were forgotten, and only the present thought of.[14]

For the first time in many decades, Clara felt a truly unmitigated joy. All the toil, all the nights of seemingly unanswered prayers, all the moments of quiet desperation that she pushed aside to continue reaching for hope, all of it was forgotten in the moment that she finally held Eliza Jane in her arms. She studied her face for glimpses of herself and her husband, Richard. "My baby," I hear her whispering. "You're here. You're here."

"Mama!" Eliza cried out as the dam in her heart broke open. Decades of compartmentalizing who she had been before she was sold from who she had become afterward crumbled. Her mother had not forgotten her. She had never stopped looking. Eliza had been haunted by the sight of Paulina's face sinking farther from view beneath the surface of the water, until she too felt like she was being pulled under by the weight of it.

But in this moment, Eliza saw her mother, not in the aquatic pools of her distant memory, but here in the flesh, warm and wonderful. Too tangible to be angelic. She was smaller than Eliza remembered, but not diminished.

Clara was described in the newspaper as above average height, strong and vigorous of frame, hair thickly sprinkled with gray, and a kindly face. The *Times* said, "She has found consolation for many a sad and lonely hour, her solace in affliction, and has said to the troubled soul, 'Peace, be still.' It has been the bright and guiding star of her hope that she should again see her child."

Despite her near blindness, hope now filled Clara's field of vision, glorious in its colors, basking in the warm sun of peace, and of contentment, and of joy.

Eliza was herself a widow, but before she lost her husband she had made Clara a grandmother several times over. Clara returned to beloved Colorado with Eliza and one of her granddaughters—perhaps the most beautiful creature she'd ever laid eyes on—in tow.[15]

If the phrase "I can die happy now" applied to anyone, it was Clara Brown. She passed away on October 26, 1885, surrounded by her daughter, her granddaughter, and a host of people who enveloped her in the kind of warmth and kindness Clara had freely given to others.[16] When asked if she bore any resentment toward those who wronged her, those who had enslaved her and stolen her money, she simply replied: "My little sufferings was nothing, honey, and the Lord, He gave me strength to bear up under them. I can't complain."[17]

Crowds packed her funeral, with both the mayor and the governor seated prominently in the front church pew. Her burial plot was donated by the Colorado Pioneer Association. A stained-glass portrait of Clara now hangs in the Old Supreme Court Chambers in Denver. She is memorialized at the Smithsonian. Dr. George Junne, a professor at the University of Northern Colorado, said of her, "People like Clara Brown are rare. She saw her role in the world not as 'I' or 'me' against 'them,' but as 'us' and 'we.' It was the way that she lived her life that garnered her the amount of respect that she received."[18]

He continued, "She took Christianity to mean for someone to be Christ-like if they were a Christian. And I joke with my students that there are people who go to the church, to the mosque, to the temple, and there are those that follow their religion. And those are not necessarily the same people."

One of the many women's clubs Clara belonged to passed a resolution after her death that read: "Resolved, that we sincerely mourn the loss of this noble woman whose many acts of benevolence made her presence like an angel's visit, and may Heaven amply reward her in the unknown land beyond the range."[19]

When people were at their most vulnerable—sick, poor, about to give birth, desperately lonely—Clara Brown could be trusted. A woman with hands and feet that embodied what it meant to be just, peaceful, good, and free. A woman with a kindly face, tall and strong, who lived out the American virtues perhaps better than any president or founding father, perhaps better than anyone whose bust is preserved in the marble statuary of a namesake library. A woman, too, who saw opportunity for herself and for others and had the fortitude to forge ahead, not knowing where the path would lead.

☆

The Next Needed Thing

————

FOUR

VIRGINIA RANDOLPH

Virginia, 1890

Virginia stood at the back of the church, her serious, spectacled face staring at the preacher in the pulpit.

"If you're with me, then sign this petition!" the preacher roared.

"Amen!" someone in the crowd responded.

Sweat dripped from the preacher's brow. "Our children are not going to be taught how to be slaves any longer! They are not any less than any of the children sitting in the white schools!"

Virginia's heartbeat was loud in her ears.

"I'll sign it!" one man cried, leaping out of his seat. The church thrummed with anger, parents eager to attach their names to the petition to save their children, to rescue them from the clutches of a caste system that shut African Americans out of opportunity and equal justice.

Virginia looked around nervously and slowly raised her hand: "Wait," she said. "Wait a second." She caught the preacher's eye.

Shhhhh, she heard the women of the church signal. *Shhhhh*.

Virginia knew she was a double agent at this meeting. Not a spy, but a person forced, by necessity, to serve two masters. And everyone here hated her for it.

Twenty years prior to that meeting in the country church, Virginia was born in Richmond, Virginia, to parents who had been enslaved.[1] The streets she played on as a girl straddled an invisible chasm between the Union and the Confederacy, between bondage and freedom, between the blue and the gray.

Virginia's father, Edward, was a bricklayer, and when he died, he left his wife with four young daughters to raise. Virginia's baby sister was but a month old, and her mother went into shock from grief and disbelief. Mama Sarah barely slept, tending to her new baby, devoting every spare moment to taking in laundry, to knitting and sewing and cooking, to make sure that her four daughters—born not into the clutches of enslavement like she was, but into the hands of liberty—had what she never did. An education.

But Virginia did poorly in school when she began at age six. "I couldn't learn my alphabet," Virginia recalled in her later years. Her teacher was so frustrated by Virginia's inability to memorize and repeat *ABCDEFG* that she eventually gave up and just gave her a book to read, and found that she could. "By the end of the term, I received a medal for the highest honor."[2]

At eight, Virginia was forced to get a job to help make ends meet. She walked to her neighbor Mrs. Powell's house in the predawn hours, and started the fire, swept the floors, washed the dishes. When it was time for school, she left to attend third grade, and then fourth and then fifth, returning to Mrs. Powell's each afternoon after completing her lessons to resume her housework.

Mama Sarah worked outside the home, but she also washed and ironed clothes for five white families, sometimes staying up all night to make sure the dresses and work shirts were done on time. "Cleanliness is next to Godliness," Sarah often repeated to her passel of growing daughters. "Just do the next needed thing," she reminded herself when her feet throbbed and her back refused to straighten. *Make sure your children have better than you did.*

Imagine, then, the pride that swelled in Sarah's chest when Virginia attended Richmond Colored Normal School and became a qualified teacher at age sixteen.[3]

It was technically illegal for Virginia to get a job as a teacher at sixteen. But she found a school in Goochland County desperate for a warm body in the classroom, and she talked her uncle into vouching for her. He promised the school he would keep an eye on the teenage Virginia.

Virginia believed that she was born in 1874. Her parents were emancipated as adults, and it's probable they didn't know their own legal birthdays, and highly likely they were illiterate. Remembering the precise birth year of their children may not have been a priority or a possibility. But county records show baby Virginia was probably born in 1870, and that, later, she died in 1958.[4]

Richmond was a city that just years before Virginia's birth had served as the capital of the Confederate States of America and had been home to its president, Jefferson Davis. Richmond was the city in which Patrick Henry, the founding father known as the "lion of liberty," said, "I will not, I cannot, justify owning slaves," but who never freed any of the human beings under his control. Richmond was where he launched the phrase "Give me liberty or give me death!" in an impassioned speech in 1775, while never offering liberty to the people he enslaved. Liberty was apparently only for me, but not for thee.

Virginia's last name, Randolph, was one she shared with Virginia royalty. Her ancestors were likely enslaved by one of the prominent first families of Virginia, and the people in the pews of that country church signing the petition probably knew it. For more than one hundred years before the North American colonies broke with Great Britain, the name Randolph meant something. The Randolphs of Virginia owned eleven large plantations and more than ten thousand acres of land. Their quasi-corporate conglomerate solidified their interests in shipping, farming, politics, and the law.[5] The people who could trace their enslaved ancestry directly back to a Randolph property formed an association, and held periodic reunions after manumission.

When the preacher called for people to sign a petition to get rid of Virginia Randolph, when the folks in that country church tried to rise up, Virginia felt betrayed. She was one of them. Her parents had been enslaved just like their parents had been enslaved. She was poor just like they were poor. She worked just like they worked. She wanted what they wanted: for their children to have everything they never did. Freedom. Justice. Opportunity. The fact that the congregants couldn't see it yet just meant she had more work to do.

Virginia stared into the preacher's eyes and saw into his soul. Hers was a practical, no-nonsense manner, her mouth set in a purse, one eyebrow slightly raised. Her expression said that said she did not suffer fools.

She waited until the crowd was quiet, watchful, and then spoke with a measured voice: "We are here to help each other." The room was still. "I have been appointed by the School Board as a teacher, and the church and school should be helping each other. If we are teaching right religion, we should be helping each other." She paused, feeling dozens of eyes boring into her. "Insinuations don't help."[6] She turned purposefully on her heel and walked out of the church, head high, without stopping to see how the crowd reacted.

Virginia received a note of apology from the minister. Written neatly on a folded sheet, it read, *Sorry for the trouble, Miss. God bless you.* But Pandora's box had been opened, and the congregants marched the petition calling for her expulsion down to the county office. They didn't want Miss Randolph as teacher anymore—she wasn't providing the kind of education they thought their children should have. They wanted their young ones to receive exactly the same education as the white children.

The secretary accepted the petition with a shrug, likely saying, "We'll look into it," and "Thanks for dropping this off," but she chuckled after they left. She knew that there was no one to replace Miss Randolph, and that the white powers that be loved her. No one was going anywhere.

After her beginnings as a teenage teacher in Goochland County, Virginia Randolph took a job at the Mountain Road School in Henrico County when she was only twenty, and it was there that the trouble began and the petition to get rid of her was filed.[7] Some parents kept their children home from school, believing the young Miss Randolph to be serving the wrong master.

The parents worried that her teaching methods were preparing their children for a lifetime of labor, not of learning. Harvesting wild honeysuckle vines and weaving them into baskets? Building chairs out of scrap wood she foraged from the white schools? Cooking lessons? *Who was this benefiting*, the parents thought. *Surely only the white folks, who wanted cheap labor.*

Virginia was skating on perilously thin ice.

Only a few children were attending school regularly, and she had recently scolded one of them for getting into a scuffle with another boy. The morning after the altercation, she heard her students, squirrelly after their arrival, call out, "Someone's here, Miss Randolph! There's a lady outside!"[8]

On the front steps of the one room school, she discovered the mother of the boy she had admonished the day before, and Virginia was blanketed with a sense of dread. This mother had personally whipped every teacher her children ever had. Her reputation preceded her, and here she stood, inches from Virginia, holding a stick that was taller than her body. Virginia hid her fear, nodding a polite "Good morning."

"I need to speak to you," the mother said sharply, motioning for her to come outside.

"Walk right in," said Virginia, her hand indicating that she was in control here, not the mother. "I'll speak with you in a moment." Her steady voice belied the terror in her throat. "Wait until we have devotions." Virginia began the class with Scripture verses, her eyes fixed on the Bible alone so she wouldn't have to look at the mother who was there to whip her. Virginia chose I Corinthians 13:1: "Though I speak with the tongues of men and of angels, and have not charity, I am become as sounding brass, or a tinkling cymbal."

Virginia's eyes darted across the page. "And though I have the gift of prophecy, and understand all mysteries, and all knowledge; and though I have all faith, so that I could remove mountains, and have not charity, I am nothing. . . .'"

The children recited the verses aloud as the woman waited impatiently in the back of the room. Virginia didn't allow for even a moment's break in the action. "Children," she said quickly, "I am going to pray."

"Lord," Virginia continued, frightened that this woman was about to beat her in front of her students, "Have mercy on this dear mother that has come to the school. We are so glad to see her here today." She knew the mother was waiting for a moment to seize, and Virginia wasn't going to give it to her.

"And now children, we shall sing." Virginia launched into the first verse of "I Need Thee Ev'ry Hour." She hit the chorus like she was pleading for her life:

I need Thee, oh, I need Thee;
Ev'ry hour I need Thee;
Oh bless me now, my Savior,
I come to Thee

The children thought they were done, but no. Virginia began the second verse. And then she motioned for them to join her in singing the chorus again. Desperate to fill up the time, Virginia had them sing the third verse, and then again, the chorus, and by the time they reached verse four, the children were side-eyeing each other with *What the heck is going on?* glances.

Virginia drew out the fourth version of the chorus, singing the last line slowly and with great emphasis, the clock ticking away the seconds: *I commmmmmmme toooooooooo Theeeeeeeeeeeee.*

Finally, she could read no more verses and say no more prayers. The hymn had been milked beyond its useful life. Virginia perked up her voice, as though she were going to share the most wonderful news with her class. "Now children, I know you all feel proud that this is the first mother that has been to school. She is a mother with two lovely children, and you know the hand that rocks the cradle rules the world. Children, don't you feel *proud*? I am going to ask her to speak to us."

Virginia gestured for the mother to come to the front of the class, hoping to distract her from her mission of rage. The mother moved slowly. As she approached, Virginia saw tears in her eyes. "I came for one thing," she said quietly. "And found quite another."[9]

When the mother left the schoolroom, she leaned the switch against the gate as she closed it.

And here is the part where you might roll your eyes, because you will probably think this is too syrupy to be realistic. But sometimes real things are worse than you can imagine, and sometimes they are far sweeter. Later, the mother hung a picture of Virginia in her house, bestowing upon the young teacher a place of honor on the wall. And then she began to volunteer at the school.

One by one, Virginia began to win parents over.

When Virginia first arrived at the tiny Mountain Road School, it was little more than a shack stuck in a pit of red mud. State spending on Black education across the southern United States, especially in rural areas, was sometimes less than one-third of what was spent on white children, if they spent money at all.[10] The school year was far shorter for Black children, averaging only four months a year. Enrollment and literacy rates were low. Black parents were eager for their children to become educated, but rightfully distrustful of the government's intentions in the Jim Crow South. Transportation was more than an inconvenience—it was often an arduous task, with children sometimes being forced to walk six to ten miles to and from school. Many children couldn't be spared from helping the family subsist.

From as far back as she could remember, Virginia had been taught to do the next needed thing. *Don't worry about tomorrow*, her mother reminded her, *tomorrow will worry about itself.* Virginia was always focused on the task at hand. *What I could do next*, Virginia thought as she arrived at school one morning, *is fix this godforsaken driveway.* The approach to the school was deeply rutted, the thick clay mud forming canyons that could twist an ankle if you stepped wrong. When it rained, as it did with regularity in the humid state of Virginia, it became nearly impassable.

Virginia decided to invest one quarter of her meager month's salary on gravel to keep wheels—and the children's shoes—from getting stuck in the mud. She hauled it herself, spreading it smoothly with a rake.[11]

The next needed thing was whitewashing the building, which she did, thoroughly. She planted flowers, borrowing clippings from neighbors that eventually grew into a profusion of climbing vines that covered the front wall of the school. She asked around for grass seed to create a place for children to sit and eat their lunches in the sun.

With each passing month, she did what she could with what she had. With scrap lumber, she taught the children how to build a fence around the front garden. They moved on to a more complicated arbor, planting flowers for color and vegetables for food. She held an Arbor Day celebration, purchasing twelve sycamore trees with her own money and planting them behind the school. They named the trees for the twelve apostles. (Years later, one tree had to be cut down when they were making room for a new building. Guess which one of the twelve apostle trees had to be axed. You're right. It was Judas.)[12]

And yet, despite all of her beautification efforts, some of the parents continued to grumble that her methods of teaching Black children to be "industrious" and to learn useful skills that she felt would help them find employment later was not rigorous enough. They wanted learning based on books and intellectual pursuits, exactly like white children received, and Miss Randolph wanted to educate "the hands, the eyes, the feet, and the soul."[13] To some Black parents, this was code for a second-class education for second-class citizens.

"Did you hear that she brought a cooking stove to school and taught the girls how to serve coffee and tea?" Mothers whispered to each other. It wasn't a lie: Virginia had arrived at a neighbor's house early one morning and together they loaded the still-warm-from-breakfast cooking stove into a wagon. Girls sewed themselves white aprons that covered their dresses from shoulder to near hem, washing, ironing, and starching them into crisp perfection.

We know some of these things that Virginia did thanks to her school superintendent, Jackson Davis, who was an amateur photographer. More than six thousand of his photographs are now in the library collection at the University of Virginia. In fact, many of the images we have of education in the rural South during the turn of the century were taken by Jack Davis, obviously a man who was well-off enough to travel around with a camera, taking and developing thousands of unique images. Photography has never been an inexpensive hobby. Through his eye, we see Virginia and her small charges, doing the hard work of inventing Black education for a new century.

FIVE

HENRICO COUNTY

Virginia, 1907

Jackson Davis—like other whites in Henrico County—was eating what Virginia Randolph was cooking. (And let me save you the trouble: it's pronounced hen-RYE-co.) She represented the Booker T. Washington method of education, and Washington was by far the most famous Black educator of the time period. He was the head of the Tuskegee Institute, a premier institution for industrial education, and he advocated for Black self-help. His was not the Black empowerment of rattling protests and fiery-tongued messages decrying white supremacy. He didn't serve messages of full equality and integration, but of good citizenship, literacy, and job skills, which, over time, he believed would help the economic status of Black people.

Davis reached out to a philanthropic fund that had recently been established, called the Jeanes Fund. The fund, which counted among its officers people like Booker T. Washington and William Howard Taft, was founded by a northerner who wanted to assist small country schools that served Black children in the South. In his inquiry, Jackson Davis said that if the fund would provide the money, he should like to use it for the salary of a supervising teacher, someone who would travel all over Henrico County and assist other Black teachers.

Jackson Davis already had a supervising teacher in mind, someone who was doing the kind of work he wanted to see replicated throughout Henrico County: Virginia Randolph. And when the Jeanes Fund agreed to allocate the money for what would become known as a Jeanes Supervising Teacher, this "yes" changed the course of history.

Virginia Randolph said:

> Maybe I was chosen [as the first supervising Jeanes teacher] because of desire and interest in helping my people learn how to become good and productive citizens. Maybe I was chosen because I could do things with my hands. Maybe I was a good Christian. Maybe I was chosen because I did not mind traveling in the country under the circumstances that existed during the second decade of the twentieth century.
>
> However, I would like to think I was chosen because I was a good teacher, and needed to share my knowledge and skills with others. I believe this because after my appointment, I came to realize how very different my school and community were from others in Henrico County, Virginia. . . . When Mr. Jackson Davis appointed me to look after his Negro schools . . . he started a trend never to be abandoned; namely, the trend that there will always be someone caring and looking out for the education of Negro boys and girls. I leave the convictions of my parents as the heritage—a genuine belief in the power and glory of education.[1]

Randolph was so successful in her role as a supervising teacher that Jackson Davis documented her work and sent what he called the "Henrico Plan" to thousands of other districts across the South. Requests began to pour into the Jeanes Fund: "How do we apply for funding to get our own Jeanes teacher?" (And if you're wondering why they were called Jeanes teachers, just you wait. It's a good story.)

Perhaps Miss Randolph quoted Booker T. Washington to her students: "The world cares very little about what you or I know, but it cares a great deal about what you or I do."[2] And so, when Virginia or Booker or the thousands of other teachers like them said to Black parents, "This is how our community will uplift itself. We will create our own economic opportunities," some parents agreed. They could see the wisdom in this approach, that the best way to advance in society was through hard work, and soon, that would lead to equality of opportunity.

But other thinkers at the time, like W. E. B. Du Bois, vehemently disagreed. They criticized Booker T. Washington for accommodating white supremacy, for begging for money from robber barons, for refusing to fight for civil rights, and for sacrificing true equality on the altar of industrial education and job opportunities. "The slave went free; stood a brief moment in the sun; then moved back again toward slavery," Du Bois wrote. "Children learn more from what you are than from what you teach."[3]

Early twentieth-century thinkers like Du Bois saw people like Virginia as double agents: scraping and bowing to whites to get things they wanted, like books for schools, while simultaneously saying to Black communities that they stood in solidarity with them. "No man can serve two masters," the preachers quoted from Matthew 6:24, "for either he will hate the one, and love the other; or else he will hold to the one, and despise the other."

Virginia didn't have time to settle this debate. Her focus was on the children before her, the eager bodies perched on rickety chairs, their families barely eking out a meager living. What did they need, right now? To learn to read, so they could get better jobs and raise their standards of living. To have skills that people would pay for. And if she had to act nice to some rich folks in town to get her families what was necessary, then she was not above it.

But if she was going to be successful at Mountain Road School, people were going to have to get to know her. They say it's hard to hate someone up close, and so each Sunday, Virginia began showing up at the country churches, sometimes steering her little buggy more than an hour each way to say, "Hello, good morning," to each parishioner. When the preacher would call for announcements, she would plead her case to the congregation: "Good morning, y'all. It's so nice to be with you. I am Miss Randolph over at the Mountain Road School." Sometimes there were groans. "I am here to show you what the children have been working on this week." Often, she would bring a chair that they had recaned or a platter of rolls they had baked to share. "And while we're learning the virtue of hard work, we're also learning how to read and do sums. The children like coming to school, and they need to learn. I am here after the service if you have any questions."

She showed up at every community event she could, and when I tell you that she spent *years* gaining the trust of the community, I mean *years*. Years it took, putting the miles on her feet and on the buggy wheels. Years of visibility, years of effort. Years of dropping off a loaf of bread at a sick woman's house, years of teaching the children to sew sheets, only to secretly leave them on the porch of a family who had none, refusing to embarrass them. Years of organizing a Willing Workers Club to plant flowers, whitewash the houses of the elderly, and perform other tasks for money that would go directly back to the school.[4]

Slowly, parents began to warm to her, so she expanded her programs. She formed a Sunday School at the schoolhouse and brought in a preacher. The preacher taught the Bible while the teacher helped the parents learn to read. When she realized most of her students received no medical care, she brought nurses to the school to do health checks. She arranged for a dentist to see people who needed it, paid for mostly with money the students raised by selling baked goods, produce, or handcrafts. She taught classes for parents in the evening on cooking and public-health topics. She paid home visits to anyone who caught her attention. New baby? Leg wound? Lost job? You could count on Miss Randolph to show up at your house as soon as she could.

Methodist minister John Wesley may have coined the phrase "Cleanliness is next to godliness," but the concepts of personal hygiene and spiritual purification existed for many thousands of years before Protestantism came on the scene. Virginia believed in it wholeheartedly. She told her students, "When I was growing up, we struggled. We lived in one room only. We couldn't afford fuel for the fire, but the man at the wood yard would let us kids gather buckets of wood chips off the ground and carry them home to burn. Even then, cleanliness was next to godliness."[5] The subtext of what she was telling her students was, "No excuses. If I can do it, so can you."

Virginia, who never married, saved her money. And with her money, she began to buy land, using her savings as a down payment. To cover the rest, she took out loans: "I was always in debt," she recalled years later, and as parcels of land near the school became available, an acre here, five acres there, she bought them, ultimately accruing 13.5 acres.[6] When the land was paid for, she deeded it back to the county so it would belong to the school.

By 1915, the single-room school was bursting at the seams with children wanting to learn, and they had to tear it down to build a four-room school in its place. Most of the money for the new school was raised by the school community, not provided by Henrico County. The community milled the lumber, volunteered their time, held fundraisers, sacrificed, and saved to make it happen.[7] More teachers came on board, with Virginia acting as principal as well as classroom educator.

When I learned about Virginia's property acquisitions in a Richmond newspaper article, I have to tell you, I had a mixed reaction. Part of me was deeply moved at Virginia's contribution and that she was always in personal debt so that her students would have better opportunities, so that the school could be expanded and dormitories built for children who lived far away. Virginia didn't want the barrier of distance to keep them from receiving an education.

And the other part of me was angry. I was mad that Henrico County allowed a teacher, who they paid far less than white teachers, or even Black male teachers, to spend her own money on the land she deeded to them. They just accepted it as a gift without compensation. If the land was for sale and the school needed to be expanded, Henrico County could have purchased it. They could have offered to pay Virginia Randolph the fair market value for the property. Virginia could have leased it to them and made income on the property while continuing to build equity. She could have sold that property to pay for her retirement. But they took advantage of her. They would never have expected a white teacher to buy land to further the educational opportunities of their communities. Even the dormitories were funded by Virginia and the other teachers at the school, who pooled their money in 1924 to see them built.

The worst day of Virginia's life came in 1929. By then, her little Mountain Road School had been renamed the Virginia Randolph Training Academy, and it had expanded to include multiple buildings. A kitchen was added to serve the children fresh meals, and the school now enrolled 235 students, 75 of whom were in high school.[8] Virginia had no way of knowing that the stock market would soon crash—all she knew is that her world crashed on a February day when she received word that her primary school building, the gardens, the memories, the sweat of her brow, the callus of her hands: everything was on fire.

Virginia collapsed when she glimpsed the fire consuming her life's work, the flames slowly growing in intensity, eating a hole in the roof of the wooden structure, devouring the grass and the arbor, snaking its way through everything she had sacrificed for.

She shouted at the fire, screamed at it. "How dare you! I won't let you take it!" Women gathered around her, circling her like a wagon train, enclosing what was precious in their midst, safeguarding her from having to watch everything go up in flames.

"No!" she sobbed. "Please don't take this from me . . . please."

Soon, it was gone. A newspaper report in the *Richmond Times-Dispatch* said that no "inmates" at the school were hurt, but that there was nothing the fire department could do.[9] *Her school. Her namesake.* Years—decades— of her life, reduced to a pile of smoldering ash.

One of the women yelled for a child standing nearby: "Go get the doctor."

For a week, Virginia was so distraught that she was under a physician's care, likely given a barbiturate to help her sleep. Each time she opened her eyes, images of the fire roared before them. She saw the men running for water, heard the fire engine, envisioned the children trying in vain to help, their little limbs straining under the weight of a single bucket. She gasped for air as the vise of grief gripped her small and mighty body. "Give her one of these when she wakes up," the doctor had instructed one of Virginia's friends.[10]

"No," Virginia whispered as she roused from her sleep, "please don't take this from me . . ."

"Here, mama. Here." She heard the voice of her friend nearby. "Drink this." Virginia tried to swallow what was offered, but she spluttered. There seemed to be no space in her throat for water. "You're okay," her friend said. "Take some deep breaths." Each day swallowing the pills got a little easier, each day Virginia welcomed the sweet relief of sleep that they brought. After seven days, the doctor advised that she stop taking them, but that she still needed time to take it easy.

With her mind cleared, Virginia realized there was not time to rest, because things needed doing. There were children to be taught, and she wasn't going to lose the rest of the school year. She rose from bed in the cool of the morning, the dew dampening her feet as she approached the site of her beloved school. Tears pooled in her eyes when she smelled the char of the wood that used to be her students' desks, their books, worn from wear, the papers where they practiced forming the letter Q with the perfect flourish, where they learned how to divide twelve by four. But on that morning, Virginia didn't linger. What was the next needed thing? To finish the school year so her students wouldn't fall behind. To support the teachers she guided in their important work. They had lost a lot too.

Virginia, who had for several years been the Supervisor of Negro Education in Henrico County, asked herself every day, "What is the next needed thing?" And soon, the answer came: make plans to rebuild the school. Some of the money came from the families themselves, collections taken up in offering plates at school and in the churches, bake sales bringing in nickels and dimes, exhibits of household goods the children made, with all proceeds benefiting the school rebuilding fund.

Some of the money was kicked in by Henrico County, and some came from a wealthy northern philanthropist. The new school building went up, brick by brick. This one would have a library and an auditorium. The construction was finished by 1930, but it would never replace what was lost. "I worked so hard, and just to think I could not save either building. God knows what I feel. I will never get over it," Virginia lamented.[11]

I would be remiss if I failed to mention that Virginia not only created a thriving educational community for African Americans in Henrico County; she also took in children. The 1930 census says she had fourteen adopted children, and at various times she had as many as twenty.[12] To be sure, adoption in 1930 often meant something different, and possibly less permanent, than it does now. It's quite likely that she either took in children who couldn't stay with their own families because of abuse or poverty, or that families gave Virginia temporary custody of their child so they could attend school. Adoption in 1930 most often did not mean the complete severing of ties with a child's birth family. It meant that someone was caring for a child not their own, either in the short term or for the long. One of Virginia's former pupils, Mildred Holley, counted eighty-seven children, including herself, who lived with Virginia at one time or another. In recalling it, her voice cracks: "I don't think I would have finished school or anything else if it hadn't been for her."[13]

Some children came from as far away as New York to attend the Virginia Randolph Training Academy, and Virginia didn't just teach them to multiply and write their names, she mothered them. She worked with the court system to create a program for youth who were in trouble with the law, setting them on the straight and narrow and ensuring they attended school. She boarded teachers who didn't have anywhere to live, and she appears to have permanently adopted one daughter.

How did she support all of them, when she herself admitted to never having any money? One way was selling bread. She got up at 4:30 a.m. to bake, kneading dough and pulling steaming loaves out of the oven before the sun rose, but by her fifty-fifth year as a teacher, she had cut back to baking and selling bread only two days a week—Saturday and Sunday.[14]

In 1938, Virginia made a move to buy a fifty-acre farm and farmhouse adjacent to the school. She intended to use the farmhouse as a boy's dormitory, and the fields to teach the boys how to farm. The Great Migration had sent hundreds of thousands of African Americans to the North and the West, to cities like New York and Chicago, where they sought economic opportunity and to leave behind the discrimination they faced under oppressive Jim Crow laws. Farming had understandably been discarded by the vast majority of Black Americans, in part because they were denied the opportunity to purchase property, but Virginia wanted to show her rural students how to be self-sufficient.

Dr. Samuel Chiles Mitchell, a professor of history at the University of Richmond, wrote an article in the *Richmond Times-Dispatch* in 1938 encouraging the county to help Virginia pay off the mortgage on the farm.

He wrote, "She has paid, so far, about $14,000 on this farm, and as yet, owes about $6,000, covered by a mortgage. It would be a gracious act if the supervisors of Henrico County, Manager Day, and the Board of Education, could see their way clear to lift this mortgage, which is breaking the back of Virginia Randolph. Mark you, all the property she buys, she deeds to the county. It is ours."[15]

Dr. Mitchell wasn't even advocating for Henrico County to pay the fair market value for the farm, he was merely advocating for them to cover little more than a quarter of the cost, and then the land would be theirs. Two years later, the newspaper reported that the county agreed to pay the remaining $5,000 of the mortgage (by that point, she had paid $15,000), and that Virginia "embraced" County Manager Day when he gave her the money to pay off the mortgage.

I gather Virginia likely saw this differently than I do, but . . . the audacity. The audacity of Henrico County to take the money of an elderly woman and then act like they were doing her some kind of giant favor by helping her pay off one quarter of the mortgage on the land that was soon to be theirs.

So often stories like Virginia Randolph's point out the incredibly selfless act of an individual, and make no mistake, I can think of few people more selfless than Miss Randolph. We are taught to admire the impact they had on their community, and we should, because her impact cannot be measured. But we ignore the racist systems that led to Virginia turning over what should have been her life savings back to the county, and for them to willingly take it from her, without compensation. Henrico County didn't give Virginia $5,000, they paid $5,000 for a fifty-acre farm and a house, and she, an underpaid teacher who had to bake bread to cover her living expenses, paid the rest.

There is still a Virginia Randolph educational campus in Henrico County today. And it was conceived of, worked for, and paid for by a woman whose name deserves to be in the pantheon of great American educators. Samuel Mitchell wrote in 1938, "Her work ranks with that of Booker T. Washington. It has lacked the spectacular element that attaches to the great principal of Tuskegee; but in significance, it surpasses, in some ways, even his achievements. Virginia Randolph has done the common thing in an uncommon way. . . . The work of a single woman is a focal point in the social history of the South."[16]

Virginia was so beloved that her methods and philosophy of schooling spread far and wide. She traveled and trained other teachers on how to approach education as something that must address the whole child, their family, and the community at large. She viewed schools not merely as a place to gain literacy but as tools to fight systemic poverty.

In the reports that she wrote about the schools she visited, she outlined her philosophy:

> This work should begin in the primary grades and continue as long as the children remain in school. The destiny of our race depends, largely, upon the training the children receive in the schoolroom, and how careful we should be. The great majority of the children in the country schools will never reach a high school, therefore we must meet the demands of the schools in the Rural Districts by introducing this phase of training in every schoolroom.
>
> It must be impressed upon the minds of the pupils that "Cleanliness is next to Godliness" and when this law of Hygiene is obeyed, they have conquered a great giant. They must also see that their schoolroom is neat and attractive with curtains at their windows, pictures on the walls, stoves kept neatly polished, and the grounds neat and clean, have a book on the "Laws of Health" hung in the schoolroom and each child be made to make himself familiar with it. The teacher should also give instructions along these lines which will be of great benefit because the teachers are models for the school-room.[17]

Virginia didn't retire from teaching until 1949, after nearly sixty years of devoted service, each day doing the next needed thing. She was born during Reconstruction, after the Union was nearly wrenched in two, but held. She lived through World War I and the worldwide flu pandemic—the two events killing seventy million people across the globe in a few short years. She watched the Great Depression whisk livelihoods and homes out from under the feet of millions of Americans.

She worked as Hitler invaded the Sudetenland, as the United States was attacked at Pearl Harbor, as millions of Jews were killed across Europe, as the United States dropped atomic weapons on Japan. She saw her Black friends and neighbors get drafted into a military that was segregated, and she saw them come home changed men.

Virginia heard the news of the 1954 Supreme Court order that required schools to be integrated, and saw neighboring Prince Edward County, a mere seventy-five miles away, close their public schools for five years, paying for private religious school tuition for white students, and none for Black students.

By the time Virginia's frail body gave out in March 1958, she had seen Rosa Parks refuse to give up her seat and a bus boycott in Montgomery, Alabama, that lasted far longer and achieved far more than anyone imagined was possible. Her namesake elementary school and high school had seven hundred students. More buildings were added, including a home economics cottage that is now a small tribute museum. As one of her students, Louise Cunningham, said when the new brick building was dedicated: "The story of the growth of a one room school on a red clay hill . . . is truly as fascinating as an old medieval legend.

"A modern architect can present, upon request, the plans for the building, but the master copy was drafted in the heart of a quiet, determined . . . girl, who had a vision of today."[18]

Virginia was later reinterred at the site of the campus that still bears her name. Her headstone reads: "She helped people of all races. A pioneer educator, a humanitarian, and a creative leader in the field of education. Her influence throughout the world will continue to live."

Though this story conjures long-ago times when buggies crossed the dirt roads of segregated Virginia, history is alive. Some of Miss Randolph's former students now play with their own grandchildren, enjoying the verdant spring and the muggy summer weather. One of them, Richard Harris, said, "Miss Randolph was a warrior for what she believed in. Miss Randolph was a warrior for Black boys and girls. She would get on the stage and she would give us a pep talk, 'You can do it, you can be somebody. Education is your way out.' You could hear a pin drop. And even as kids, we knew that was wisdom we should listen to."[19]

And history professor Samuel Mitchell wanted the public to know this: in 1908, when Photographer/Superintendent Jackson Davis wrote about the accomplishments of Miss Randolph and created the Henrico Plan, he began with a sentence that Mitchell says has become part of the history of America.

"I have secured Miss Virginia Randolph as the teacher."[20]

That single act did more for tens of thousands of children and teachers all over the South, more for justice, more for peace, more for goodness, and more for the liberation of Americans than anyone could have imagined.

☆

America the Beautiful

SIX

KATHARINE LEE BATES

Cape Cod, 1859

A s one of his final acts, Katharine's father baptized her. Though he didn't know it in 1859, there was a tumor growing on his spine, a malady that caused excruciating pain for which there was little remedy. By the time baby Katie was four weeks old, he was dead. Left behind was his wife, Cornelia, the four children she would now have to provide for on her own, and the Congregationalist Church he had pastored on Cape Cod.[1]

Tracing her family tree back to the 1400s, with relatives who sailed for the colonies in 1635, Katie knew she came from a long line of people who moved others with their words. They were poets, lecturers, ministers, and letter writers, a community of ancestors from which to draw inspiration. Though she didn't know it yet, she would join this flock of Lees and Bateses as a woman of letters, aware of her "glimmering crew of dear and queer ancestral ghosts."[2] It was, in fact, what Katharine Lee Bates was born to do: to bring poetry into the world.

They say that when a mother gives birth, her new baby is her baby. When another child comes along, that baby becomes the baby, and the older child is moved up the line to the position of older sibling. Except for the youngest child. They always stay the baby in the eyes of their mother. Perhaps it's one of the reasons older children feel their youngest sibling gets away with murder? (Also, by the time the youngest child comes along, mama is *tired*.)

Katie was the baby, always and forever. While her older siblings were doing chores and off trying to earn money to keep their family afloat, Katie was writing in little notebooks, reading under a lilac tree, and playing with her best friend, Hattie. And yes, her mama *was* tired. Cornelia was exhausted growing vegetables on her small plot in the ground, caring for her children, and sewing for other women in Falmouth. "Where is rest to be found in this weary world?" she wrote to a friend. "I am growing a good deal in sympathy with the poor woman, who, when she was asked what was her idea of Heaven, said, 'to be able to put on a clean apron and sit down.'"[3]

Cornelia's older son, Arthur, helped keep the family in slightly less dire straits—he harvested cranberries and trapped muskrats, he caught herring and sold it to fishermen for bait, he hunted to put food on the table. The weight of being the family caretaker bore down heavily on the young boy, even though his mother did her best to prevent it.

The sea roared around the Bateses in its constant refrain. The ocean was the white noise of sleep, the warm breeze of summer, the icy spray of winter's chill. It was also the ever-present anxiety of fishermen setting off for a day's work, and the agony of those whose loved ones didn't return. Katie immortalized their town of Falmouth in her notebooks:

Never was there lovelier town
Than our Falmouth by the sea.
Tender curves of sky look down
On her grace of knoll and lea . . .

The poem goes on to reference the

Happy bell of Paul Revere,
Sounding o'er such blest demesne[4]

The Congregationalist church Katie's father left behind was the first
in Falmouth, and it's still an active congregation. It's a quintessentially
New England meetinghouse, right out of a picture postcard: white, with
a steeple. And in the steeple rings a bell forged by the one and only Paul
Revere. You probably know him as a silversmith working in Boston when
the American Revolution was in its infancy. And he was that. But he was
more. Paul Revere was a dentist. But also he made gunpowder. Paul Revere was a goldsmith. But also he engraved bookplates. Paul Revere had
sixteen children with two different women. But also only five of them
outlived him. Paul Revere was a freemason. But also a spy. Paul Revere
rode to Lexington and Concord one night in April. But also he made bells.

For all the things one could learn about Paul Revere, *he rode a horse
and shouted at people* is perhaps one of the least interesting. Revere wasn't
even the only one who rode a horse to warn troops in the distance that
the British were coming. A teenage girl did it, too, and she rode twice as
far, in the rain. She got a personal thanks from George Washington. But
Sybil Ludington didn't have a famous poem written about her, so hers is
not the name we remember.[5]

Paul Revere was the son of a Huguenot who left France because of
religious persecution. His father, Apollos Rivoire, landed in the colonies,
alone, at age thirteen. He decided to Anglicize his name to Paul Revere,
a moniker he later bestowed upon his son. Revere the elder was a goldsmith and a silversmith, a profession he taught to Revere the younger.[6]

Had Paul been born the second son, he might have gone on to college.
But he was the oldest boy, and when his father died too young, it was his

duty to carry on his father's business. He became excellent at his craft, during a time when nearly all silver buckles and tea sets were bespoke and afforded only to the wealthy. This allowed Revere to move about the upper echelons of society in ways other tradesmen could not—he was more than just a man who worked with his hands. He was an artisan, and he earned a modest but comfortable living for his growing family.

Revere started forging bells late in life, after his storied career as a dentist/silversmith/spy/midnight rider. In early America, to obtain a bell for your church or school usually meant sending away for it and taking delivery many months later, the instrument voyaging across the sea from England.

The bell in Paul's own church community had cracked, and he offered to try to fix it. It's apparently quite the endeavor, making bells. One can't just pour some metal in a mold and call it good.

For starters, bells are heavy. The largest of Revere's bells weighed over two thousand pounds, but the one he made atop Katie's home church weighed around eight hundred.[7] The bell has to be able to support its own weight, withstand extreme temperature swings, and handle being struck. Most importantly, bells have to sound right. Imagine hitting another hunk of metal with a hammer: A railcar? Your stove? It would sound like a bang, not like a substantial, resonant tone that covered the surrounding village in sound waves. A bell needs to sound like a bell, not cannon fire.

Paul Revere's bell in Falmouth, Massachusetts, was cast in 1796. The church still possesses the original receipt, written in Revere's handwriting. It says they paid $338.94. The bell waits for its cue, its chance to ring out the Sunday meeting, as it's done for more than two hundred years. It rang on the day of Katie's father's funeral in 1859, and again when the women of the congregation draped their mourning shawls over the windows after Abraham Lincoln was shot. The outside of the bell reads, "The living to the church I call, and to the grave I summon all."[8]

Katie was a bespectacled girl who grew into a bespectacled woman. Portraits of her make Katie seem serious and stern, when, in fact, there was never a dull moment in her company. When a peddler stopped by her home to offer his wares, Katie tried a pair of glasses, and to her astonishment, she could see. "There are leaves on the trees!" she exclaimed. One of her friends said that her glasses seemed to stay perched on her face as if "by a miracle."[9]

From the time she was a young child, Katie was pondering life's existential questions, like "Why do boys get to play outside and girls have to stay in and sew?" Her hatred of sewing was a recurring theme in her life. What she wanted was to learn. Book learning. She wrote that her fondest wish was to be able to read and write and go to school as much as she wanted. "I would study and study. I would know what makes the beautiful colors all around you, dear old setting sun, and I would learn all about the nations on the other side of the globe you are going to shine on now. . . . I would study and study and study and know and know and know."[10]

Her intelligent childhood mind didn't quit. "So the great question of women's rights has arisen," she wrote in 1866. "I like women better than men. I like fat women better than lean ones. . . . Girls are a very necessary part of creation. They are full as necessary as boys. Sewing is always expected of girls. Why not of boys."[11]

In her diary, she wrote out a will, divvying her possessions should anything untoward occur. She gave her friend Hattie some things, her sister some others, and she concluded the will by saying: "To my schoolmates, I give and bequeath my love, and urge them to remember the words 'life is uncertain.'"[12]

And it was.

Cornelia eventually moved her children away from Falmouth on Cape

Cod to what would later become Wellesley in central Massachusetts, to help her ailing sister. As Katie grew, everyone could see that her bright mind needed something more than a life of stitching. She wanted to attend college.

Women in the 1800s were prohibited from enrolling in many universities in the United States, but small groups of dedicated people changed that. They set out to create a system of women's seminaries and colleges, the original of which are referred to as the Seven Sisters. These were highly selective institutions with admission requirements very similar to those of all-male universities like Harvard.

Wellesley, a Seven Sisters school first chartered in 1870, had a sprawling and luxurious campus perched on a pastoral piece of former farmland. Katie was admitted to one of the first classes of attendees. Her favorite part of campus was the library, which she described as a gem, "arranged in alcoves and superbly finished throughout in solid black walnut . . . with cozy nooks and corners . . . sunny windows, some of them thrown out into deep bays; with galleries, reached by winding stairs."[13] It was regarded by many as one of the finest buildings in America at the time. The founders, Pauline and Henry Durant, spent a million dollars building the campus.[14]

Henry Durant expected women who graduated from Wellesley to be fully on par with graduates of Harvard and Yale, and his watchwords were, "Aspiration! Adventure! Experiment! Expansion! Follow the gleam!"[15]

Women's health was poorly understood at the time, and it was a common belief among men that pursuing too much education made a woman unfit for childbearing, as it diverted too great a blood supply to the brain and away from reproductive organs. Durant refuted this, arguing that a proper education strengthens the body and mind.

One of his goals was to produce a generation of female scholars who could fill the gaps left by the 750,000-plus men killed during the Civil War. To that end, Wellesley would be the only college in the nation that would have an all-female faculty, which was no small feat, given how few colleges awarded degrees to women who might become professors.

Durant was religious and required attendees to practice daily Christian devotions. Wellesley, he said, would embody "the revolt which is the real meaning of the Higher Education of Women. We revolt against the slavery in which women are held by the customs of society—the broken health, the aimless lives, the subordinate position, the helpless dependence, the dishonesties and shams of so-called education. The Higher Education of Women is one of the great world battle-cries for freedom; for right against might."[16]

Katie loved to write, and Wellesley loved her for it. She was elected class president and earned the nickname "Katie of '80," a title she held for the rest of her life. Her work began to be published regularly, including in prestigious periodicals like *The Atlantic*, which started to actively champion the writings of women. She was enamored with the work of the world-famous poet Henry Wadsworth Longfellow, and through her connections at *The Atlantic*, made his acquaintance. He told her that he had seen her poem in the magazine and liked it.[17]

Longfellow believed that to flourish as a nation, America needed its own writers. Its own literary tradition, those who knew the crests of the Atlantic's waves on the stark landscape of New England, those who knew the beat of liberty that kept time in the chests of Americans. Longfellow's work, including enduring pieces like "The Song of Hiawatha" and "The Courtship of Miles Standish," spoke to this uniquely American perspective.

And, of course, he wrote "The Midnight Ride of Paul Revere."

Perhaps Katie took Longfellow's compliment to mean that she had what he had: the courage and vision to become a great American poet, whose work wasn't just *about* America, but *for* America.

Like all women of the time, Katie's life choices were constrained by societal norms and expectations about what kinds of jobs were acceptable for women to hold. She turned to the profession of many millions of women before her: that of teacher. She didn't particularly enjoy the "suffocating atmosphere of a winter schoolroom,"[18] but she was delighted when Henry Durant offered her a position at the new Dana Hall School, the official prep school for girls who wanted to attend Wellesley College.

She continued writing, and she made a purposeful decision to center women in her poems and stories. She made famous the concept of Mrs. Claus in "A Story of Christmas Eve," and she told the editor of the *Boston Evening Transcript* that her wish was that American writers would be able to portray American women as they really were: "The Yankee smartness, the quick tact and intuition, the dry humor and love of fun, the restless, eager curiosity, the spirited independence, the sparkle and gleam that play over the surface of earnestness and energy, thoughtfulness and devoutness, passion and intensity."[19]

A new genre of literature was emerging in this time period, which for the first time began to treat childhood as a special period of life. Following in the footsteps of Louisa May Alcott and other New England writers, Katie continued to grow her body of literary work for both children and adults, and the publications she appeared in allowed her to reach tens of thousands of readers. Though her work was published next to Walt Whitman's in prestigious periodicals, she knew she would never make money unless her writing could be published in books.

When Katie was twenty-six, she gladly accepted the offer of Alice Freeman, the new president of Wellesley, to become an instructor on its faculty. That's not to say, though, that she felt qualified or ready. Despite her Ivy League equivalent education and significant publishing experience, she wrote to a friend that "I am dreading next year horribly. I am a regular coward and I would like to take to my heels and run for it."[20]

Wellesley grew, and Alice Freeman recruited other stellar female professors to meet the burgeoning demand. When Alice Freeman left

Wellesley, her final act was to promote Katie to the position of assistant professor of Literature, which helped seal Katie's career as an academic.

More than anything, Katie sought to help shape Wellesley in the vision of Henry Durant: "Gather around it all wisdom and all knowledge. Bring to it the light of all science and all truth. Study over it; pray over it; live in it; love in it; suffer for it."[21]

On a trip to visit a friend for Christmas that year, Katie was exposed to smallpox, and the subsequent quarantine allowed her enough time to write a novel for young readers, called *Rose and Thorn*. It won $700 in a writing contest, which gave her the funds to take a year off from teaching at Wellesley and to spend the year in Europe.[22] At last, her writing was propelling Katie into a larger world, well beyond the narrow confines of New England.

SEVEN

KATHARINE LEE BATES

England, 1880s

K atie set sail for England on a ship called *State of Nebraska*, and the weather on the voyage was terrible. She arrived injured from being tossed about on the boat, and sad to have left her loved ones behind for an entire year. She wrote that she arrived "blue and black and blue."[1]

In England, she explored the libraries and the countryside alike. She found a room in the British Museum dedicated to the surname Bates, and in it was delighted to discover her very own book, *Rose and Thorn*. Haunting the Gothic cathedrals, she wrestled with her faith, knowing that she believed in *something*, but unable to decide what it was exactly. There was too much presumption in theology, Katie thought. She was both jealous and suspicious of people who trusted what they were taught about God.

Meanwhile, back in the United States, new waves of immigration were remaking the face of America. Many were worried that the newcomers would take their jobs, and too often, people found themselves working in abysmal and dangerous conditions. Perched from the vantage point of the wisdom and riches of Oxford, Katie saw America differently, and clearly: the American ideal of democracy was fragile.

After Katie's year abroad, she returned home strengthened with new resolve. She earned her master's degree from Wellesley and took her place as the head of her department. But she still felt stifled by the societal expectations placed on women: "We can calculate eclipses, but we are not free from the tyranny of the needle."[2] *Again, with the sewing.* Being a female scholar had unique demands—not only were they expected to research and teach but they still had to undertake all of the domestic duties, unlike their male counterparts. Even if a woman was unmarried, she was still expected to cook and clean and stitch at home, while a man would have gotten someone else to do it for him.

Wellesley culture was unique. Here was a group of highly educated and talented women, all teaching other talented young women, and most of them, like Katie, were childless and unmarried. Many became each other's best friends, spending holidays in the common spaces of the college and traveling together in the summer. And it was here at Wellesley that Katie met her lifelong companion, Professor Katharine Coman.

Katie and Katharine lived together for over twenty years. They wrote letters to each other that are decidedly romantic. Some scholars have said that when taken in its totality, Katie and Katharine Coman were obviously in love and "together" together. A minority of others have landed in the column of, it's possible they were together, but there is no way to know for sure, because the nature of female friendship plus the Wellesley culture was very different than anything we experience today.

At the turn of the twentieth century, two women who lived together as partners were sometimes referred to as being in a "Boston marriage," with the subtext being that they were quietly in a romantic relationship.[3]

When Katie was away in England, she wrote letters to Katharine that said things like, "For I am coming back to you, my Dearest, whether I come back to Wellesley or not. You are always in my heart and in my longings. I've been so homesick for you on this side of the ocean and yet so still and happy in the memory and consciousness of you."[4]

Katharine Coman studied history, and had a particular interest in labor rights. Her research about economic history was groundbreaking—she was one of the first historians to use government documents like labor statistics in her books. She was politically active and adventurous, with a strong face and a prominent chin cleft. Katharine also had something that Katie longed for: a steadfast faith in God. Katie wished she could be sure like Katharine was. She knew that her restless mind might be stilled by a knowing faith, but belief was too elusive.

EIGHT

KATHARINE LEE BATES

Chicago, 1890s

The nation was headed toward a severe economic downturn in the 1890s, which at the time people referred to as the Great Depression. This unrest contributed to growing nativist ideas and anti-immigrant sentiment, and led to the passage of laws restricting immigration from Asian countries. Corporate monopolies were helping the rich grow richer as they paid their workers less, and corruption was at an all-time high. Grover Cleveland had been reelected president on the promise that he would help ferret out the corruption that had taken root in Washington.

In 1893, the World's Columbian Exposition was set to open in Chicago. People often wonder why we call Washington, D.C., the "District of Columbia," or why an event like this was called a "Columbian" Exposition. It has nothing to do with the country of Colombia and everything to do with Columbus, the explorer. Columbia was the female form of the name Columbus, and so "Columbia" was sometimes used as a female personification of America. (Think about the woman holding a torch aloft at the beginning of any film made by Columbia Pictures. That's her.)

Advertisements for the Expo screamed SELL THE COOKSTOVE

IF NECESSARY BUT COME.[1] Katie and Katharine were scheduled to teach summer workshops in Colorado—a chance to marry their love of travel and their need for extra funds and intellectual stimulation. (To the same extent that Katie hated sewing, she loved travel. She went abroad regularly, and the list of countries she visited was quite long.)

Their train left Massachusetts and took them first to Niagara Falls, which was the site of Nikola Tesla's incredible electrical innovations in alternating current electricity. It jostled them to sleep as they headed to see the expo, which was also billed as the White City, its alabaster structures glowing in the new light of incandescence.

The fair was huge and astonishing. There was a Liberty Bell constructed from oranges, and another from wheat, and also: the real Liberty Bell. (Why stop at just one Liberty Bell?) There was a map of the United States fashioned from pickles and a replica of the Statue of Liberty made from salt.

The Pledge of Allegiance was written especially for the fair, recited by children around a flagpole, designed to be adopted by schools nationwide to promote what some would call patriotism, and others would call a reflection of xenophobia.[2] Francis Bellamy, the author, said he was concerned about all the new immigrants pledging loyalty to their own countries of origin, and this was meant to remind them that they owed their loyalty to America only.

The fair was the United States' signal to the world: *Anything you can do, we can do better.* America, at just over one hundred years old, was fully independent, ready and willing to claim the prestige it felt it deserved to have bestowed upon its name for its artistic, technological, and commercial innovations. President Grover Cleveland said of the expo, "I cherish the thought that America stands on the threshold of a great awakening . . . as by a touch the machinery that gives life to this vast Exposition is now set in motion, so at the same instant let our hopes and aspirations awaken forces which in all time to come shall influence the dignity and the freedom of mankind."[3] He pressed a button, and in doing so set off a commotion of whistles, bells, cannons, guns, fountains, applause, and machinery.

Wealthy Bertha Palmer was the head of the "Board of Lady Managers" and was in charge of creating a building with displays to promote the accomplishments of women. She hoped it would encourage women to "step down from their pedestals, because freedom and justice for all are infinitely more desired than pedestals for a few."[4] (We also have Bertha Palmer, whose husband owned a famous Chicago hotel, to thank for the invention of the brownie, arguably one of the best treats of all time. Inside the Women's Building, box lunches were served, and Bertha Palmer directed the chef at the hotel to come up with a dessert that could withstand the jostling of delivery and the heat of the summer.)

Statues of activists loomed over the throngs of people visiting the Women's Building—Susan B. Anthony, Elizabeth Cady Stanton, and the like—and murals of women picking the fruits of Knowledge and Science decorated the walls. Exhibits demonstrated the abysmal working conditions and low wages of women, so that women could advocate for the systemic reforms that were needed. Perhaps for the first time, Katie was able to fully envision the importance of Katharine's work on labor rights. The building's library had seventy thousand volumes written by women, and orchestras performed works by female composers.

The impression made, Katie and Katharine departed Chicago and continued their journey west, across the plains and into Colorado. As their summer school drew to a close, they had the chance to ascend Pike's Peak on a cog tram, to visit Garden of the Gods, and to breathe in the landscape that was unlike anything they had seen on voyages anywhere else, with craggy sandstone rocks rising like giants out of the forest. It was a landscape that Clara Brown had helped pioneer just a few decades before.

There was nothing else like it on earth, Katie was sure, and to know it was here, in her own beloved America, stirred something inside her chest.

Katie took out her notebook, as poets do, and jotted down some lines, which she would forever describe as a moment of divine inspiration. It was perhaps the closest she had ever come to the religious faith she yearned for. She said the words "sprang into being," or they "floated into her consciousness."[5] But soon, the journey home would begin, and the notebook was tucked away. The lines didn't see the light of day for some time.

A year later, Katie revisited her travel notebook, pondering with fresh eyes what worked and what didn't. She finished off the remaining stanzas and submitted the poem to *The Congregationalist* magazine, a publication for churches like the one where her father preached all those years ago.

A short time later, she received a letter congratulating her on the poem's acceptance for publication, and she eagerly waited for the edition that contained her newest work to arrive, along with a check for five dollars.

The date was July 4, 1895.[6]

Katie's published poem was immediately beloved by Americans far and wide. It went viral before anyone knew what going viral meant. Reprint requests rolled in, which she granted for free. She began receiving letters from people insisting that the lines should be set to music, urging her to consider how much better a song would be if she helped a few lines rhyme more melodically. Deluged with requests, Katie rewrote some of the lyrics to make them easier to sing.

Once her updated version was published, a Baptist minister named Clarence Barbour read them, and he got a bee in his bonnet. This poem just had to be a song. Barbour and his wife turned to their church hymnal to look for a tune that matched the metrical index of the poem. After a number of false starts, Barbour and his wife found "Materna," and "at once I felt that this was the tune to which the words could be most wisely joined," he said.[7]

"Materna" was written by Samuel Ward, a natural-born musician who took up the accordion at six and began playing the organ so skillfully that he was hired by a Manhattan church at age sixteen. He had no formal training but taught lessons to students, directed choirs, and supported himself and his family with his musical endeavors.

Ward found inspiration in unusual places, the most famous of which was Coney Island. As he and a friend, Harry, sailed away after a visit in 1882, Coney Island gleaming like Venice in the distance, he turned to Harry and said, "If I had something to write on, I'd put down a tune that has just come to me."[8] Harry scrounged through his pockets, eventually removing a linen cuff from his shirt and handing it to Sam. Ward scratched out a staff on the piece of fabric and wrote the melody that danced through his mind.

The tune was a new setting for the hymn "O Mother Dear Jerusalem," which was already famous and sung throughout Britain and the United States.

O mother dear, Jerusalem,
When shall I come to thee?
When shall my sorrows have an end?
The joys when shall I see?

A decade later, "Materna" was published in books of Episcopal hymnals, and the choir Ward directed at Grace Episcopal sang it.

One afternoon, as Samuel walked through downtown Newark, New Jersey, he heard the angelic sounds of children singing. He recognized "Materna" and stopped and listened, moved by the melody. When he got home, he told his wife wistfully, "It really is a lovely hymn."[9]

———

Lake Avenue Baptist in Rochester, New York, likely became the first congregation in the world to sing Katie's poetic verses set to Samuel Ward's melody. It was such a hit with the congregants that the elementary school principal included it in the commencement exercises the following week. It spread throughout Rochester, then the rest of New York and the rest of the country.

In 1911, Katharine Lee Bates, our Katie, published the final version of her best-known masterpiece, one that struck a chord in the hearts of Americans, as conflict darkened the doorstep of Europe. A conflict that would eventually burst into the flames that would consume Europe and singe America too.

> O beautiful for spacious skies,
> For amber waves of grain,
> For purple mountain majesties
> Above the fruited plain!
> America! America!
> God shed His grace on thee
> And crown thy good with brotherhood
> From sea to shining sea!

Though her poem was bringing joy across the country, the next few years were dark ones for Katie and Katharine. They were living together in a house that they had designed and dubbed the Scarab, working at their dream jobs at Wellesley, content with their charming pets and their wide circle of friends. But everything changed in 1912, when Katharine Coman found a lump in her breast.[10]

Cancer was a word spoken about in whispers in the early twentieth century. Some people mistakenly believed it was contagious, others found it shameful. Doctors recommended that Katharine undergo a radical mastectomy, which involved removing all of her breast tissue, the surrounding lymph nodes, and large portions of her pectoral muscles. At a minimum, Katharine would be permanently disabled with the loss of much of her chest. She also faced the very real possibility of living the rest of her life in crippling pain.

Katie became the first known person to write a breast cancer narrative, as she watched her beloved suffer through the surgery. Katharine recuperated at home, surrounded by their collie and their friends. She never returned to her full quality of life, but she had it better than most breast cancer patients of the time, who were typically shuttered away in darkened rooms, hidden from society.[11]

Once, I found myself sitting in the warm September sunshine on the lawn of the White House, the porticos of the West Wing guarded by dozens of serious men and women in sunglasses and suits. The seal of the United States draped the familiar columns before me, the Washington Monument stood sentinel at my back. I listened as James Taylor invited everyone to sing Katie's words set to Samuel's melody of quiet majesty. Tears blurred my vision as his kind, familiar voice began, and around me, all the assembled voices of politicians and dignitaries, workers and aides, joined in, hesitant at first, and then with growing conviction, giving voice to the ideals and dreams that we all nurse in our most secret American hearts.

The themes Katie loved are all there: the beauty of nature, the hope for the future, the unlimited potential of America. She vividly remembered the news of Lincoln's assassination when she was a child. As an adult, she marveled at the miracle of a radio broadcast from Antarctica.

O beautiful for pilgrim feet,
Whose stern, impassioned stress
A thoroughfare for freedom beat
Across the wilderness!
America! America!
God mend thine every flaw,
Confirm thy soul in self-control,
Thy liberty in law!

Each stanza begins with an appreciation of what America is and has done. It crescendos into a moment of passion for her beloved country, and ends in a prayer for the future.

O beautiful for heroes proved
In liberating strife,
Who more than self their country loved
And mercy more than life!
America! America!
May God thy gold refine,
Till all success be nobleness,
And every gain divine!

Unlike "The Star-Spangled Banner," which is difficult to sing and deeply rooted in military imagery, "America the Beautiful" is about the land of America and her people.

O beautiful for patriot dream
That sees beyond the years
Thine alabaster cities gleam
Undimmed by human tears!
America! America!
God shed His grace on thee
And crown thy good with brotherhood
From sea to shining sea!

Katie asks us to work for justice, embrace peace, to do and be good, and for us to love liberty. And for that, she says, we will someday be rewarded in a place undimmed by human tears. (By the way, "Thine alabaster cities gleam" is a direct reference to the White City of the World's Columbian Exhibition.)

Over the years, Katie received many letters from people sharing what "America the Beautiful" meant to them, but her favorite was this: on the day the Germans surrendered in the Great War, soldiers serving in France heard about it at the eleventh hour of the eleventh day of the eleventh month. The fighting had been brutal, but all at once the sound of nothingness rang out across the countryside. "A bewildering silence fell. The soldiers stood speechless, staring at one another, or dropped to the ground. Then they saw on a hillside a battalion in formation and heard them singing 'America the Beautiful,' and they all came to life again, and sang it with tears on their faces."[12]

The National Hymn Society pressed Congress to make "America the Beautiful" the national anthem. "It expresses the highest and deepest emotions of patriotism, not in any spirit of militant aggression and world-conquering imperialism, but with a profound gratitude and affection for the country, the government, and the traditions that have made us what we are."[13]

World-famous American opera singer Jessye Norman felt the same. "It doesn't talk about war," she said in 2012. "It doesn't talk about anything but this land, and the joy that we should have in being in this land."[14]

Katharine Coman died in January 1915, as the blistering winter winds of Massachusetts buffeted the house that she and Katie shared. Katie leaned close to her bed, knowing the moment was drawing near. "Underneath are the everlasting arms,"[15] Katharine whispered. Katharine, whose faith was always stronger than her own. Katharine, who always felt certain about who she was and where she was going.

Before she passed, Katharine penned a note to Katie. "I have no fear, Dear Heart, for Life and Death are one, and God is all in all. My only real concern to remain in this body is to spare you grief and pain and loneliness. But I should not leave you comfortless. I would come to you as my mother comes to me in my best moments when my heart is open to her. The breezes come in off the meadow where the song sparrows are piping. Sure God is love."[16]

Even when you know someone is dying, even when you can see they are suffering and you wish for them not another moment of painful breath, nothing can really prepare you for *the* moment. Not the moment they depart this life, but the moment you realize you must continue to exist, even though they are gone. Why do the birds go on singing, as though nothing has changed? Why do the children continue playing as though everything has not just been ripped asunder? "I don't know why this heart of mine should go on beating when Katharine's heart is ashes," Katie wrote in her diary. "But it does."[17]

She wrote to Katharine's relatives, who by this time felt like her family too, and said, "I seem to find Katharine again, not in vision, but within myself, the courage in my grief, the comfort in my weariness, and the guidance in my perplexity. We must not cease loving and working, we who sorrow, for our Beloveds are pressing on in bright new paths of service, and it will never do for us to be left too far behind."[18]

In 1931, President Herbert Hoover signed a bill into law making "The Star-Spangled Banner" the national anthem. But that didn't diminish the role Katie's song played in the minds and hearts of Americans. After Pearl Harbor was attacked in 1941, members of Congress met with FDR until after midnight to discuss what the American response should be. As the congressmen departed, a small crowd gathered outside the White House and began to sing, their voices raw and tearful under the dark sky. It wasn't "The Star-Spangled Banner" that moved them in the December chill as the country stood at the threshold of another world war. It was "America the Beautiful."

Katie never sought the spotlight. She rode her bicycle all over Welles-ley, drinking in the fragrance of spring and the crunch of leaves beneath her tires in autumn. She became fluent in Spanish and began to translate

Spanish literature into English, her mind motivated by the desire to know and know and know.

She stayed out of the battles over the national anthem, never advocating for her lines or offering an opinion when a group held a contest to choose an original melody for the verses. (They received twelve hundred entries, and in the end, chose none. None could live up to Samuel Ward's now familiar tune.) Katie became an unwitting celebrity, finding herself thrust onto national stages she never anticipated, never accepting the credit for her work's success.

The enduring appeal of the song, she said, "is clearly due to the fact that Americans are at heart idealists, with a fundamental faith in human brotherhood."[19] Katie approved nearly every reasonable request for her lyrics to be reprinted—in hymnals, schoolbooks, newspapers, and in performances. Keeping up with her correspondence was nearly a full-time job, and she had a steady stream of visitors who came to Wellesley wanting to meet her in person.

In March 1929, Katie, who was nearly seventy, contracted pneumonia. She slowly grew feeble, and soon it became apparent that she was very sick. Her friends took turns staying with her, bringing her tea, reading to her in the quiet of the evening. She asked to hear "At Last" by John Greenleaf Whittier.

When on my day of life the night is falling,
And, in the winds from unsunned spaces blown,
I hear far voices out of darkness calling
My feet to paths unknown

Over the course of her entire life, Katie made a total of five dollars for "America the Beautiful," the fee she was paid when her poem was published in *The Congregationalist* magazine in 1895. The poem, she said, was made possible by her older brother, Arthur, who took over some of the roles of father when their own father died. It was Arthur who paid for her to go to Wellesley, and it was Wellesley that made her who she was.

Katie wasn't the suffragist picketing the White House encouraging President Wilson to give votes to women, although she met him once before he became president. Katie didn't chain herself to courthouses, get arrested, and go on hunger strikes. She didn't win elections or defeat foes in battle. But what she did was—and is—important. Her words light the way of truth: our shared history as a nation and the direction in which we should be heading.

Katharine Lee Bates died on March 28, 1929, the sound of Whittier's poem reverberating through the room like the soft tolling of a Paul Revere bell. Just the previous month, Virginia Randolph had watched, helplessly, as the school she loved burned. And now Katie would be eulogized at the one she devoted her career to.

At her funeral, Samuel Ward's melody began in its gentle murmur before lifting to its crescendo. A friend rose to eulogize her, saying, "To have put the expression of the highest and deepest patriotism into the mouths of a hundred million Americans is a monument so noble and enduring that it seems as if no poet could possibly ask or expect anything more complete."[20]

A bronze tablet at Wellesley bears her name. And beneath it:

SCHOLAR   PATRIOT   POET

Who gave enduring speech to the love of
Americans for America

The bell in the bell tower atop her father's Congregationalist church in Falmouth, Massachusetts, still rings out each year on the anniversary of her death, reminding us all of the power of one woman's words to articulate the highest ideals of the American soul.

☆

Forward Out of Darkness

———

NINE

INEZ MILHOLLAND

New York, 1910

G oddess," the fellows whispered to each other, craning their necks to follow Inez as she walked by.

"Amazonian beauty," another remarked.[1]

With her mane of dark hair, piercing light eyes, and an eye-catching figure, Inez Milholland attracted men's attention wherever she went. Women, though sometimes envious of her looks, loved the inspiring words that tumbled boldly from her lips.

Inez was a new kind of woman. Audacious. Sure of herself. Intelligent. Under her 1909 Vassar yearbook picture were the words: "Fascinating— but a trifle dangerous for household use."[2]

For decades, Gilded Age women had been corseted by a cult of domesticity, by notions that true femininity must suffocate a woman's independent thoughts and beliefs. Women didn't need things like an education. What they needed was a man and a family. But that wasn't enough for Inez.

Inez stood on the precipice of change. When Inez looked to the future, she saw suffrage for women, prison reform, and the end of racial and sex discrimination. By 1910, Inez was attending law school at New

York University, one of only a handful of women to do so.[3] Her plan was to use her legal education to fight for justice. To throw off the shackles of gendered expectations. She would don a cape, mount a horse, and ride down Pennsylvania Avenue like the general of an invading army of new women toward the White House, if that's what it took.

And it did.

Inez was a Milholland, raised by parents with serious progressive principles. Her father, John, helped found the NAACP, and counted Ida B. Wells as a personal friend.[4] Although John Milholland was raised desperately poor, he made a small fortune from pneumatic tube systems, which were deployed by the likes of the United States Post Office. Milholland was no Carnegie, no Rockefeller, but he did well enough to have a home in New York City, a farm in the country, and a townhouse in London.

John and Jean Milholland raised their three children to be exactly who they wanted to be. The family frequently hopped from America to Europe and back again as their whims and business dealings required.

If you want to picture what life was like for the Milhollands in London, I like to think about the 1964 Disney classic *Mary Poppins*. (Possibly minus the magical chalk drawings and the talking parrot umbrella.)

Why does the Banks family need a nanny to begin with? George Banks is very busy at the bank, doing man work in a suit, and Winifred Banks is a suffragette, fighting for votes for women, which obviously occupied much of her time. In the movie, Mrs. Banks comes home with her Votes for Women sash, chattering excitedly about how one of her friends got hauled off to prison, while another chained herself to the wheels of the prime minister's carriage, and wasn't it just the most glorious meeting?

My favorite line from "Sister Suffragette"—perhaps one of the greatest lyrics written by the Sherman brothers and delivered perfectly by Glynis Johns—is, *Though we adore men individually, we agree that as a group, they're rather stuuuuuuupid.* The look on Johns's face, with her huge doe eyes and her stilted vibrato, is priceless.

Inez became one of the most recognizable suffrage workers in U.S. history, garnering the kind of press usually reserved for celebrities in society at the time.

Charles Dana Gibson's illustrations of the ideal woman at the turn of the century seemed to be modeled after Inez Milholland—a woman who was tall and slender but voluptuous, with flowing long hair and smooth skin.[5] A woman who was delicate in beauty but who enjoyed adventure. Women the world over strove for the Gibson aesthetic, much like women of the 1990s were propelled by the impossibly slim figure of Kate Moss, or later, the preternatural curves of Kim Kardashian.

Inez was always giving the press a new story. INEZ TO ORGANIZE LABOR STRIKE. INEZ ARRESTED ON WAY TO OPERA. INEZ DRIVES SUFFRAGE WORKERS IN HER CAR. Cars, of course, were new. But a car driven by a woman? So new it was difficult to imagine.

Every time Inez was in the press, she appeared in opposition to the patriarchy. "We have found that protestation did no good," she once announced. "Friends, we must revolt!"[6] When you picture the height of the suffrage movement, of women marching in parades, of picketing and pamphleteering, picture Inez. Because while she was not the organizer of many of these events—those duties fell to people like Carrie Chapman Catt and Alice Paul—the organizers wanted her there, out front, being photographed.

And though women like Milholland, Catt, and Paul did much for the cause of women's suffrage, that advocacy didn't extend to Black women, who were often intentionally excluded from the movement. One reason why so many people, particularly southern Democrats, opposed suffrage for women is because they knew it would give Black women the right to vote, and that, they just couldn't abide. Giving them the right to vote would upset the entire power dynamic that the United States was founded upon, and the rock upon which it still rested: the supremacy of white men.

Many white women went along with it: suffrage was so important to them that they were willing to leave Black women behind in order to gain the right to vote for themselves. Because they knew that a huge part of the country's opposition to their suffrage was opposition to Black women being enfranchised, white women were often willing to not just look the other way but to intentionally exclude Black women for the purposes of appeasing white men.

Black women were usually not allowed to march in suffrage parades, or they were relegated to the back, permitted to participate only after all the white women had their turn. Black women formed their own clubs, their own political action groups, and their own suffrage organizations. They weren't quiet about wanting suffrage for themselves, suffrage for all, *universal* suffrage, even when white women were unwilling to go that far.

Many southerners saw the connections between the suffrage movement and the antislavery abolitionist movement and wanted nothing of it. But in order to succeed in their quest for voting rights, white women needed the support of southern leaders in Congress and in statehouses. Some even tried to entice southerners by essentially saying, "We know y'all don't like the fact that Black men can vote, so why not mitigate the damage Black men are doing by giving white women the right to cast a ballot?" Susan B. Anthony famously once said, "I will cut off this right arm of mine before I will ever work or demand the ballot for the Negro and not the woman." Suffrage newsletters assured white male voters that they would work to uphold poll taxes and literacy tests to keep the "wrong"—aka Black—women from voting.

Milholland was a member of the NAACP, and in some cases, she insisted that Black women be allowed to participate in suffrage events. She took on Black clients as a lawyer, although some records indicate that she fell into using racially derogatory language when speaking to a Black client.

According to historian Linda Lumsden, the *New York Press* proclaimed that Inez "was an ideal figure of a typical American woman," which says much when you read between the lines. The ideal suffrage worker wasn't elderly, she wasn't a woman of color, and she didn't have an ordinary appearance. "No suffrage parade was complete without Inez Milholland," the *New York Press* said, noting that Inez was wearing a "tight-fitting white satin gown which clings to her with the same tenacity with which she clings to the suffrage cause."[7] Even then, newspapers talked more about what women wore and how they looked more than what they had to say.

But Inez knew the power that her attractiveness gave her. She allowed people to envision how a woman might be feminine *and* think for herself. How she might be desired by men *and* cast a ballot. No longer was the Votes for Women message relegated to teetotaling scolds hell-bent on removing all fun from public life, as some men believed. Suffrage was now sexy.

Inez's fame brought more attention to the suffrage movement than anything women of the previous six decades had done. She became so popular that she started getting fan mail from overseas with her picture pasted on the outside of the envelope and the words "New York USA." No other address required.[8]

In May 1911, Fifth Avenue was jammed with one hundred fifty thousand onlookers, all there to watch as thousands of women paraded through the streets of New York demanding the right to vote. Inez was leading the way, carrying a large yellow banner emblazoned with:

Forward, out of error
Leave behind the night

Forward, through the darkness

Forward into light

Forward, Inez believed. She said, "Suffrage is a gift no one can confer—it is a right."[9]

Inez's most infamous appearance occurred in 1913, at the suffrage march planned for the day before President Woodrow Wilson's inauguration in Washington, D.C. Women intended to parade down Pennsylvania Avenue, along the exact route Wilson would take after being sworn in.

Inez wore what can only be described as a Wonder Woman visits *Lord of the Rings* Rivendell elvish costume, eager to make the newspapers and draw attention to the cause of suffrage.

She had learned to ride horses at her family's country property, so Inez confidently sat astride Grey Dawn—a towering, handsome white horse. Her riot of dark hair was emblazoned with a shining star, and her body was draped in a cape that was clearly meant to billow in the wind as she rode up the avenue, making for a dramatic photograph.

In a letter to her friend Lucy Burns, Inez described the costume she was going to be wearing at the parade as "something suggesting the free woman of the future, crowned with the star of hope, armed with the cross of mercy, circled with the blue mantle of freedom, breasted with the torch of knowledge, and carrying the trumpet which is to herald the dawn of a new day of heroic endeavor for womanhood."[10]

Slowly the parade began, wending its way through the District of Columbia to culminate in a dramatic suffrage tableau on the steps of the Treasury. Inez rode ahead of a float laden with a gigantic placard that read: WE DEMAND AN AMENDMENT TO THE CONSTITUTION OF THE UNITED STATES ENFRANCHISING THE WOMEN OF THIS COUNTRY.[11]

(If you're wondering what a "suffrage tableau" is, look no further than the scene in *The Music Man* where the mayor's wife, Eulalie Mackecknie Shinn, leads her friends, who are all dressed in Grecian costumes, through a series of elaborate poses. "One Grrrrrecian urn," Eulalie trills, rolling her *r*'s. The women all stop, holding their pose, as though they were being featured on the side of a Greek vase. Then they begin moving again, *shuffle shuffle shuffle shuffle,* until Eulalie says, "Two Grrrrrrrrecian urn." *The Music Man* was set in 1912, and tableaus were a type of historical skit/reenactment. Strangely, they've fallen out of favor.)

The spectators of the 1913 parade, many of them men intent on maintaining the male-dominated power structure of society, began to heckle the marchers. It started slowly at first. A whistle here, a catcall there. They made fun of older women as they marched past, shouting, "We came to see chicks and not hens!" Egged on by their comrades, some men flicked lit cigarettes at the women, others spat. Then the crowd began to surge out of control.

Before she knew what was happening, Inez found herself hemmed in by the sea of angry spectators, men packed so tightly together around her that Grey Dawn couldn't walk. It's a testament to the horse and his rider that he didn't spook, rear up, and take off, as he was surrounded by thousands of angry men who were furious that women were demanding what already rightfully belonged to them—equality and freedom.

"You ought to be ashamed of yourselves!" Inez shouted at them. To the police, who were sitting idly by, Inez yelled, "If you have a particle of backbone, you will come out here and help us to continue our parade instead of standing there and shouting at us!"[12]

But the crowd was too riled up, and the police were too late in trying to gain control of them. The United States Cavalry had to be called in, galloping from across the Potomac and directly into the unruly throngs. Spectators scattered, marchers fell, bloodstains bloomed across fresh white dresses. Ambulances wailed back and forth to the hospital nonstop for over six hours, transporting injured women. Helen Keller was so rattled and upset by the events that she was unable to appear as scheduled at the tableau.[13]

The next day, newspapers around the country published horrifying stories of violence and harassment at the hands of men who would deny women the vote. One of the organizers, Dora Lewis, said, "We were jostled, humiliated, insulted, and deprived of the right of protection. In our ranks were the foremost women of America, college women, social workers, lawyers, physicians, wives of Senators and Representatives, and all these were allowed to be insulted and their lives jeopardized by crowds of drunken men. The police would not even rope off the streets for us . . . the militiamen who were present along the route were all drunk."[14] The granddaughter of Elizabeth Cady Stanton was hit by an intoxicated man while the nearby police did nothing. Another attempted to scale a float and throw a woman off it. Hundreds of demonstrating women had bruises creeping across their bodies and faces the next day. The only group that even attempted to help the marchers fend off the swarms were a troop of Boy Scouts.

After the parade, people immediately called for the chief of police to be fired. Newspapers ran images of what the crowds looked like during the suffrage parade compared to what they looked like the next day during the inaugural parade—in one, crowds clog the streets in chaos. In the other, the newly sworn in president is helped to proceed in an orderly fashion down the same road, the crowds standing neatly behind the lines set up by the police.

The Women's Political Union, a suffrage group, sent a telegram to Woodrow Wilson that arrived shortly before his inauguration. It read: "As you ride today in comfort and safety to the Capitol to be inaugurated as the President of the people of the United States, we beg that you will not be unmindful that yesterday the government, which is supposed to exist for the good of all, left women, while passing in peaceful procession in their demand for political freedom, at the mercy of a howling mob on the very streets which are being at this moment sufficiently officered for the protection of men."[15]

Congress held weeks of hearings afterward. The Senate later wrote in one of their reports about the suffrage parade:

> It is unfortunate that a quiet, dignified parade, composed mostly of women, could not be held upon the best-known avenue in the Nation's capital without interference or insult. . . . We cannot condemn too strongly the conduct of those who thus interfered with the parade and jeered at the marchers. We regret that the parade was not fully protected. . . . Some of the uniformed and more of the special police acted with apparent indifference and in this way encouraged the crowd to press in upon the parade. These made little attempt to control or check the crowd, and in some instances, must have observed acts and conduct which should have called forth stern measures on their part, without doing anything to prevent the same.[16]

Inez Milholland was one tens of thousands of women who worked for seventy years to gain the right to vote. She wasn't one of the women, like Alice Paul, who spent months in jail strapped to a chair with a tube shoved down her throat being force-fed out of her hunger strike. She wasn't the brains behind the "Winning Strategy" of Carrie Chapman Catt, who would go on to found the League of Women Voters in 1920. You may think Inez was the pretty face of an often rugged movement, but in the coming years she would face a gruesome trial for the cause to which she was ready to give her entire life.

TEN

MARIA DE LOPEZ

California, 1911

For more than ninety minutes, Maria stood on the seat of her car in the plaza, pelting passersby with her "votes for women" message. She wasn't the only woman in America to create a spectacle for the purpose of the suffrage cause. But she was the first to do it in Spanish.[1]

"Maria." People whispered to each other, pointing at the woman they recognized with her broad-brimmed hat and the vehicle festooned with yellow buntings.

Maria Guadalupe Evangelina de Lopez grew up surrounded by the farmland and orange groves of the burgeoning San Gabriel Valley. Her father, a Mexican immigrant who worked as a blacksmith, purchased an adobe house on the grounds of the San Gabriel Mission, a structure that still stands today.[2]

De Lopez often went by the nickname Lupe, and she, too, was a new kind of woman. Her hair didn't cascade adventurously down her shoulders like a Gibson girl, no, but Maria was smart, racking up degrees and becoming (likely) the first-ever Latina professor at UCLA. The Spanish Department she taught in eventually enrolled more than 650 students, and she worked as a translator and teacher, expertly switching between the multiple languages she mastered.[3]

She did other things few women of her time would have dared to undertake. Not only was she going to college and driving a car, she was traveling abroad. Alone. And then offering public lectures about what it was like to traverse the Andes.

When her father died in 1904, Maria moved back to the long, narrow adobe house she had grown up in, the bells of the mission and the smell of orange blossoms welcoming her home. She opened her house to her students, hosting holiday teas in Spanish that recreated what life was like on a California mission in the nineteenth century and inviting students to board with her.

Unlike what you might have learned in your elementary school textbooks, North America was not settled only by British colonists in places like Massachusetts and Virginia. Spain and France were all up in North America's grill, and while the British subjects were still arguing about whether they should kick King George to the curb, missions were being built in what would become the states of California and Texas. The San Gabriel Mission was founded in 1771. Yes, before the ultimate breakup letter declaring American independence was sent across the Atlantic to despotic King George III.

And of course, that is not even counting the indigenous communities that lived in North America for many thousands of years before the arrival of Europeans. There are Pueblo ruins in New Mexico that are a thousand years old. Well-organized civilizations existed here long before anyone settled New Amsterdam or Jamestown or even before Columbus sailed the ocean blue.

To prove the point that North America didn't need to be discovered by Columbus because people already lived here, a Native American man named Adam Fortunate Eagle flew to an international event taking place in Italy. In preparation for his trip, he began to research the "discovery" of Italy, much like American students learn of Columbus's "discovery" of the Americas. But he found there was no such myth, no tale of a heroic aha moment on the part of an explorer.

Fortunate Eagle reasoned the same should be true of North America. What right did Columbus have to discover a place that was already occupied? So when he got off the plane in Italy, he was dressed in his full Native American regalia, carrying a spear (it was the 1970s; spears were allowed on planes). At a press conference he said facetiously that he was extremely excited to have discovered this land called Italy, and that he was establishing a government agency to oversee his discovery.[4]

The Italians got it. They took the joke, and Fortunate Eagle was invited to meet the pope. When the pope held up his ring so Fortunate Eagle could kiss it, Fortunate Eagle held out his hand instead, his finger heavy with a ring made from American turquoise. I imagine what was happening in their minds as they held out their hands to each other.

"You may kiss my ring."

"No, you can kiss MY ring."

"I am not kissing your ring, I am the pope."

"Well, I'm not kissing your ring, I just discovered Italy."

Eventually, the men smiled and shook hands instead, each side refusing to do any smooching. But the point was made: Adam Fortunate Eagle was featured in the international news with his "America did not need to be discovered by Europeans, it was already occupied" message.

Maria was a club woman. And yes, that means she went to club meetings. The women's club movement began in the nineteenth century and flourished in the early twentieth, as women sought community, education, and organization. Clubs existed for a variety of purposes, but often they were involved in some kind of civic engagement or community service. It was the club women of Southern California who helped establish a juvenile court system and raised awareness and funds to hire probation officers. It was the club women who helped organize kindergartens and playgrounds. It was the club women who fought for labor laws, and it was the club women who organized for women's suffrage.[5]

Maria was in at least six clubs and was the president of at least one of them. She helped organize a group of female professors and worked to help elect the first female president of the California Teachers Association. It was Maria who was out there festooning her automobile and passing out pamphlets that had suffrage information written in Spanish. "POR QUE?" the pamphlet quizzed. "Why must women have to wait for suffrage?" The answer the pamphlet gave was:

WOMEN Need It.
MEN Need It.
The STATE Needs It.
Women Ought to GIVE Their Help.
Men Ought to HAVE Their Help.
The State Ought to USE Their Help.[6]

In August 1911, an article written by Maria appeared in the *Los Angeles Herald*. There's a large photograph of her that accompanies the article: her hair is parted in the middle and pulled back, her cheeks are full, a slight smile on her lips.

In it, she says, "A democracy, we have been taught for many a year, is a government of the people, by the people, and for the people. What is a man?" she asks. "A man is a person. What is a person? A person is a human being—a person has a soul. Is woman a human being? Yes, a woman is a human being. Has woman a soul?" she asks. "Yes, woman has a soul."[7]

She goes on to lay out her case that men and women are equal, because they are both human beings. We can't have a democracy without men, and we can't have a democracy without half of the democracy's citizens—women, she says.

While Maria loved teaching Spanish, things were happening on the other side of the world, and she couldn't resist the siren song of adventure and service. Rather than sitting home and watching news reports about the war unfolding in Europe, Maria decided she would do something, packing her belongings and boarding a train for New York.

In New York, she learned how to be an ambulance mechanic, with Los Angeles newspapers reporting that she had passed her mechanic exams with a grade of 95.[8] (I know, cue the shocked menfolk: "I never realized it was possible for women to do complex things!") She even began learning to fly airplanes.

On May 26, 1917, the *Los Angeles Times* ran a picture of her and an article that read: "Ambitious. From Schools to Trenches. Los Angeles Girl soon will leave for France. Former teacher here passes ambulance tests. Hopes also to complete her aviation studies. Noted local teacher to go to war."

Maria said, "It's just a chance whether I will ever return, but I am ready and willing to make the sacrifice for my country. I have no one depending on me, and my country needs me, so I must go. The idea of flying and of going to France thrills me. The call cannot come too soon, even if before I have finished my course in flying. I am anxious to be giving my services and to be doing something for my country."[9]

Maria went to France, likely sometime in 1918. A number of famous men, like Walt Disney and Ernest Hemingway, served in the same capacity as Maria—ambulance drivers in World War I.

Walt Disney was too young to enlist like his older brothers, so he altered his own birth certificate to make himself eligible to drive an ambulance for the Red Cross in France. At the time, you only had to be seventeen for ambulance service, whereas you had to be eighteen for military service. Walt missed shipping out with his unit because he became very ill as the worldwide flu pandemic raged.[10] He was so sick that the doctors at the ambulance driver training program said that if he had any hope of making it, he needed to go home, because if he stayed with all the other sick people, he would surely die.

Walt was carried up the steps of his home on a stretcher, where his family nursed him back to health, and he was eventually able to leave for France. He sailed on a converted cattle ship, and recalled the journey as most unpleasant—turns out that crossing the Atlantic on a ship made for cows is not a first-class voyage.

While in France, he worked on his artistic skills, painting helmets for Americans who were heading home. He would paint realistic bullet holes, enabling soldiers to make it seem that they had killed a German and taken his helmet as a prize. Walt then sent much of the money he earned back to his family.[11]

At the outset of WWI, the U.S. military was quite small compared to other countries of similar size. The government partnered with the Red Cross to provide ambulance services, one of the many public-private partnerships it undertook during the war. Eventually, the United States stopped recruiting men to work in the ambulance motor corps and instead drafted them into regular military service. This helped create the opportunity for women to serve overseas in roles other than that of nurse.

After Maria arrived, she received her duty assignment at a hospital that was run by women. The United States refused to allow women who were trained physicians to serve in WWI. There were roughly eighty female doctors who were like, "I would like to serve, please send me," and the United States essentially said, "No, thanks anyway."[12]

So what did the women doctors do? Sit back and complain that the government was allowing soldiers to suffer instead of using the willing and able services of trained surgeons? No. They fundraised to go on their own. They got donations from wealthy women who sponsored them, they organized and worked, and they paid their own way. The National American Woman Suffrage Association even used its funds to pay for a hospital facility in France, although they changed the name, removing any reference to suffrage because they knew that it may not be popular with antisuffrage activists. When they got to France, France was like, "Yes, please, we will take all the help we can get—if you are a surgeon, we don't care what gender you are."

Ambulance drivers had to be qualified mechanics (often the vehicle of choice was a retrofitted Model T), because there was no garage to just drop your ambulance off at should something go wrong. Women like Maria had to be willing to dodge bombs and men with machine guns. They had to know enough first aid to stabilize a patient before they were loaded into the ambulance and brought back to the hospital. They had to be okay with seeing arms blown off and shrapnel that gravely disfigured a face. They had to be willing to be alone on a road that was likely in horrible condition, trying not to fall into car-size potholes, making their way across bridges weakened by warfare, all without street signs.

When Maria arrived at her duty station in France, the ambulances had not yet made it, so she was assigned an alternate job in the interim working for the French government, finding herself stationed in an old château, its once stately rooms filled with wounded soldiers. Not long after her arrival, Maria heard her first booms of warfare, the château shaken by German bombardment. On and on the bombing continued, lighting fire to the building, chunks of plaster raining down from the ceilings.

Maria and three other women ran toward the fire and the sound of weapons to pick up and move soldiers out of the building that the Germans seemed intent on destroying. With *I am ready and willing to make the sacrifice for my country* echoing more loudly than the whoosh of blood in her chest, Maria worked through the night.

The next morning, word spread quickly about what the women had done—how they ran not from the danger, as many men assumed they would, but toward it. How they thought not of saving their own lives but of laying them down so that others might be saved. Maria was in her late thirties, doing work reserved for strong young men half her age.

Maria received a commendation for bravery from the French government. And then she kept going, driving an ambulance, dodging bullets and potholes, until the war ended.[13]

When she returned from France, she married a professor of French, and she continued to host students and visitors at the adobe house she had grown up in, ringed by a picket fence, the bells of the mission tolling in the distance.

———

ELEVEN

REBECCA BROWN MITCHELL

Idaho, 1856

Suffrage wasn't an idea that sprang up overnight. Women like Inez Milholland and Maria de Lopez climbed onto the shoulders of the people who came before. Much of what the generation of new women was able to accomplish was because of women like Rebecca Mitchell, who made sure the women of the West could vote long before Inez and Maria were even old enough to understand what suffrage was.

Rebecca was a young widow, the mother of two tiny sons, when she was informed that under Illinois law, all of her property, with two small exceptions, no longer belonged to her. When her husband died in the 1850s, nearly everything they owned, right down to the clothes on her own back, became property of the state. If she wanted to keep her trunk of wedding gifts, the dishes on which she fed her children, the chairs upon which they sat, she would have to buy them back from the government of Illinois. With the exception of the family Bible and a hymnal, she had nothing of her own.[1]

Coverture laws, like the one in force in Illinois, said that women were legally "covered" by a man. If she was single, her father was meant to oversee her, and if she was married, the job fell to her husband. Women had few rights of their own—not to own property, not even legal rights to parent the children she birthed. In Illinois, if a couple divorced, the man got to dictate the terms of custody, and if he wanted to keep a woman from seeing her babies, he could. If a woman was deemed too much trouble, was too opinionated or intelligent, if she had what a man regarded as any emotional instability, he had the legal right to take her to an asylum and institutionalize her. While Rebecca Brown Mitchell wasn't institutionalized, she was imprisoned, as she called it, in the iron cage of the law.[2]

Rebecca married again, this time to her husband's brother, a union that was ultimately doomed and ended in separation, but not before they had two daughters together. One of her daughters, not more than five years old, died, leaving Rebecca to raise three children on her own.[3]

Rebecca wasn't a new kind of woman like Inez or Maria—she was from an older generation, the one that felt the weight of oppressive gender roles squarely on their shoulders. Rebecca wanted to attend college to become a minister, but she said she was rejected repeatedly, "hedged out by public opinion and sex prejudice." She "chafed in silence, for at that time, women were to be seen and not heard."[4]

Eventually, she found a missionary training program that was willing to accept a woman who was estranged from her husband. Rebecca felt the pang of wanting to do something meaningful with her life, of wanting to escape the ghosts of her past and start afresh. The West was calling.

By now, in 1882, Rebecca's sons were grown, so she and her teenage daughter, Bessie, boarded a train from Illinois and settled in for the long journey—over the Mississippi, out past the prairies, across the Continental Divide, winding through the Rockies and the red rocks of Utah, and into a place that felt like it needed her more than she needed it: Eagle Rock, Idaho, the town that would later become Idaho Falls.[5] Like many towns of the West in the nineteenth century, towns like the one where Clara Brown lived in Colorado, Eagle Rock consisted of little more than a handful of shanties, a few saloons, and company houses built by the railroads. Eagle Rock perched on the banks of the Snake River, whose currents sprang from fissures in the rock, the water so ferocious that it tumbled into foam, its force an ever-present roar.

Rebecca was forty-eight years old and covered from neck to foot in heavy taffeta fabric. On the morning of her arrival, she stepped off the train and into a whole new world. She and Bessie began by trying to find a hotel or a furnished room to rent, which they quickly discovered did not exist.

They had not come this far to turn back now, so they began knocking on doors, eventually inquiring at every single home in Eagle Rock. Most of the residents were friendly but poor, and didn't have space for a woman and her nearly grown daughter in their meager accommodations.

Eventually, someone told her about a shanty—a shed, really—near the back of a saloon. Rebecca and Bessie borrowed a broom, stuck a single candle in a beer bottle, spread their blanket on the floor, and went to sleep. The next day, Rebecca went back to every house in the town, again knocking and introducing herself, this time inviting the townspeople to send their children to school.

Which school would that be? you might be wondering. "The school Rebecca conjured out of thin air in a shed," I would reply. On weekdays, Rebecca taught academic subjects, and on Sundays, she taught Christian Sunday school. The shed was an accommodation of the most "primitive kind imaginable, with no furniture save for two benches, which served at night for a bedstead and by day for seats for the larger pupils."[6] The smaller children sat on boxes. Before long, Rebecca had forty children crammed into her rundown shed wedged between saloons. Rebecca told her little flock, "All things are possible to those that believeth," which was Mark 9:23, one of her favorite passages from the New Testament.

Teaching in a shed wasn't lucrative—more than once she felt desperate financially—and as winter approached, she knew she couldn't make it in this northern climate with so little warmth. The cracks in the walls were so large that sunlight peeked through, and it was impossible to keep the growing piles of dirt and the sounds of hoofbeats out of the haphazard structure. Men from all the surrounding saloons stumbled in various states of inebriation near her door, but despite the hardship, Rebecca "never halted, doubted, or hesitated," convinced that she was doing the Lord's work.[7]

Living on the western frontier was more expensive than Rebecca had bargained for, and she dashed off a letter home begging for financial assistance from friends and family. She was a self-supporting Baptist missionary, which meant that it was her job to find people to send her money. She would have to wait weeks, at best, before she heard back, and to make matters worse, her daughter was sick. After dropping off the letter at the post office, praying it would arrive quickly, a man appeared at her door.

"Can I help you?" Rebecca asked Frank Reardon, one of the people in town who was better-off financially than many others. Frank replied that he was there to pay his son's tuition.

Except the tuition wasn't due yet. He had no reason to show up that day.

"Mr. R., why do you do this?" Rebecca asked. "Did you know I had spent my last cent, and now you come to pay your tuition before it is due?"[8] Frank held out the money, and Rebecca felt certain that this was a moment of divine providence. Hadn't she just dropped off the letter? Wasn't she desperate to buy her daughter something to help her condition improve? That settled it for Rebecca. This was her sign. She named the school Providence Mission.

When winter arrived, colder and snowier than she had dreamed possible, Rebecca knew she needed a safer place to live. Her work had ingratiated her with the community enough that she was able to find a small but better-insulated location for living in and schooling children in the community. But she knew that this too was temporary, and that she had to secure funding to build a larger building that could be used both as a church and school.

Rebecca worked for two solid years to scrape together the funds for her mission. Two years of teaching and appeals and fundraising from people she knew back in Illinois before she was finally able to dedicate a small chapel. When the space was finished, it also housed the new public school district that Rebecca helped found.[9] Eagle Rock was experiencing a population boom, nearly tripling its residents by 1885, three years after her arrival.[10]

Rebecca sought even more education, this time pursuing a formal teaching certificate. She helped open schools in neighboring communities and secured a pastor for the church she raised money to build. Bessie was now married, and Rebecca, a mature woman in her fifties, finally felt free to "drop her work and enter the open door."[11]

By 1891, she set her sights on government, on the belief that America's best days were ahead of her, on the idea that the marginalized needed to be treated fairly by society and the legal system. She would begin, she thought, by lobbying the Idaho legislature to achieve action on her three primary goals:

1. Raise the age of consent for girls from ten to eighteen. (Yes. *Ten*.)
2. Secure women's suffrage in Idaho.
3. Reform Idaho's prison and parole system.[12]

You can see where Rebecca's fire for empowering women comes from: her own experiences being legally stripped of all her possessions, being told that if she wanted *her own clothing* she would have to pay the government for it. Being denied access to the education she desired as a result of nothing more than her gender.

Rebecca was part of the temperance movement, which was inextricably linked to suffrage in the United States. As America's cities grew and prospered, they became more densely populated and allowed for the proliferation of a popular pastime, mostly for men: drinking. Bars, pubs, saloons, and gentlemen's clubs sprang up on every corner, selling a substance that impaired judgment, lowered inhibitions, damaged health, and that forced women to pick up the pieces of addiction. Liquor was profitable. And it harmed families, Rebecca and groups like the Women's Christian Temperance Union believed.

The WCTU thought that if they could make alcohol illegal, men would be required to turn their attention away from the bottle and back to their homes. If they could make alcohol illegal, men would not be able to squander their wages, leaving their children to beg for food at the charity kitchens. If they could make alcohol illegal, fewer women would find themselves beaten for a minor perceived infraction on a Friday night after the pub closed.

But the women of the WCTU believed that in order to make alcohol illegal, women would need to be able to vote—men were not going to vote against their own self-interest. So the two movements, temperance and suffrage, grew together, two stems of the same vine. The suffrage workers of the time knew that equality is one of the cornerstones of justice, and justice one of the cornerstones of peace.

The WCTU sent representatives to Idaho to train local chapter members in advocacy. They taught them how to speak to audiences and how to make persuasive arguments, and Rebecca soon found herself rising through the ranks of suffrage and temperance workers, becoming the president of the state's WCTU organization in 1891.[13] She was an in-demand speaker, and logged many miles through mountain passes, braving the dark and the danger while traveling around Idaho, Utah, and Montana to encourage women to work for the right to vote.

Women would gather for Rebecca's evening lecture, setting out a plate of cookies they brought to share, offering each other cups of tea, making small talk about their families and the weather. Most had not been in a classroom setting in decades, if ever, and some worried that they were ill-equipped to learn in this way. Rebecca strode in, skirts rustling, her friendly, straightforward demeanor attracting attention. Even when she became elderly, she had a taut jawline and plump cheeks, her thin lips set into a type of audacity uncommon for a woman of her time.

On the chalkboard, she drew a column labeled JUSTICE, and set the column upon a base that was labeled TRUTH and RIGHT. She said there should be "one standard of moral, legal, civil, and personal rights for all without discrimination."[14]

She then drew a light shining upon the column of Justice, the light of the Golden Rule. It illuminated the column from all directions. "Justice is inflexible," she said. "It does not lean to the right or the left. Justice and truth are fixed eternal principles, but mankind has leaned away from this tower, until the standard lies prone upon the earth, at right angles with justice, the will or the passions of men being recognized as the law."[15]

She described for the audience how, thus, men hold the lives of their wives in their hands, in the same way that he holds the lives of the animals he owns. She said, "Women are bought and sold and driven like cattle, or even worse."[16] Rebecca's vision was to realign mankind's view of justice, so that it no longer lay prone upon the earth but rose up to its rightful place, squared with the immutable standards of what is true and what is right.

It would happen slowly, she predicted, but each increment would bring us closer in line with the standard: first, men must not be permitted to kill their wives, even if they are allowed to sell them. (I know, I know.) Then, a woman may gain the right to eat in his presence and speak to him. It could then progress to a woman being consulted about whom she wished to marry, even if she was treated like an enslaved person afterward. Step by step, Rebecca proffered, the whole of humanity would be lifted out of the deepest degradation and moved upward toward the perpendicular column of Justice.

"There is not a Nation in all the world," Rebecca taught, "Christian or non-Christian, that gives to the daughter the same moral, legal, educational, and parental rights that the son claims for himself and keeps."[17]

"Let Idaho be among the first," she said. "Wyoming, Utah, and Colorado have all agreed that women should vote. Let Idaho join them."[18] Being at the forefront of progress has always come with a certain amount of fear—you're asking people to abandon comfort for the sake of growth. It's like asking people to follow you into the wilderness for the promise of a better tomorrow. Some people would rather stay where they are, because home is comfortable. Home is safe. Change is scary.

Legislators in Idaho said that if the citizens wanted women to vote, they would have to amend the state constitution. The women of the WCTU would have to convince the men to let them have the ballot. When the morning of election day in 1896 dawned, storms rolled through the sky and through the hearts and stomachs of the women who had fought and organized for so long. They made a schedule to ensure there was always someone to stand as close to the polling place as possible. They hired little boys to stand outside with signs that read, "Vote for your mother."[19] They gave out free coffee, and met men with a kind word and an ask to please vote for the amendment.

"It's not my ticket, it's not my ticket," they heard over and over.

Some men told them, "Women have too many rights as it is."[20] The cruel comments cut like the cold wind of the stormy day.

When the election ended and the ballots were tabulated, the women sat for a moment in stunned silence. They had done it. It had worked. They had convinced nearly 66 percent of the men of Idaho to extend them the vote. "Praise God from whom all blessings flow!" the newspapers read.[21]

The State Board of Canvassers then tried to claim that the victory wasn't good enough, and that they needed an even bigger majority than the one they had just secured. Suffrage worker Kate Green appealed their decision in court.[22] Attorney William Borah argued heartily for the high court to permit the amendment to be added to the Constitution, which was ironic, because later, he would oppose the Nineteenth Amendment enfranchising women nationwide.

More than a month after the election of 1896, the Idaho Supreme Court came back unanimously: the amendment enfranchising women stood. The women of Idaho would be voting in the next election.[23]

The suffrage fight had been won in Idaho, but Rebecca didn't stop. She put herself on the ballot to be an elector in the Electoral College, and she did something else that gained her national attention, something that no one anywhere in the world had done before: she asked to be the chaplain of the Idaho legislature.[24]

When she first approached her contacts in the legislature about becoming the official chaplain—whose job it was to pray for the lawmakers and to provide counseling or other spiritual direction as they sought it— the men of Idaho said, "I've never heard of such a thing."

"Why not do the unheard-of thing?" Rebecca asked.[25]

And what a question that is. Why *not* do the unheard-of thing? Why *not* do what no one else is doing? Why *not* leave behind the old ways that are no longer serving? Why *not* be the first?

Humans aren't so much afraid of failure as they are of having people watch them fail. The shame doesn't come from not scaling the summit, it's from the people who judge you for not having succeeded. So you have to admire Rebecca, who was likened to a tiny tornado, a woman in her later years, who most definitely was being judged. She was judged for having a failed marriage, for having the audacity to start a school the day after she arrived in Eagle Rock, for founding a church and deciding she wanted to be a chaplain, for going back to school as an adult, for advocating for temperance and suffrage, for deciding that instead of retiring, she would become a crusader.

Rebecca didn't get the chaplain job. People watched her try and fail, and some undoubtedly judged her for it.

The next year, she went to bat for the appointment again, having spent considerable time getting to know the legislators who were in the position of power to make the call. This time, when the legislative session opened, it was Rebecca whose voice filled the room, lifting a prayer to the almighty, as the men listened with bowed heads. Rebecca was the first female chaplain of a legislative body in world history.[26]

She received letters of congratulations from all over the United States, and she said, "As worn as I was with the long battle for citizenship, I was cheered by the honor given me in my old age, a kind compensation for long weary miles of stage travel and storm and cold."[27]

When she took her post in 1897, she found that "the jeers of men were forgotten, the haughty looks of women who had all the rights they wanted, faded away as a cloud before the sun. . . . Not for myself did I care so much . . . but for Womanhood was victory dear to my heart."[28] Men and institutions that had stood in the way of Rebecca Brown Mitchell had learned to stand aside or come to grief over their opposition. She was sixty-four years old.

Oh, did you think she stopped there? Of course not. Boxes of books stored under her bed? *Might as well start the Idaho Falls Public Library*, she thought. Eventually, community members were able to get a Carnegie Foundation grant and build a proper library building.

The city of Idaho Falls doesn't have the infrastructure to beautify its public spaces? *Might as well start a Civic Improvement Club and grow some trees.*

No historian has come to write the story of Eagle Rock/Idaho Falls? *Let me get right on that.*

Why not do the unheard-of thing, indeed.

When Rebecca died in 1908, her strength having been slowly sapped by tuberculosis, an article in *The Wilsonville Review* mentioned that the WCTU was planning a marble monument to her. The *Review* wrote, "While a monument of marble would serve to perpetuate her memory, far richer monuments are the churches she has fostered, the schools she has founded, the libraries she has opened, the Sunday schools she has established, and men and women who are better men and women for having come in contact with her influence."[29]

Rebecca took a train across the country to live in a shed. She was never the type who aspired to a marble bust of her face in a hushed memorial hall somewhere. Instead, I think she'd love to know that some of the institutions she nurtured, the schools and the churches and the libraries, the places that continue to help their communities learn about justice and truth and right—these are the most fitting monuments to the woman who finally picked the lock of the iron cage of the law.

On Christmas Day, a few months after her death, *The Idaho Republican* published a resolution that said Mitchell was "ever ready to proffer the hand of aid and the voice of sympathy to the needy and distressed . . . a woman of heroic courage, faith, and fearlessness, in championing every right and righteous cause and whose self-sacrificing spirit will ever be an inspiration to all who knew her."[30]

In 2022, Idaho erected a statue to commemorate women's suffrage. Cast in bronze, the *Spirit of Idaho Women* depicts a lithe figure with an outstretched hand. Behind her stand twelve sets of shoes, those of the generations of women who came before, each decade of suffragists treading the path to enfranchisement. In her hand, she extends a shoe to the women of the future, inviting them to continue in the work that was begun by those with the courage to let people watch them fail.

TWELVE

INEZ MILHOLLAND

The West, 1916

In between her headline-grabbing turns at the forefront of suffrage marches, Inez's private life had unfolded as well. She finished law school and secretly eloped with a Dutch man named Eugen Boissevain. Even though Inez was a new kind of woman, she and Eugen longed for a child. Many of the letters between them detail this fondest wish, one that was never realized.

By 1916, the struggles of the national suffrage movement were beginning to bear fruit. Women had gained the right to vote in eleven states, all in the West. Why the West? A few reasons stand out:

1. Territorial organizers wanted more settlers so they could gain statehood. Correction: they wanted more *white* settlers. And they figured that if they wanted more white men, they could get them by enticing white women to move to the territories. In the words of Maria Portokalos in *My Big Fat Greek Wedding,* "Men may be the head of the household, but women are the neck." Wherever the women looked, the men were sure to follow.

2. Organized activism. Suffrage shows us the importance of organization when seeking to make change. Without the newspapers and lobbyists, the events and the publicity, the connections and the infrastructure, voting rights for women would have taken decades longer, if not more.

3. Coalitions. People with a common goal worked together. In Oregon, for example, twenty-three separate suffrage groups coalesced around pulling for the same thing. Black women and Chinese women, Jewish women and Quaker women, women who supported prohibition and women who ran saloons—rather than trying to go it alone, they formed a united front.[1]

The western states were a good start, but they weren't enough. Suffragists wanted a constitutional amendment, and their work picked up a feverish pace. In furtherance of their goal, they formed a new political party: the National Woman's Party. One of their goals was mobilizing the women of the West, who could vote, to get rid of Woodrow Wilson in the next election, since he was seen as one of the primary obstacles to progress.

They began to step up the pressure. Suffragists attended every speech Wilson gave, and one woman, Mabel Vernon, interrupted him multiple times while he was addressing the American Federation of Labor on July 4, 1916. She yelled, "Mr. President, if you sincerely desire to forward the interests of all the people, why do you oppose the national enfranchisement of women?"[2] Later, after Wilson refused to respond, she called again for him to answer the question. She was promptly escorted out by the Secret Service.

Later, Mabel Vernon would attend one of Wilson's congressional addresses.

She situated herself in the balcony, in the direct sight line of the Speaker's podium. Pinned underneath her skirt was a banner, which, at precisely the right moment, she unfurled from the balcony of the House of Representatives. "MR. PRESIDENT WHAT WILL YOU DO

FOR WOMAN SUFFRAGE?" the banner demanded.[3] The suffragists in attendance sat quietly, expectantly, waiting for Wilson to look up from his written remarks.

Murmurs rippled through the room, members of Congress craning their necks to see what had happened. Finally, Wilson looked up and saw the banner. He smiled broadly and immediately returned to reading his prepared statement. As the women were escorted out, a representative greeted the press outside the Capitol with prepared statements listing the names of the women involved and offering them up for comments and interviews.

The women did not try to conceal their identities, didn't come armed, didn't break any glass or invade any private offices. They weren't there to kidnap members of Congress; no faux gallows waited outside the building. They came peacefully, stayed in the section designated for visitors, and left peacefully, confident that they had made their point. Suffrage leader Alice Paul smiled happily at reporters and remarked, "It was a most excellent demonstration. Certainly we may in the future adopt various methods not dissimilar from the one we used today to keep Congress reminded of our cause."[4]

Alice Paul's National Woman's Party held its first convention in the summer of 1916. If they could mobilize the four million women who had gained voting rights in the West, that was one-third of the votes needed to elect a president. What they needed was to inspire women in solidarity to know that their highest loyalty was owed not to the Republican Party or Woodrow Wilson, but to *women*, and convince them that voting against the interests of women was morally wrong.

Inez Milholland took the stage in Chicago at the first convention of the National Woman's Party, dazzling the audience with the force of her fame. "I believe," she said to the assembled crowds, "and every woman of spirit and independence believes, that women are human beings with a definite part to play in the shaping of human events. . . . we must say, 'Women first!'"[5]

The crowd erupted.

The *Deseret News* reported that the convention's attendees had a motto of "Duty first! Duty to other women; duty to the many millions living in the slave states."[6]

For the first time in history, women had organized themselves into a political force to be reckoned with. A new battalion was assembling at the edge of the battlefield for equal rights. But before the year was out, Inez Milholland, who had survived a violent mob in Washington, D.C., would be a martyr for the cause.

Leader Alice Paul planned a speaking tour, one that would take suffrage workers on an ambitious journey across the western states in October 1916, just before the presidential election where they hoped to unseat Woodrow Wilson. Inez Milholland Boissevain, one of the most popular speakers in the party's arsenal, reluctantly agreed to headline the tour. She had been feeling ill for some time, so her little sister, Vida, agreed to come along for emotional and physical support. Vida would help make sure Inez slept and ate, that her clothing was organized, and that everything was in order on each stop from Kansas to California.

But no matter how much she slept, Inez never felt rested. Her throat was on fire. Her neck hurt whenever she moved her head. When she and her sister boarded the train for the first eighteen-hour leg of their journey, Inez hoped to wake up at the first tour stop refreshed. Instead, she was worse. The sisters sent for a doctor. After examining her, the doctor told Inez that her tonsils were infected, and had been for some time, which was probably why she felt so run down—her body was trying to fight the infection. Aside from that, the doctor said, Inez was as healthy as a horse. As soon as possible, he said, you will need to get your tonsils removed. But in the meantime, he said, "Here, take these," handing her strychnine and arsenic pills, common (though deadly) treatments for infection in the decades before penicillin.[7]

Privately, Inez struggled with depression. Her career in the law had languished. The child she yearned for didn't appear. But forward she forged, adrenaline allowing her to dazzle onstage and then collapse into bed afterward. Vida was a classically trained singer, and she entertained audiences with her voice while waiting for Inez to take the stage, sometimes in a large hall, sometimes at an intimate ladies' tea, and sometimes on the back terrace of a train car. "After each meeting," Vida said, Inez "wilted and looked like a ghost."[8]

But before every event, Inez would rally. Newspapers described her delivery as having a "dramatic charm," and that what she had to say was "fearlessly expressed."[9] Another noted that she was "as beautiful as her pictures promised," and that her personality was "magnetic."[10]

At one speech in Boise, Inez shouted, "What is your answer, women with the ballot? Are you going to lick the hand that smites you like the hounds?" And, "Women should assert their power. If women don't respect themselves, no one else will."[11]

Rebecca Mitchell had been dead for eight years. But Inez's position on that stage, encouraging enfranchised women—like the women of Idaho—to set aside their party preference and vote in the best interest of women nationwide? That was only possible because of the decades of labor that Mitchell and women like her put in, the path that was cleared for the people who came behind.

"It is women for women now, and shall be until the fight is won!" Inez declared. "How can our nation be free with half of its citizens mute and unadvised? In union alone is strength!"[12] Inez rallied her listeners, bringing them what she felt was a message of hope.

Some trains didn't depart until 2:00 a.m., and some arrived at 5:00 a.m. The lack of consistent rest, the strain of being in the public eye, of having to look and speak the part at all times, contributed to Inez's malaise. "We travel every night, get up early every morning, and keep on the go all day," Inez remarked to a dinner guest in Multnomah, Oregon. "I cannot see how I can keep going, but I just have to."[13]

Inez thought of the tens of thousands of women who were waiting for her at the coming stops. She thought of her own family and friends in New York who could not vote yet. In fact, *Inez herself* could not yet vote. She thought of the all the Black women in the South who would never be granted the right to vote from their state because of racial prejudice. Inez insisted on pressing forward. She had come too far to turn back now. Forward.

By the time they arrived in Montana, Inez had a fever. She glittered on stage, with *The Butte Daily Post* reporting that her "personality . . . [was] no less striking than her personal beauty." She told her audience, "Our self-respect as suffragists demands that we repudiate the political party that has consistently ignored the claims of women."[14] But in private, her head "had on a tight iron cup of pain," her throat hurt so badly it was nearly all she could think about, and she was so weak she could only stand with assistance. They summoned another doctor. This one prescribed strong coffee and more strychnine.[15]

Strychnine is used today as rat poison. It's a neurotoxin, and works by binding to receptors on nerve cells, which then makes them more susceptible to stimulation with lower levels of neurotransmitters. It was used medicinally at the time as a stimulant, which is why doctors would have prescribed it to Inez, whose stamina and energy were flagging. One small problem with strychnine: it is deadly at even a very low dose, and the difference between a medicinally effective dose and a deadly dose is tiny. The muscles you use to breathe can contract so strongly that they suffocate you to death.

The grueling tour continued on, but Inez's spirits were buoyed by the crowds that loved her. Ever the media darling, Inez's uncanny ability to captivate a room impressed all the newspaper writers who were dispatched to report on her doings, and when they saw her in person, they continued to marvel at her beauty. The attention she was bringing to the cause was vital. No one else could do what Inez was doing.

Inez arrived in San Francisco strung out on very little sleep after a blur of dozens of stops. True to form, her fatigue didn't stop her from wowing a crowd of fifteen hundred people before departing by train later that evening for Pasadena, near where Maria de Lopez lived. A train accident elsewhere on the tracks delayed Inez and Vida's train. They didn't even board until 3:00 a.m. The next day, tour organizers had to substitute another speaker for Inez at an event for the Pasadena club women.

After the mishap of Pasadena, Inez pressed on to speak at Blanchard Hall, another Los Angeles venue. Blanchard Hall had a capacity of eight hundred. One thousand people crammed the auditorium, with hundreds more turned away at the door for lack of space. "President Wilson, how long must this go on?" Inez implored from the podium. "President Wilson, how long must women wait for liberty?"[16] She raised her arm to demonstrate the sweep of her argument, her compelling voice carrying through the hall.

And then, without warning, she collapsed into a "dead faint." *The Los Angeles Times* described how she "crumpled like a wilted white rose and lay stark upon the platform."[17] Women rushed to her side and carried her offstage. Fifteen minutes later, Inez was back, this time sitting in a chair to talk to the audience. "I have tonsillitis," she explained. "Don't worry about me."[18]

The next morning, Inez's companions summoned another doctor, who immediately called in Dr. Catherine Lynch to examine her. No amount of strong coffee, sleep, or strychnine had cured Inez, and her collapse left Vida legitimately concerned for her sister. By now, Inez's gums were bleeding and she was too weak to stand. Lynch took one look at her and called in a throat specialist, who determined that her ailment was now affecting her heart. "If you don't have surgery immediately to remove your tonsils and several infected teeth," they told her, "you will die. Period."

Inez and the organizers of the tour were desperate to continue. The election was but weeks away, and this was their last chance to plead their case—to set free the disenfranchised women of America. But when Inez became so weak she could barely sit up, Vida finally took charge. She was used to being the younger sister to the beautiful and magnetic Inez, but she refused to let her sister die from her lack of action. Vida insisted on admitting Inez to the hospital.

Once Inez was examined at Good Samaritan Hospital in Los Angeles, she was given IV hydration, and blood tests revealed the real culprit behind Inez's failing health: aplastic anemia, a chronic illness in which one's body is unable to properly make new red blood cells. Inez's blood counts were half what they should have been. Her teeth were operated on, but doctors deemed her not well enough to undergo the tonsil procedure. They hoped she would improve enough in a few weeks that she'd be able to withstand the second surgery. There was no choice now, the rest of the tour had to be called off. Inez was distraught, shivering and feverish beneath mountains of blankets, unable to get warm.

The news of her illness hit the papers, and the world waited with bated breath. Dozens of telegrams arrived for Inez every day. Reporters crowded the hospital hallway, eager for any news they could glean. Updates of her condition were published around the country.

Two weeks had now passed since Inez was hospitalized. Despite trying to boost her blood counts with food and hydration, her anemia was still too severe for her to undergo the needed tonsil surgery. She required a blood transfusion.

Transfusions in 1916 are the same as they are today, in that a person gets blood via an IV. But they are different in nearly every other way. For example: for Inez's first transfusion, Vida sat on a chair next to her, and blood was taken directly from Vida's arm and put into Inez's. Inez rallied, but then relapsed. Vida donated again, weakening her own condition considerably.

Inez's husband arrived, and together, Eugen and Vida kept Inez company in the hospital. Vida was forced to deliver the bad news to their parents: things were not looking good. You should come.

When Inez's parents arrived, doctors barred them from seeing her, except for when Inez was asleep—they felt that too much stimulation would harm Inez's chance of recovery. More transfusions were ordered, with four friends that shared her blood type offering up donations. Each yielded the same results: a short rally followed by a relapse.

Three weeks after entering the hospital, her fever spiked to 106. She had developed pleurisy, an inflammation of the chest lining, and every excruciating breath had to be worked for. Inez kept insisting she would improve, promising her parents that she was going to be better any day. She saw another suffrage worker who came to visit, and Inez whispered her encouragement, "It's not going to be so hard now. Women have shown their power."[19] Wilson had won reelection, despite Inez's best efforts, but progress on suffrage was being made at the state level.

Inez's body was giving out, purpled all over in dark bruises, but her mind remained clear. Her family grew grief-stricken, and her husband beside himself. "Shall I come with you?" Eugen asked, desperate.

"No," she told him. "You go ahead and live another life."[20]

A few hours later, on November 25, 1916, Inez Milholland Boissevain died. She was only thirty years old.

At once Inez became the Joan of Arc of the suffrage movement, a martyr for the cause of liberty. An obituary ran on the front page of *The New York Times* the next day. Suffrage workers sprang into action planning a memorial befitting such a hero, and one month later, on Christmas Day, she was memorialized in Statuary Hall inside the U.S. Capitol. She was the first women ever honored there, and she was the first person so honored who wasn't a member of Congress.

When I say that the National Woman's Party wanted to send a message with this tribute, that is an understatement. They wanted a *spectacle* of suffrage. They wanted Congress and President Wilson to see what they had done to Inez, how the only reason she undertook this excruciating journey to begin with was because they continued to deny women the right to vote. Washington, D.C., would see suffrage from every angle that Christmas Day. Suffrage leaders swathed the Capitol in banners and buntings in the colors of the suffrage movement: purple, gold, and white.

Over one thousand people left their Christmas plans behind to take part in the service for Inez Milholland. Security had to turn people away at the door. In the House of Representatives office buildings across the street, a boys' choir assembled and processed into Statuary Hall, chanting the words on the banner Inez had carried, now held aloft by renowned suffragist Alice Paul:

Forward, out of error
Leave behind the night
Forward through the darkness
Forward into light

Lucy Burns held a banner that read: "As he died to make men holy, let us die to make men free." *The Washington Post* reported that other banners cited Scripture, saying, "Greater love hath no man than this, that he lay down his life for his friends."[21]

Elizabeth Kent, wife of California senator William Kent, said that Inez was "blithe and valiant and unafraid to be herself, even though she knew that self . . . would not be understood by the many with eyes on today."[22]

Suffragist Maud Younger eulogized her, saying, "Inez Milholland is one around whom legends will grow up. Generations to come will point out Mount Inez and tell of the beautiful woman who sleeps her last on its slopes."[23]

(In 2019, the Department of the Interior renamed a peak in the Adirondacks in her honor. You can visit Mount Inez in the town of Lewis, New York.)

"They will tell of her in the West, tell of the vision of loveliness as she flashed through on her last burning mission, flashed through to her death, a falling star in the western heavens," Maud Younger continued. "But neither legend nor vision is liberty, which was her life. Liberty cannot die. No work for liberty can be lost. It lives on in the hearts of the people, in their hopes, their aspirations, their activities. It becomes part of the life of the nation."[24]

The moment of Inez's passing opened another area for women to demonstrate their bravery and worth on the world stage. Only four months after her death, the United States officially entered the Great War. The U.S. military recruited some twenty-two thousand female nurses to serve overseas, but there is one group that stands out in my mind who never get the credit they deserve: the Hello Girls.

THIRTEEN

FRANCE

1916

The United States may not have had a fantastic military when World War I broke out, but what it did have was a booming telecom industry. Companies like American Telephone & Telegraph crisscrossed the country with wires, seizing the opportunity to capitalize on what they undoubtedly saw as the wave of the future: the telephone. At the time, placing a telephone call didn't require dialing anything, you simply picked up the receiver, and an operator would be waiting for you on the other end, cordially asking for the number you wished to ring. You were then connected using a series of signals, interchanges, and a bit of magic to someone half a continent away, or even down the street.

Once the decision was made to enter the war, the U.S. government began working with AT&T to assemble telecom equipment that would be needed overseas. But telephone and telegraph lines were only part of the communication system the military needed: someone had to operate the switchboards. Most people who worked as telephone operators in the early twentieth century were women.

Because they would be working in France, the women who were to serve overseas as telephone operators also had to speak French fluently.

When applications for the positions opened, the government was deluged with women wanting adventure (and of course, a steady paycheck and the ability to say they did their part in the war). Ultimately, only 223 women were chosen for a duty that had massive and lasting impacts on the world.[1]

If I asked you how women ultimately gained suffrage in the United States, you would probably point to people like Inez Milholland. And you would be right. But the women who took possession of the ball and ran, dodging bullets, being denied pensions and military benefits, braving fire and hypothermia, to move that ball the remaining yards over the finish line? It was the "Hello Girls," even though they didn't know it yet.

Woodrow Wilson felt that women who worked for suffrage were "abhorrent," and that they should not be engaged in things like speaking in public.[2]

"No," he said to the demands of suffrage fighters.

"No," he said to the paraders and picketers.

"No," to the members of Congress in favor of suffrage.

"No," to the letters and telegrams from suffrage activists.

So what changed his mind? Historian Elizabeth Cobbs argues that the Hello Girls who risked their lives on the front lines of the military battles, operating telephone switchboards under abysmal conditions with speed and efficiency, slowly chipped away at Wilson's resistance. Over time, Wilson began to realize that we couldn't ask women to serve their country and not give them a say in how it was run.

One of the best-known Hello Girls was a take-charge gal with a baby face named Grace Banker. She was one of the more than seven thousand women who applied to work for AT&T and the Signal Corps, much like ambulance drivers worked for both the Red Cross and the Army.[3] When she finally received word back about her application, the Army asked for Banker's educational and work history, her medical history, and a photograph—because, of course, one's appearance was of great importance in such trying times. Grace, who had worked for AT&T for several years by the time the United States became involved in the war, was ultimately chosen to be the leader of a unit of female telephone operators in France.[4]

Before shipping out, groups of women assembled in New York, received some basic training, got fitted for their uniforms, and put together their kits. Women were given a list of things to purchase and bring with them, including iodine, sewing tools, gloves, and bloomers. They were also issued a uniform, which recruits later reported feeling very stylish in, that included a coat, skirt, hat, and more. But the telephone operators were required to pay for their own uniforms, unlike everyone else Uncle Sam was hiring.

And the price? Around $300, which is more than $7,000 in modern money.[5] I can't think of another uniform that would cost $7,000, except for perhaps a suit someone would wear to work on the International Space Station. Seven thousand whole American dollars. Did all of the recruits have $300? Of course not. AT&T said they'd front them the money and then deduct it in increments from their paychecks.

Speaking of paychecks, the female members of the Signal Corps, the Hello Girls, were told they were part of the American Expeditionary Forces, and would be able to receive military benefits, like a pension. They swore an oath to the Constitution like everyone else. They wore (incredibly expensive) military uniforms. Yet when they applied for benefits available to others, like War Risk Insurance, they were told they weren't eligible because they were contract employees.[6]

But the Hello Girls were never given a contract of any kind to sign. This meant that when women returned home, they were denied—over and over for decades—any kind of military benefits, even though enlisted men who worked in an office in New Jersey and whose lives were never at risk were eligible to get them.[7]

During the interim, after the telephone equipment landed and before the Hello Girls arrived, French women helped the military place phone calls on the exchanges. It took, on average, a full sixty seconds for calls to be connected. After the Americans arrived, it took twenty.[8] "Number, please," they asked, with an expert mix of efficiency and warmth. Men reported that just hearing an American woman on the other end of the line gave them hope and made them feel like they were capable of turning the war around.

The women operating telephone switchboards in Europe, sometimes in gas masks, their nerves jangled by the booms outside their windows, were far removed from Inez's suffrage fight. They knew it was happening, certainly, but they had to focus on the task at hand: connecting calls to win the war. "I just managed, managed, managed," Grace Banker later said.[9] And these were not ordinary calls—in many cases, the calls were matters of grave security, and the Hello Girls had to exercise complete discretion. The threat of court-martial hung over their heads.

Telephones allowed men at the front to communicate their positions, which was particularly useful when they were trapped. From cellars and trenches, men were able to make phone calls using portable phones that didn't require electricity, give the appropriate passcode, and be connected with someone who might be able to send in reinforcements or devise a plan.

But funnily enough, phones weren't the only way men at the front communicated with each other. They also used birds. Pigeon birds. Carrier pigeons, which are the thoroughbred horse of the bird world. Capable of flying twelve to fifteen hours per day without a break, covering five hundred to seven hundred miles at speeds of thirty to sixty miles per hour, the cocks and hens of the U.S. Pigeon Intelligence Service delivered many an important message in a moment of trouble.[10]

(There's no question that Bert from *Sesame Street* would be proud of the U.S. Pigeon Intelligence Service.)

When presented with the idea of using pigeons to carry messages, in addition to telephones, the Army at first was like, *Mmmmmmmm, let's pass on the birds. We've got enough to deal with without adding pigeons on a ship across the Atlantic into the mix.* (Forget snakes on a plane, this was birds on a boat.) I was like, "Why are fully grown adult human women paying seven thousand dollars for an outfit, but somehow we have money for birds?" But hey, that's just me. No shade to the pigeons, I love birds.

Very few military men had any pigeon skills. So even once the Army was like, "Let's go with the pigeons," they had difficulty finding people to help train, feed, and house them. When they eventually recruited two men—David Buscall and John Carney—to head up the pigeon program, it took some time to train other soldiers into the wizarding world of pigeoneering.[11]

Pigeons had their feathers marked with paint—boys were blue and girls were red—and they learned that they only got food at their roost. If they were hungry, they needed to get back home. And home, in the case of WWI pigeons, was a car chassis retrofitted with cages for individual birds. Men heading out into the front lines carried a bird with them in a wicker backpack, and if they needed help, they would write a message on a slip of paper, affix it to the pigeon's ankle, and set it free.

Pigeons were so excellent at finding home that they could immediately begin winging their way back, no matter the time of day, no matter how hungry they were, no matter if there were bombs and guns being fired all around them. Once they made it home, the message was read and relayed to the appropriate people, often by telephone, and the birds got some food.

The Army eventually acquired around 4,400 pigeons for their use during the war, and had twenty mobile lofts that the birds would return to.[12] Germans who became aware that both the British and the Americans were using birds began to shoot at every pigeon they saw, hoping to intercept important messages.

The most famous moment in pigeoneering involved a bird named Cher Ami, whom I affectionately call Cher. Cher was presumed to be a girl and was treated as such, but genetic testing after his death later demon-strated his maleness.

A group of American troops found themselves completely fenced in by Germans in October 1918. Hunkered down on the side of a slope in a ravine, mortar fire began to rain down on the men, who knew that if they exposed their position to the Germans, they were toast.

The Americans soon realized they were taking fire from their own military, who couldn't see them in the ravine. The stranded troops had only one pigeon left—the others had already returned messages or been killed by the enemy. So Cher was fitted with a pigeongram that read, "We are along the road parallel 276.4. Our own artillery is dropping a barrage directly on us. For heaven's sake stop it."[13]

As Cher left the backpack basket, he first flew to a nearby tree and waited, disoriented by the sounds of mortar shells and gunfire around him. One of the men of the Lost Battalion, as it was later called, ran full tilt toward the tree, shaking the branches, trying to get Cher to fly away. Cher fluttered from branch to branch, momentarily unsure of what to do next. The soldier screamed at him to go, hurry, fly away, knowing the lives of his unit were on the line.

Finally, Cher took off from the tree branch. He was immediately spotted by the enemy, who took aim at his small pigeon chest. BOOM. Cher felt the bullet pierce his breast. A flurry of feathers followed him to the ground.

Breathing heavily, Cher considered his surroundings. *Am I . . . alive?* he might have wondered. After a few moments of rest, it dawned on him that the landscape of warfare surrounding him could hardly be birdie heaven. Staying where he was meant certain death, so Cher tested his wings, flapping strongly to see if he could get off the ground.

The moment came in which Cher realized he had no choice but to try. Ignoring the ripping feeling in his chest, he pumped his wings, and soon found himself three, six, nine, thirty feet in the air. Everything up here seemed familiar. He could feel the magnetic fields of the earth beneath him, steering his little pigeon compass over the sights and smells of the battlefield below.

Up, up, up his wings took him, too high for any bullet to reach. It took no time at all for the invisible forces that rule the earth—the forces that create auroras and were being studied by the likes of Einstein, who was tucked away in a flat in Berlin during the Great War, the forces that creatures like him had always felt and experienced and known as real—to guide him from the currents above to that one tiny, specific dot far below.

Cher began to dive, his compass telling him he was home, the pull growing stronger as he picked up speed. The smells and sounds of his roost drew nearer and nearer, until his flight wisdom told him it was time to brake and land softly on his perch.

"*Cher Ami!*" his keeper crooned, taking stock of the injured bird. He read the message attached to his ankle, and immediately the army commanders picked up the phone. "*Number, please?*" they heard as they executed plans to aid the trapped unit. Cher had done it, but it was not without cost. Emergency veterinary services were needed. A large portion of Cher's breast had to be removed, and so did one of his legs.[14]

By the time the Lost Battalion was rescued, the men had been in the ravine for days. Of the six hundred men that went in, only 194 reportedly walked out without assistance.[15]

The press had a field day when it heard Cher's story, and the public ate it up. *The New York Herald* wrote, "Cher Ami is her name, and that she proved herself truly a dear friend of liberty is attested by the circumstances that she left a leg in the Argonne; that across her dauntless breast there is a ghastly scar that marks the trail of a German bullet that spilled her blood but failed to chill her spirit, and that she wears the symbol of her homeland's gratitude for her brave and able service—the Distinguished Service Cross, conferred upon her by Gen. Pershing himself."[16]

When the war ended, Cher sailed the Atlantic as few birds in history have done, riding in the cabin of John Carney and undertaking a press tour upon arrival. The media hailed Cher Ami as a hero who was a "faithful servant" who "never complained."[17] And that's how eventually, when Cher Ami's life was cut short by his war wounds, he ended up in the Smithsonian, where he remains, his bulgy eyes peering out from behind the glass.

Tellingly, Cher enjoyed more retirement benefits than the Hello Girls. That didn't change until 1977, when Merle Anderson of the Signal Corps, with the help of lawyer Mark Hough, finally got the attention of Congress. Hough put his cards on the table, essentially saying, "We will sue you and we will win, or you can take action on your own and give the handful of remaining Signal Corps members their due."

The Army treated them as members of the military when they were in Europe, he said. They wore military uniforms and insignia. Some, like Grace Banker, received military awards, and even the most senior commanders believed they were in the military and acted accordingly. The lawyer pointed out that it was actually illegal for people to wear military uniforms and insignia in this context if they were not in the military, and it was the Army who told the women they had to wear (and *pay* for) the uniforms.

Congress finally listened, and passed a bill granting the Hello Girls their official military status, a bill that the newly elected Jimmy Carter signed into law.[18]

By the end of the Great War, Woodrow Wilson's posture toward suffrage had softened considerably. On September 30, 1918, he went to Congress and said, "This war could not have been fought, either by the nations engaged or by America, if it had not been for the services of women. . . . Are we alone to ask and take the utmost that women can give—service and sacrifice of every kind—and still say that we do not see what title that gives them to stand by our sides in the guidance of the affairs of their nation and ours? We have made partners of the women in this war; shall we admit them only to a partnership of sacrifice and suffering and toil and not to a partnership of privilege and of right?"[19]

Two more long years wore on before the Nineteenth Amendment was finally passed by Congress and ratified by enough states to be added to the Constitution. Make no mistake. For the suffragists like Inez Milholland, who gave her very life, for the members of the military who were willing to give theirs, for women of every belief and stripe: justice and freedom—suffrage—was not granted, it was seized. Suffrage was not a gift bestowed, delivered in a basket on a doorstep. Suffrage was the hard-won harvest of seventy years of toil.

☆

An Orientation
of the Spirit

———————

FOURTEEN

ANNA THOMAS JEANES

Philadelphia, 1822

If you google Anna Thomas Jeanes, you'll see there is but one portrait of her, painted after she died. While she was alive, she didn't believe in having her picture taken or her portrait painted. She wears a simple black dress, a thick white shawl pulled over her shoulders. Her gray hair is tied back and covered with a lace cap. Her expression is kind. Knowing. Her gaze says that seeing you is a very pleasant sight, indeed.[1]

Anna spent her childhood as the apple of her father's eye, doted upon and given simple privileges that reflected her upbringing in nineteenth-century Philadelphia. As the last baby of the family, baby number ten, every new milestone was a delight to her parents. She was marvelously bright, reading fairy tales before she could even begin school.

But by the time Anna made her earthside debut in 1822, only six of her nine siblings were alive, and by the time Anna was four, her mother was also dead.[2]

Anna's father was well-off. Born before the Revolutionary War, he made his money as a merchant of imported goods, and the family lived near the Philadelphia harbor in a handsome home that was well appointed but lacking the ostentatiousness of wealthy New York society.

The Jeaneses didn't bedeck themselves in jewels. They didn't go on the Grand Tour to revel in the palaces of Europe. They dressed mostly in black cotton, finding even dark silk too garish for their modest Quaker convictions.

Mary was Anna's older sister by several years, and she stepped into a maternal role after their mother died. The Jeanes children devoted themselves to learning. Several of Anna's siblings were quite successful in their own right—one of her brothers was a doctor and three were merchants. Only one of the six children who lived to adulthood ever married, and that marriage only produced one child, who died in infancy.

Anna's brother Jacob, the doctor, started Hahnemann Medical College, which would later become part of Drexel University.[3]

Her brother Joseph was fascinated by fossils. It's long been a source of amusement to me that some of the greatest thinkers in history, the people of the Enlightenment, the humans who wrote the Constitution and founded the world's oldest democracy, didn't know about dinosaurs. Though scientists had started complex systems of classification of animal and plant life, and understood that the fossil record illustrated life on earth that had long since gone extinct, the field of what would be called paleontology wasn't officially defined until 1822. (That didn't stop Thomas Jefferson from being obsessed with mastodons, though.)

Yes, over the years, farmers and builders had dug up large bones and seen things they didn't understand. But paleontology wasn't a field until the nineteenth century. No one was out there Ross Geller-ing fossil identification. (By the way, did anyone actually buy the idea that Ross on *Friends* had a PhD and worked at a very prestigious facility? Come on now.) As part of the nineteenth-century enthusiasm for the natural sciences, the Jeaneses were highly instrumental in building the fossil collection of the Philadelphia Academy of Natural Sciences.

One record says Joseph Jeanes helped donate 248 bird species from Africa and Mexico. Another says he donated a "fine suite of California shells," while Anna donated some glass models of mollusks.[4] They donated elephant skulls, and Joseph was one of a few dozen men who contributed to help purchase a collection of more than a thousand human crania.

During this time, Joseph Leidy, one of the world's famed naturalists and the father of vertebrate paleontology, was working at the Academy of Natural Sciences, now a part of Drexel University. In the 1830s, John Estaugh Hopkins was digging around in a marl pit in New Jersey and uncovered some *very* large bones. Marl, by the way, is a mineral-rich clay, and people used it as fertilizer. Hopkins gave some of the curious bones away to friends, but kept one of them at his house as a source of amusement.

More than two decades later, a man named William Foulke was dining at the home of John Hopkins, when he saw this giant bone sitting out. Foulke was interested in these sorts of things, and he was like, "Excuse me? What is this and why do you have it?"

"I dug that up in a marl pit a piece back," imagine Hopkins saying, taking Foulke to the place where he had found the fossils.

Excitedly, Foulke sent word to Joseph Leidy, and before long they had excavated a nearly complete Hadrosaurus skeleton and put it on display at the Academy. The dinosaur, now known as *Hadrosaurus foulkii*, is still housed there.[5]

The Jeanes family lived mere blocks from other famous Philadelphians of the time—like women's suffrage activist Lucretia Mott, one of the earliest pioneers of women's rights and an organizer of the Seneca Falls Convention. It's likely Anna Jeanes and Lucretia Mott knew each other—not only were they neighbors, they were both Quaker women, and the Society of Friends was closely knit. They probably attended the same meeting house.

Quakerism was founded in the mid-1600s in England by a man named George Fox. It grew out of Protestantism, but it was a version of Christianity unlike any other. And because of its unique beliefs and practices, Fox and his followers were severely persecuted in England. They were beaten and imprisoned, and it's no wonder that Quakers wanted to escape and made their way to the colonies. William Penn himself, one of the Quaker founders of Pennsylvania, was imprisoned in the Tower of London more than once.

When Penn was a teenager, his family was visited by a Quaker missionary, and Penn said that "the Lord visited me and gave me divine Impressions of Himself."[6] Penn lived a privileged life, including being in the court of King Louis XIV, but he was kicked out of his wealthy family's home because he decided to follow Quakerism.

Why were the Quakers so hated in England? For starters, they refused to do things like bow to their superiors or remove their hats in deference, because they believed in the equality of all people. This was, of course, a direct affront to the king and the aristocracy. They refused to pay tithes and would not swear an oath, both of which were quite problematic in 1600s Britain.

Eventually, after multiple bouts of sitting in jail, William Penn went to the king and the Duke of York and was like, "Hey. Let's make a deal. Why don't you leave us alone and let us depart from this dreary little island?"

The king said, "Sounds good to me," and eventually Penn became the world's largest private landowner. The king and the Duke of York sold Penn forty-five thousand square miles of territory in America.[7] (Not acres. Miles.)

Penn started calling the area—he hadn't even been there yet—"Sylvania," which means "forest" in Latin, and King Charles II added the Penn in front of it, which is how we got the name Pennsylvania.

But it wasn't like all the Quakers of Europe were prepared to leave everything they had and start over again. Were there houses available for purchase on these forty-five thousand square miles of land in America? No. What were they going to find there? "Sylvania," remember? Woods. The Lenape tribes, whom they knew nothing about, were they going to want us to live there? To leave Europe would mean constructing an entirely new life from scratch. How are we going to feed our kids while we're on a boat earning zero pounds sterling?

So William Penn wrote a compelling description of the new land he wanted the Quakers to inhabit. He described this new utopian community in Pennsylvania, where everyone would be free to practice their religion as they saw fit, and no one was going to be imprisoned in a tower for not taking off their hat. The promise of this freedom appealed to many Quaker families and also to religious minorities like the Amish and Mennonites in Germany. Soon, Penn had parceled out hundreds of thousands of acres to willing Christian immigrants from Europe.

William Penn died penniless back in England in 1718. He was a terrible business manager who was cheated out of much of his fortune. But one thing he did was refuse to force Pennsylvania's Quakerism onto everyone else. He wanted to be free to practice his faith how he saw fit, and while it would have been easier to just set up Pennsylvania as a Quaker colony, he resisted on principle.

Other than the hats and the tithes, the oaths and the equality, what exactly did Quakers believe? For that, we turn to a Quaker historian, a man that Anna Jeanes knew well, Howard Malcolm Jenkins. He presented at the World's College of Religions in 1893[8] and described what he called "The First Five Principles of Quakerism," which were:

1. The Supreme Being, to whom we attribute the supreme qualities of Goodness, Love, and Mercy.
2. The Divine Immanence, in which God directly reveals himself to the perceptions of Man, that his light shines into our souls.

3. The Scriptures, which record the visitations of God to the souls of men in the past, and our reverence for them creates desire for the truth and enlightenment they contain.

4. The Divinity of Christ, and he is regarded as the highest possible manifestation of God in man.

5. The Christ Rule in Daily Life, which includes love, not hatred; brotherly kindness, not oppression; moderation, not excess; simplicity, not ostentation; sincerity, not pretense; truth, not deceit.

Some Quaker beliefs blended well with other forms of Christianity, but the Quaker belief about the Divine Immanence, sometimes called an Inner Light, a Divine Spark, or the Light of Christ, puts all humans on equal footing—people of all colors, races, and genders. And while it's true that this is one of the reasons we sometimes find the Quakers at the forefront of the women's suffrage movements and working for the abolition of slavery—they believed every single human is an equal vessel of God—William Penn himself was an enslaver. And his biographer Andrew Murphy says he "displayed no signs of a troubled conscience over it."[9] It would be many decades before the Quaker Society of Friends would officially oppose enslavement.

Anna never worked outside the home, and she was cared for financially by her father, and then by her brothers. She took painting classes. She wrote two books, mostly for the benefit of her small circle of friends. But by November 1894, all of Anna's family was dead. Because none of her siblings had living spouses or children, that meant that Anna inherited all of her family's wealth.[10]

At the age of seventy-two, she was in possession of a vast personal fortune—$5 million, which is around $178 million in modern money.

What would an ordinary woman who came into sudden wealth do with her money in 1894? Take trips to the seaside? Buy a house in Newport?

Purchase all the gems and baubles that caught her eye? Bedeck herself in ostrich plume hats? Dine at the finest restaurants? Join the upper crust of Gilded Age society?

Anna was no ordinary woman, and that's exactly what she didn't do.

No, she didn't travel. In fact, she seems to have never ventured further than Seneca Falls, New York. Did she attend the Seneca Women's Convention there? Signs point to yes.

No, she didn't buy fancy headwear and custom-made clothes. Even in Anna's old age, her letters indicate disapproval of other Quaker Friends who pretended to live simple lives but who were secretly getting their pictures taken and wearing silk.

No, Anna did not spend the money on herself. Instead, she realized that her time was short, and the world was in need of much good.

Perhaps Anna was inspired by the Quaker preacher Edward Burrough, who wrote in 1659, "We are not for Names, nor Men, nor Titles of Government, nor are we for this Party, nor against the other, because of its Name and Pretence; but we are for Justice and Mercy, and Truth and Peace, and true Freedom, that these may be exalted in our Nation."[11]

How closely these sentiments would be echoed by Gouverneur Morris when he wrote the Preamble to the Constitution more than one hundred years later. And more than two hundred years later, Miss Anna T. Jeanes asked herself what she could do to bring more justice, more mercy, more truth, more peace, and more freedom to the world. Instead of spending $5 million on fancy furnishings and luxury cruises, she decided to give it all away.

So Anna began making bequests. A few causes had always been important to the Jeanes family. Anna's sister Mary, for instance, was the founder of a home for African American children who had nowhere to go—kind of like an emergency shelter.

In the annual reports, managers of the Home for Destitute Colored

Children describe the circumstances under which children came into their care, including a mother who had been abandoned by her husband. The mother was hospitalized and could no longer care for her daughter. Another report described a boy found sleeping in a railway station, begging for food.[12]

The Jeanes Six, as I call the six siblings who lived to adulthood—Jacob, Joshua, Samuel, Joseph, Mary, and Anna—stayed out of the spotlight intentionally. Occasionally, you see one of their names printed in a small blurb in a Philadelphia newspaper as having been to this annual meeting or contributing to that cause.

For example, a notice in *The Philadelphia Inquirer* from 1883 shows Mary and Samuel Jeanes as having contributed to a children's sanitarium.[13] Another article shows that both Samuel and Joseph sent money to a fund to help flood victims out west.[14]

The Jeanes Six cared about the human condition, not about naming rights. The Jeaneses were founding sponsors of the first women's medical college of Pennsylvania, their names and contributions printed in the annual reports for transparency and bookkeeping purposes. But they didn't want their picture taken at a ribbon cutting or to be interviewed by the newspaper. (And if you're from Philly, maybe you know there actually is a Jeanes Campus at Temple University Hospital. It is named after the Jeanes Six, most especially Anna, but not at her request.)

Anna cared about women's equality, but she was not one to make public speeches advocating for it. Anna is described by others as being a near recluse. Peculiar, with few close friends. She even seemed cranky at times. A story that appeared in newspapers in 1901 recounts how the people who lived in the row house next door to her played the piano far, far too much for Anna's taste, and she asked them multiple times to *Please, for the love of sweet baby Jesus, stop playing the piano so much.* When they refused to acquiesce, Anna just bought the house. Here's how one newspaper account described it:

Anna T. Jeanes, a Philadelphia spinster, who has money enough to be independent, was annoyed by a young woman who lived next door and played the piano with a persistence worthy of a better cause. Miss Jeanes did not go to the neighbors and tell them that she wished the girl would get married or paralyzed or something, and she didn't write anonymous letters. She stood the playing as long as she could: then she paid $60,000 for the house in which the girl lived, making it necessary for the latter and her parents to move.[15]

Note that $60,000 at that time is about $2.2 million today. Whether Anna paid the family a premium to vacate the premises and enjoy the peace and quiet, I know not.

Anna wanted to make a large bequest to Swarthmore College, which was controlled by the Quaker Society of Friends. But she would only give the gift on one condition: that they agreed to abandon college athletics altogether, and most especially football. Anna considered football a waste of time and a distraction from what really mattered.

Swarthmore pondered her offer for a long time and decided, ultimately, to reject Anna's money and keep athletics.[16]

The Jeaneses tried to follow the edict found in Matthew 6:3, which can be summarized as, "Let not thy left hand know what thy right hand doeth." Keep your good works a secret, and don't publicly claim credit for them. God's rewards came, the Jeaneses believed, when their work was shielded from public view.

And now, friend, it's time now for me to tell you how I met Anna. When Anna came into her vast personal fortune, she, of course, had many people vying for her funds. She refused to take meetings with most of the people who courted her, but there was one meeting she did take—with William James Edwards.

FIFTEEN

WILLIAM JAMES EDWARDS

Alabama, 1869

Wﾠilliam Edwards was born at the close of the Civil War in Snow Hill, Alabama, to a family that was soon to be emancipated from enslavement. His birth name was Ulysses Grant Edwards, but after his mother died when he was one year old, his grandmother changed his name to William. He adopted his grandfather's name, James, as a middle name later.[1]

When William was a small boy, he became deathly ill with a painful condition that caused portions of his bones to die. He could barely walk, and for a time, his main method of locomotion was crawling around the yard. Because of his illness, he couldn't live with his father, and his grandmother had since passed away as well. He was forced to stay with his aunt Rina, who could barely feed her own children, let alone him. The only full meals he ate were when his aunt and cousin gave up their food so he could have more.

Because his family had to work to subsist, William was left home alone for many hours a day, which he spent teaching himself arithmetic and reading one of the few books they had. His medical condition did not improve after several months of his aunt's care, and Rina, now desperate, went door to door, begging for nickels, impressing upon her neighbors how dire William's health was and how badly he needed a doctor.

One Sunday, a large group of people stopped by their tiny home after church. William was sitting on the ground outside, watching baby chicks play, and overheard the adults inside. "You should send him to the poorhouse," one person said.

"You've done too much for him already," said another.

"Drive him away and let him go wherever he can find shelter."[2]

The implication was clear to William: His life was not worth saving, and everyone would be better off if he were dead. Distraught, he hobbled beneath a pine tree, and for more than an hour, begged God to let him die. When the prayer was done, he laid down, folded his arms, and waited for the prayer to work. For his life on earth to end.

But no such answer came. Instead, William felt better than he had in months, and his aunt Rina was even more determined than ever to get him well. The following year, she rented a small patch of land and planted seeds, tending to her garden and selling her harvest. At the end of the summer, she had managed to scrape together five dollars to take William to see a better doctor than the one that was available nearby.

Dr. George Keyser gave William medicine, and every time he needed to see the physician again, William would bring any money his aunt had. Sometimes it was none. As William rode a neighbor's mule the ten miles to see the doctor, he would pray that a way would be made, and that the doctor would find it in his heart to give him his medicine even if he could not pay.

Eventually, Dr. Keyser told him, "You must continue to come and get treatment, even if you don't have the funds."[3] When William was well enough for surgery, Dr. Keyser told Aunt Rina that she needed to get him a place to stay that was closer to his office, so that he could be checked on every day. Rina found another woman who had previously been enslaved at the same plantation and who agreed to let William live with her while he received medical care.

Dr. Keyser's notes read:

> WJ Edwards was sent to me by his aunt, Rina Rivers, for medical treatment. He had been sick for several months from scrofula, and it had infected the bone of his left arm near the elbow joint, and the heel bone of his left foot. It was with much difficulty and pain that he walked at all.
>
> I had to remove the dead bone (necrosed bone) from his arm and heel many times. He always stood the operation patiently and manifested so great a desire to get well, I kept him near me a long time and patiently watched his case.
>
> After four years of treatment, his heel cured up nicely, and he was enabled to walk very well, and the following fall, he picked cotton. With prudence, care, and close application to cotton picking, he saved money enough to very nearly pay his medical account, and his fare to Booker T. Washington's School at Tuskegee, Alabama.[4]

William Edwards grew to be a fine-looking man, with smooth skin and a thick mustache. He did in fact attend the Tuskegee Institute, becoming a teacher and starting his own school near where he had grown up in Snow Hill, Alabama. When school wasn't in session, Booker T. Washington recruited him to take trips up north spreading the word about Tuskegee.

On one such trip—he remembers it as being in 1902, but it was probably more like 1900—Edwards received a letter introducing him to Anna Jeanes. The letter was from Henry C. Davis, a trustee of Tuskegee and friend of Booker T. Washington. Henry C. Davis was Lucretia Mott's grandson, and this is another piece of evidence showing that it's quite likely that Lucretia Mott and Anna Jeanes knew each other.

According to Edwards, Henry Davis basically said, "Hey, you should meet Anna Jeanes," and Edwards took him up on his suggestion.

Edwards said he had "many apprehensions" in dropping by Anna's home, but he found her very cordial, and "deeply interested in the welfare of my people."[5] He told Anna his life story—how sick he had been as a child and how hard he had to work to become educated.

Edwards recounted to Anna how he had a vision to build a beautiful school at Snow Hill, one that could house three or four hundred students who could learn industrial education as he had. When he returned home, he found a check from Anna for $5,000. (To put this in context, this is $186,000 in modern money.) Every year for the next few years, Anna sent more, in amounts ranging from $300 to $2,000.[6]

By the early 1900s, Anna had grown frail. She had invested a large sum to build a facility for elderly Quakers so that aging people could be cared for with dignity and without living in poverty. Each apartment in the boarding home had its own bedroom, living room, and bathroom, and many large living areas were shared so people could visit each other without being lonely. Anna herself moved into the boarding home, called Stapeley after her family's former country estate, and she lived in exactly the same type of accommodations as everyone else.

Sometime in 1905 or 1906, Edwards called on Anna at the boarding home, and the nurse on duty said she was not up to seeing anyone—she was too infirm. "Please, just take her my card," Edwards likely implored. A few moments later, the nurse reappeared and told him he could go upstairs to see Anna.

Enfeebled by advanced age and cancer, her tiny body growing smaller by the day, Anna said to Edwards, "I have been deeply interested in what thee has been telling me all these years about the little schools. I would give largely to them if thee thinks that thee could get Dr. Washington or Dr. Frissell to come see me."[7]

Edwards relayed the message to Booker T. Washington, and to Hollis

Frissell, the president of the Hampton Institute, the school Booker T. Washington had attended. Soon, Anna had given them a check for $11,000.[8] Anna decided she wanted to help rural Black schools, and she established a fund to make it happen. Unlike many northern philanthropists who gave money to causes that benefited the Black community, Anna Jeanes did not have the motivation of preparing a workforce or keeping people in a position of subservience. She would soon be nearly penniless and dead, and she knew it.

Booker T. Washington wrote to Secretary of War William Howard Taft, saying,

My Dear Secretary Taft:

You have no doubt received notice from Dr. Frissell that the trustees of the Jeanes Fund will meet in New York June 6th. Then it is the plan to adjourn to Philadelphia, mainly as a compliment to Miss Jeanes, and for the purpose of seeing her.

When in Philadelphia a few days ago, I mentioned to her that you had accepted a place on the board and she seemed exceedingly pleased. She is an old lady over eighty-five years of age, and I am sure that nothing would better please her than for you to call, with the rest of the members of the board, if you, in your busy life can possibly spare the time to do so. And I very much hope that your plans will enable you to do this.

Very truly yours,

Booker T. Washington[9]

William Howard Taft, future president and Supreme Court justice, visited Anna at Stapeley as requested. James Dillard, who later became the president of the Jeanes Fund, was also in attendance, and said that

Taft "presented the matter in the kindliest manner," and that Anna had a "very swollen right hand," and could not have weighed more than eighty or ninety pounds. Dillard said that Anna "talked in the brightest and most cheerful way," delighted that this eminent man shared her enthusiasm for philanthropy and education for all.[10]

Anna died in 1907, a quiet end to a seemingly quiet life. She never marveled at the Rocky Mountains, never experienced the warmth of the Pacific Coast, never saw the cathedrals of Europe. She never married. She had no children. She lived alone, save for some hired help. But quiet lives can sometimes leave the loudest echoes.

Anna Jeanes left over a million dollars—over $33 million in today's money—to be used exclusively to benefit rural schools that served the Black community. She entrusted Booker T. Washington, Hollis Frissell, and the businessmen of the General Education Board—men like Taft and Andrew Carnegie—to decide exactly how to spend it.[11]

Anna's bequest was one of the first times that a northern philanthropist insisted that the board of governors of a fund be of mixed race, and that Black men be among the primary determiners of how the money that was to benefit their community be used. Anna believed that people could decide for themselves what their community needed, and that people of all races should have equal seats at the table.

It took a while for the board to decide how to make best use of Anna Jeanes's money. It couldn't be used for anything related to higher education, she insisted. Small, rural schools only. She stipulated that financial advisers help invest the money so that the fund could continue to grow. Other than that, she said, it's up to you. Before her death, she refused press interviews about the massive donation. She didn't want any ceremonies or hype. Again, typical Anna.[12]

After Taft was elected president, he continued to serve on the board of the Jeanes Fund, which met at the White House to discuss plans for distributing the money.[13]

Now, let's get something out of the way: this was 1908. Anna, Booker T. Washington, William Edwards, and William Howard Taft were not talking about desegregating the schools. They were having discussions about how to help educate the children and grandchildren of formerly enslaved people, but they were not advocating for full racial equality in public life. Many believed that segregation was the nature of society, and while Booker felt that someday it might end if African Americans worked hard enough to make themselves acceptable to the white community, that someday was not 1908.

From our vantage point, this is ludicrous. Booker T. Washington has long been criticized for engaging in respectability politics—that if Blacks just acted the way that white people wanted them to, then there could be racial harmony. Washington, some feel, was participating in the system of white supremacy.

I get it. I really do. And if this is your view, you're not wrong. But I'll also add an AND to these sentiments. The system was inherently racist, AND Booker and Anna were doing what they thought was best at the time. The system continued to uphold white supremacy AND they thought this was the path toward changing that. From their perspective, what was the alternative? Should they *not* educate these children? Should children continue to be illiterate while they tried to change the minds of millions of adults who believed in the superiority of white people? How could they raise a generation of children to help change the system if the children couldn't read because their parents couldn't read?

So I see your concern, and I acknowledge it. I encourage you to frame these conversations not just from the present but from the past as well.

Money from Anna's fund underwrote all of Virginia Randolph's work as a Jeanes teacher in Henrico County, Virginia. Soon, many other school districts had their own Jeanes supervising teachers traversing the rutted country roads, bettering the communities in which they worked. Within a handful of years of the establishment of the fund, Virginia Randolph was traveling far and wide training more teachers in her methods, and soon, those 118 Jeanes teachers were teaching 1,000 more.[14]

Jeanes teachers were expected to do everything. And I do mean everything. Nearly all of them worked every single day with no days off. Activities ranged from "helped five women can 132 quarts of pears" to "served as a judge at the county fair" to "assisted at the diphtheria clinic" to "spoke at churches on the importance of school attendance" to "assisted in examination for dental clinic" to "helped with teaching arithmetic 7, language 5 and arithmetic 3" to "attended school board meeting."[15]

In one month, a teacher might travel as many as thirteen hundred miles around the area to which they were assigned, all while developing curricula, and organizing career days, United Nations festivals, and choral groups. Driving a buggy on muddy roads to make fundraising visits so schools could purchase books; keeping careful records of the facilities they oversaw; and planning and executing graduation ceremonies, water-testing programs, community cleanup campaigns, and mobile health programs.[16]

The Jeanes Story, published by former Jeanes Teachers in 1979, has a complete list of all of the teachers, including pictures of some of them. The overwhelming majority are African American women, but a tiny handful are men. A surprising number are named Beulah, Eula, or Lula. Most of the pictures appear to have been taken in the 1950s, and many of the teachers wear cat-eye glasses. They almost all sport lipstick, earrings, and necklaces. Several wear corsages or brooches.

How much they have seen, I thought. Dr. Evelyn Sharp smiles, seated near a typewriter. She had no way of knowing that future generations of teachers would stare at her picture, wondering what she was like. Ethel

Bell sports a "you have got to be kidding me" expression, which every teacher I know has honed through years of practice. Lillian Edwards's face says "I'm not mad, I'm just disappointed," and Clara West's dimples make her seem like she was the fun teacher, with the easy laugh. Florida Robins most definitely knows everything but will only be sharing that information with you on a need-to-know basis, while Margaret Louise Hooks will instruct the class on the proper use of the library card catalog. If I had a secret, one I was afraid others would find out, I would find Catherine Bozeman, and I know she would never betray me.

They knew their work was important. But they had no way of knowing the true, lasting impact they had on generations of students, on the American South at large, and, consequently, on America as a whole. In one of his reports fourteen years into the existence of the Jeanes teacher program, William Dillard, the president of the Jeanes Fund, wrote, "There have been no nobler pioneers and missionaries than these humble teachers. They have literally gone about doing good."[17]

The Jeanes teachers continued their work into the 1970s, with most counties ending their programs before then, as school integration became more widely practiced.

The working environment for Jeanes teachers began to change in the 1950s. Many did not feel safe taking public transportation and instead drove their own cars. Teachers who traveled by train sometimes found themselves subject to arrest or beatings.

One scorching August day, a Jeanes Supervisor embarked on a journey from Florida to Louisiana. To reach her destination, she had to switch from a plane to a bus. Opting for a more comfortable ride on the last leg of her homeward trip, she settled into a seat around the middle of the bus. Her comfort was short-lived, as she was forced off the bus in a small town more than a dozen miles from her final destination.

A highway patrolman stopped the bus and ordered all passengers to disembark for a luggage search. Out of all the passengers, only two were singled out to be taken to the local jail—both of them Black women, and one of them the Jeanes Supervising teacher. In jail, both women were subjected to cruel verbal abuse. Just before she was released, one white person said to the Jeanes teacher, "It's truly disgraceful how they treated you."

But another, influenced by hate and prejudice, tried to make it seem like the Jeanes teacher had done something egregious. They asked, "What did you do, get into in an argument on that bus with a white woman?"

In recounting her story, the teacher said, "The real lesson to be learned is that beneath the surface of remarks similar to those made by the second person lurks a psychosis capable of building or destroying a nation."[18]

As the KKK rose for a third time in the 1950s amid violent opposition to African Americans seeking access to equal rights, many of the skilled Jeanes teachers were eliminated, and some school systems decided that instead of integrating, they would just close schools for Black children and pay for white children to attend private religious schools.

But I love what one Jeanes teacher, Mildred Williams, said on this topic: "Gloom and pessimism must not overshadow the good which has grown out of the several years of the Civil Rights laws. Optimism must prevail and persistent movements continue, using every useful weapon at hand to make the dream, as stated by one of America's most recent forthright Black leaders [Dr. Martin Luther King Jr.] a reality. He said, 'I have a dream that one day, on the red hills of Georgia, sons of former slaves and the sons of former slave owners will be able to sit down together at the table of brotherhood.'

"Progress is usually born out of struggle. Old doors close, but new ones will open."[19]

Progress is usually born out of struggle. But struggle doesn't always mean progress, does it? What do we need to add to struggle to create progress? The answer is hope. Hope, which attorney and author Bryan Stevenson told me is not a feeling but an orientation of the spirit. Hope is a choice that we make each morning, and we do not have the luxury of hopelessness if we want to see progress.

The United States itself was born out of struggle. The Quaker migration was born out of struggle. The incredible achievements of the Jeanes teachers were born out of struggle.

Progress doesn't arrive unbidden, carried on the back of a silvery bird, deposited on our doorsteps during the night. Progress is birthed. It is conceived of and labored for. It is the work of multitudes.

None of us can do it all. But all of us can do something. And it might as well be the next needed thing.

SIXTEEN

JULIUS ROSENWALD
Illinois, 1862

ittle did Samuel Rosenwald know that when his boat pushed off from Europe, he would soon find himself living down the street from a future president. He also couldn't have anticipated that when he left behind the oppression in the region that would become Germany, before long, men in white hoods would terrorize communities across his adopted homeland. He could never have imagined that his baby son, born at a time when the United States was nearly wrenched apart by war, would become wealthy beyond the wildest dreams of any immigrant, most especially one who began his life in the United States as a peddler.

In the summer of 1862, Samuel's wife, Augusta, kept their solidly middle-class Illinois home tidy, watching their son, Benjamin, play on the sidewalk half a block from the Lincoln family.[1] Augusta had to have been deeply uncomfortable that summer, her back aching from late-stage pregnancy, anxiously hoping that this baby, unlike the one that came before, would live.

Baby Julius, born in the bedroom of a house that is now part of the Lincoln National Historic Site, was too young to remember the newspaper headlines announcing LINCOLN IS DEAD, too young to remember the manhunt for John Wilkes Booth and his co-conspirators, too young to remember his uncle, good friends with Honest Abe, being chosen as one of the men to help return Lincoln's body home to Springfield, Illinois.[2]

JR, as Julius preferred to be called, left high school after two years, moving to New York to work with relatives in the garment industry. He discovered that he was proficient at the art of selling suits: summer suits, winter suits, suits for courting a lady friend, suits for business meetings. Suits to be buried in, and suits to be married in.

Did JR get married in one of the suits he sold? There's no way to know. But when JR married Augusta Nusbaum in the spring of 1890, photographs show he was not very tall, solidly built, his wavy hair parted smartly to one side. His wife, nicknamed Gussie, had a handsome profile, and like most Gilded Age women, she wore gowns with puffed sleeves, her hair drawn back into a flattering coif.

After being married under a chuppah in a Jewish ceremony, Gussie and JR boarded a train for the newly fashionable honeymoon spot of Niagara Falls.

Four years before JR and Gussie took a train to Niagara Falls, a young man with a boyish, clean-shaven face took possession of an abandoned package at the railroad station where he worked in North Redwood, Minnesota. The young man had been raised in rural Minnesota and helped out at his father's wagon shop, and as he was coming of age, he befriended another famed man of the Minnesota prairie: Almanzo Wilder, who would later marry author Laura Ingalls.

The package the boyish young man took possession of was a shipment of gold watches, meant for a jewelry store, but the shop owner had refused the delivery. Opening the unclaimed freight, the young man contacted the manufacturer, who agreed to let him sell the watches on his own. With the help of other railroad station workers, he quickly sold all of the watches to passersby, earning a tidy profit. He didn't have the markup of a retail location, but what he did have was the charm of a youthful face telling you the watches were absolutely the most stylish items *du jour*.

Within six months, the young Richard Sears had made $5,000.[3] He realized he was onto something, so he left his job at the railroad, moved to the big city of Saint Paul, Minnesota, and hung out a shingle advertising his watch company. He was twenty-eight years old, and this moment in retail history was only possible because of trains. Railroads clipped across the continent with enough speed to make purchasing things via mail order practical for the first time, and along with the rail lines went many miles of telegraph cable, which facilitated sending orders far faster than waiting for mailed letters to be carried by horse.[4]

Sears eventually realized that if he really wanted to make a go of things—selling watches and more via mail-order catalog—he would need to be where the action was. And the action was at Chicago's new rail hub, where he could receive and ship things more quickly. He took on a partner who knew how to repair watches, and soon discovered he had a real propensity for writing copy that appealed to the everyday American. "Don't be afraid you will make a mistake," his catalog soothed. "We receive hundreds of orders every day from young and old who never sent away for goods. Tell us what you want, in your own way, written in any language, no matter whether good or poor writing, and the goods will be promptly sent to you."[5]

It's a humble origin story for an Amazon before Amazon existed, for a founder before founders blasted to space in bizarrely shaped rockets. But it's how a young railroad worker started what would become Sears, Roebuck & Co., the largest retailer that had ever existed on the planet. The making of R.W. Sears Watches, and later Sears, Roebuck & Co., was—and is—the stuff of retail legend. Alvah Roebuck, the watch repairman, exited the business a few years after its founding, but Sears kept the name for continuity purposes.

By 1895, his business was going gangbusters, but it was suffering from a lack of organization. Sears was selling merchandise before he even or-dered it, and the mail-order department didn't have a system that could accurately ship inventory. People were receiving things they didn't want and sending the goods back without paying, because Sears allowed peo-ple to pay when the item was delivered.

The business had potential, but the potential was being limited by a lack of capital to create an inventory and shipping system that made sense. Sears began to wrack his brain for a business partner who could help. *What about that one guy with the pneumatic tubes?* Sears thought. Aaron Nusbaum was enterprising, and he had money to invest. Nusbaum had tried to sell Sears a system of pneumatic tubes for his shipping floor, hoping he would want to *whoosh* messages from one side of the room to the other, like at a bank drive-through.

Sears didn't want any tubes, but he did want Nusbaum, who had recently heard that Marshall Field, the owner of a department store named after himself had lost a trainload of merchandise somewhere on a rail line, somewhere in the country. Field was offering a hefty reward to anyone who could find it. *I gotta find that railcar,* Nusbaum thought.

And he did. He found it in Indiana. When he went back to Marshall Field with news that his railcar had been found in a random railroad siding, Field was so grateful that he did Nusbaum one better than giving him a chunk of cash. He offered him the option to run the soft-drink concessions at the World's Columbian Exposition, which came to Chi-cago in part because of Field's financial support.[6]

The White City was created from scratch, not far from where Julius Rosenwald lived, designed by the nation's best architects and thinkers to attract a large number of people from around the world.

When Aaron Nusbaum signed the agreement to provide soft drinks, he knew it was going to be lucrative. But he didn't know it was going to be $150,000 lucrative, a sum of $5 million today. With his newfound wealth, Nusbaum invested in pneumatic tubes, and eventually Richard

Sears approached him with an offer: Would you like to pay $75,000 for a partnership in my business, Sears, Roebuck & Co.?

Aaron Nusbaum was Julius Rosenwald's brother-in-law. Aaron liked the idea of investing in Sears, but he wasn't sure about spending half his money in one fell swoop. Aaron began asking other family members if they wanted to put up some of the money and go in with him to buy a portion of the business that would eventually just become known as Sears.

JR was like, "I am interested. They owe me a bunch of money anyway." And it was true: Sears owed JR money for a shipment of men's suits they had ordered and sold in their catalog. This decision, y'all. This decision to invest $37,500 in a young company with potential but an organization problem? That was one of the best decisions made in the history of business.[7]

When Aaron Nusbaum and Julius Rosenwald joined Sears, Roebuck & Co., they knew they couldn't attach their names publicly to the company. The company's primary demographic was rural farmers, who at the turn of the century would not have been keen to order from a company run by Jewish people. Sears and Roebuck were names that sounded more solidly "American."

Antisemitic sentiment wasn't new. It was one of the forces that pushed JR's father out of Europe, but it was growing in the United States, and Rosenwald and Nusbaum couldn't take any chances.

"What do you need?" the Sears catalog asked. Or better yet, "What do you want?" Because whatever your heart desired, it could likely be found in the thousand-plus-page Sears Wish Books. Cream separators? A refrigerator? Leather shoes? A boar bristle brush? A kit to build a house? No matter your color, you won't be refused service here. Within a few years, Sears was making money hand over fist. The company figured that the average American had several competing catalogs at their house, and they purposely made the trim size of theirs just a little smaller than their competitors. Logic said that when Edith in rural Kansas neatly stacked the catalogs in her home, the smallest one would go on top. They wanted the first catalog under your hand to be Sears.[8]

Sears, says historian Louis Hyman, was unintentionally undermining white supremacy with its catalog business. While larger cities might have had a wider selection of stores, rural communities often had one general store, and the owner often doubled as the postmaster. Rural general stores were not Targets, where you could spend an hour or more browsing. Goods were kept behind counters. You had to go in and specifically ask for an item. White shopkeepers often stood between Black consumers and the things they needed.

Mail order was changing everything, brought on by federally mandated rural postal delivery, trains, and catalogs. White shopkeepers began to refuse to sell stamps to Black families, or they threw away letters addressed to Sears, aware that the catalog gave Black shoppers options they otherwise didn't have.

In response, Sears created postage-paid cards and directed people to give the ordering cards directly to their letter carriers, completely cutting out the rural postmasters. Shopkeepers in the South began to spread the rumor that Sears was Black, in an effort to keep white supremacists like them from patronizing Sears.[9]

And still, Sears, Roebuck & Co. grew.

To keep pace with demand, Sears built a new shipping facility in Chicago. So large was the expanded location that multiple trains could run through it. It had a beautiful cafeteria and a small hospital.[10] But not everything was rosy at the company headquarters: Aaron Nusbaum didn't get along with Richard Sears. Richard Sears gave JR an ultimatum: pick me or pick your brother-in-law, Aaron. Sears and JR decided to buy out Aaron Nusbaum, and Nusbaum was so hurt that the relationship between him and his brother-in-law was irreparably damaged.

Then, Richard Sears developed health problems, forcing him to leave the company, which meant that JR, the man who attributed 95 percent of his success to luck, was now solely in charge of the world's largest retailer.[11]

As JR's fortune grew, he saw to it that his children had the best education money could buy. His beloved wife dressed beautifully. But he made so much money so quickly that it wasn't possible to spend it all. JR was faced with the one problem we would all like to have: *Dear me, what SHALL I do with all this money?*

JR and Gussie became good friends with Jane Addams and other prominent Progressive Era reformers, and they were frequently asked for donations to various causes. And they did give. JR made many bequests to various Jewish charities and causes. He was highly instrumental in the development of YMCAs around the country (yes, despite the YMCA being a Christian organization). Blue skies smiled down on Rosenwald as he approached fifty. But what he didn't yet know was that he was about to fundamentally change America.

SEVENTEEN

BOOKER T. WASHINGTON

Virginia, 1856

Booker started life without a last name. His mother was enslaved, which meant that he was enslaved. His father was an unidentified white man.[1] As a child, Booker was not permitted to go to school, but he walked the daughters of the family who owned him to their one-room schoolhouse, feeling that he would give anything to be able to step inside. Instead, he waited by the door, overcome by the notion that going to school would be "about the same as getting into paradise."[2]

After Booker's mother was emancipated following the Civil War, there was still no hope for regular schooling, so dire was their poverty. The family relocated to West Virginia, where Booker's stepfather, Wash Ferguson, had a job at a salt factory, a job he later made Booker work at from before the sun rose until it set behind the West Virginia mountains. Wash kept all of his stepson's wages.

The first thing Booker ever learned to read was in that salt factory. It was the number 18, Wash Ferguson's number, which was written on the outside of the barrels to show how many receptacles he had packed. Booker knew those characters, the one and the eight, meant something important. And he was still desperate to step foot in paradise: a school.[3]

Booker did eventually attend school at age nine, over his stepdad's protests. He realized that it was the norm for students to have a first and last name, so he took the first last name he could think of: Washington. At age sixteen, having worked packing salt, in a coal mine, and even as a butler, Booker heard of a school for Black Americans in his home state of Virginia.

He saved every penny he made as a teenager, but discovered he didn't even have enough for the roughly four-hundred-mile journey from Malden, West Virginia, to the Hampton Industrial and Normal School. He slept wherever he could, sometimes hitching a ride on a freight train, stopping to work when the hunger gnawing in his belly couldn't be sated by food that he foraged. He walked most of the way, and when he arrived at the school, he didn't look like the kind of students they admitted.

He presented himself to the woman in charge, a white woman named Mary Mackie. Because African Americans had been denied the opportunity for education for hundreds of years, testing their knowledge as a requirement for admission was largely pointless. Instead, Mackie wanted to see if he was the kind of student who was willing to work hard. She told him to tidy a nearby classroom. Booker knew this was his chance, so he cleaned the classroom. And then he cleaned it again. And then he cleaned it a third time. Over and over, he swept the floors. The blackboards gleamed.

Finally, he pronounced the room clean enough and nervously waited while Mackie ran her handkerchief over the top of the blackboard, along the baseboards, around the clock, and over the door frame. All of them were spotless. Booker was offered admission. And a position as the school's janitor to pay for his tuition.

Hampton was founded by Samuel Armstrong, son of Hawaiian missionaries. Armstrong came to the United States to attend college, and left college to enlist in the Union Army, where he commanded all-Black regiments of troops. He saw that, despite being excellent soldiers who fought valiantly and trained rigorously, few of them could read. Lack of literacy was not because of a lack of ability, it was because generations of enslavers greatly feared what could happen if Black people became educated. Enslavers made it illegal to teach enslaved people to read, and consequently, few of their parents knew how to read, even if they were free. Education was liberation, and the enslavers knew it.[4]

After the Civil War, Armstrong convinced the American Missionary Association to support beginning an industrial and normal school for African Americans. (For centuries, teacher preparation programs were called "normal" schools. The idea was that the colleges prepared teachers by instructing them on the "norms" of pedagogy and curriculum.) Armstrong believed strongly in the vocational model of schooling, reasoning that after hundreds of years of enslavement, white people should be responsible to help guide the formerly enslaved, to help them find employment, and to assist in the development of their moral character.

Booker was immediately taken with Armstrong's philosophy. Other Black leaders of the time were not. In Booker T. Washington's autobiography, *Up from Slavery*, he described Armstrong as "a great man—the noblest, rarest human being it has ever been my privilege to meet." Booker eventually joined the faculty at Hampton.[5]

A friend, John Denison, wrote a tribute to Armstrong in an 1894 edition of *The Atlantic*, the same magazine that published the likes of Katie Bates. He said, "With astute insight, Armstrong not only saw exactly the character and function of the African nature; he took in the organic value of a New England Deacon, a Boston millionaire, a Quaker philanthropist, and a Virginia legislature; he understood the gearing by which they could be united; he understood the relation of Providence to organisms of all kinds."[6] That Quaker philanthropist was Anna Jeanes.

Armstrong, however, did not believe that the Black students he was educating should be allowed to vote, and he encouraged the Black community to divest itself from the hard-won political gains they had made throughout the South after the Civil War ended. In *The Education of Blacks in the South*, historian James D. Anderson recounts how Armstrong felt that "the votes of Negroes have enabled some of the worst men who ever figured in American politics to hold high places of honor and trust."[7] Armstrong encouraged Black leaders to refuse elected office, at least for a few generations, until whites could steer them into the kind of moral framework they believed would benefit them.

Notably, the framework that Samuel Armstrong and his acolytes used as a model for Black education was "fundamentally different from and opposed to the interests of freedmen," says Anderson, and Armstrong "developed a pedagogy and ideology . . . that did not challenge traditional inequalities of wealth and power."[8]

Here again is the AND, the nuance that we must embrace with history. Our minds want to categorize people into one of two camps: Good or evil. Angel or demon. Most often, that viewpoint denies people the fullness of their humanity and can overlook positive contributions or ignore negative impacts. The fact is that Sam Armstrong had paternalistic and harmful ideas, and he was also beloved by thousands, including students like Booker T. Washington.

Armstrong answered the call from Alabama officials looking for a white leader for their new Black industrial school in Tuskegee, Alabama. Armstrong basically told them, "I can't recommend any white people. But I know a Black man who would be perfect for it."

When Booker arrived at Tuskegee in 1881, he found absolutely nothing. Alabama allocated some money for teacher salaries. But they gave zero dollars for buildings or materials or books. In order to make this school a success, Booker was going to have to come up with the money himself. He threw himself into fundraising, speaking for ten minutes in Atlanta, only to hop on a train and head to Boston. He spent *years* working on Andrew Carnegie to donate the money for a library. He befriended wealthy whites, who were taken by his humble attitude and his ability to make them feel like they were doing something truly important with their money.

Washington's autobiography was originally published in installments in *The Outlook*, a weekly Christian magazine. The ensuing book sold thirty thousand copies in two years. Since its publication, *Up from Slavery* has never been out of print. A friend recommended the book to Julius Rosenwald, and after JR read it, he found himself inspired in unexpected ways.

Rosenwald first met Washington at a luncheon in 1911. He invited a few dozen prominent Chicago business leaders to join him at a new hotel overlooking Lake Michigan. The day was hot, and the men gazed out over the water, sweat soaking their backs. Booker was the first guest of color at the new hotel.[9]

Two months before the luncheon with JR, Booker had been assaulted on the streets of New York, beaten with a walking stick by a man who said he was alarmed by the sight of a Black man near his apartment. When the police arrived, they didn't believe that the man who had been attacked, whose face was now dripping blood, was the famous Booker T. Washington. The front page of *The New York Times* read: "Booker T. Washington, head of the Tuskegee Institute for Negroes, was beaten last night in the hall of an apartment house at 111/2 West Sixty-third Street by Albert Ulrich, a white resident of that house. Ulrich pursued Dr. Washington along Central Park West to Sixty-fourth Street. In his flight he fell several times and was kicked by others who had joined the pursuit without knowing who the fleeing man was. His scalp was cut in two places, his right ear was split, and his face was cut and scratched."[10]

At the Chicago luncheon, JR addressed the assembled business leaders: "Whether it is because I belong to a people who have known centuries of persecution or whether it is because I naturally am inclined to sympathize with the oppressed, I have always felt keenly for the colored race."[11]

Later that same day, Booker and JR attended a gala dinner with four hundred people. They dined on cream of asparagus soup and Neapolitan ice cream, and JR introduced Booker to the crowd. Booker spoke of how any inferiority of Blacks was not intrinsic but came from the fact that they had been enslaved for two hundred fifty years and had no education. He mentioned that in the forty-five years since emancipation, Blacks had built thirty-five thousand church buildings across the South with their own money, and that Blacks would support the YMCAs that Rosenwald had donated money to establish.

JR was modest, saying he didn't believe he needed to be thanked for his donation, but that he liked donating to YMCAs because they had the ability to bring races together. He said, "There is no problem which faces the American people that has more importance than this problem of how to have these two races live congenially and try to uplift each other."[12] He surveyed the audience, which was about two-thirds white and one-third Black, and felt good that his work seemed to be having an effect.

I don't want to paint the picture that JR was without blemish: in letters to his wife, Gussie, he wrote about how he took Booker to tour the Sears plant the day following the luncheon and gala, and he ate with him and a Black physician in the cafeteria. He referred to them as "culled," or "darkies," and said he noticed that his workers were curious that he was "showing two 'n*****s' around." He put the N-word in quotation marks.[13] Samuel Armstrong used the same kinds of language in his writings and conversations.

Within a short time, Booker T. Washington and Julius Rosenwald began writing to each other. JR rented a train car and visited the Tuskegee Institute, bringing his wife, rabbi, and other Jewish friends. What he saw at Tuskegee impressed him—he found it better than any facility for whites he had ever seen, expressing that what Booker had done had "inspired [him] beyond words" and that Booker had engaged in "the greatest work of any man in America."[14] JR joined the board of Tuskegee and began donating money.

Back in Chicago, race relations began to occupy more of JR's thoughts and conversations. He said, "A harelip is a misfortune, a club foot is a deformity, but side whiskers are a man's own fault. And race prejudices are side whiskers that are a man's own fault."[15] JR was invited to join the newly formed National Association for the Advancement of Colored People, which he did, even arranging for the Chicago chapter to meet at his temple. He served on its board and gave speeches on its behalf.

Booker T. Washington wrote to Teddy Roosevelt, who was also on the board of Tuskegee, saying that he was excited JR had agreed to sit on the board, and that JR was among the strongest men who had ever joined it.[16]

On another visit to Tuskegee, Booker drove JR through the countryside, where they passed a shack, at significant risk of collapse, a single window hanging on for dear life. Booker pointed out the shack and told JR that it was a school, and it was representative of what the state of Alabama provided to Black children.

White northern philanthropists had made inroads with Black education, he explained, describing the work of women like Anna Jeanes. But it was difficult to do good work when students had to hold an umbrella over the teacher when it rained. JR was aghast. Many of the places in the South where school was taught were worse than stables that housed farm animals.

The following month, JR sent a letter to Booker marked "personal." In the letter, he posed a question: "If I gave you $25,000, how would you spend it?" (For context: this is nearly $800,000 in modern money.) Booker replied that the money would be a godsend, and that it would accomplish more than anyone could even realize.[17]

By the time JR turned fifty, he was richer than any child of a working-class immigrant could ever have imagined. *How should I celebrate this milestone?* JR wondered to himself. In the quiet of the evenings, he talked with Gussie about taking a special trip. And he would vacation, but JR was envisioning something even more grand. He decided instead to do what Oprah and Ellen would later become well-known for. But instead of YOU GET A CAR AND YOU GET A CAR, he decided on a version of YOU GET A CHECK AND YOU GET A CHECK. He and his family had everything they could ever want in life, and what good were vast piles of wealth doing locked up in a bank?

So he made grants to Hull House, to Jewish charities, to an orphanage, to a tuberculosis sanitorium, and to the Tuskegee Institute, eventually parting ways with $687,000 of his fortune, which is now worth more than $21 million.[18] Though he had long been generous with his time and money, after turning fifty, he felt lighter, less encumbered by the weight of riches. (And yes, I know you're thinking *I would really like to be encumbered by the weight of riches right now. Weigh me down, massive fortune! I can take one for humanity!* I understand.)

Some time later, JR received another letter from Booker. Turning it over in his hand and sliding a letter opener beneath the flap, the paper that spilled out contained a proposition that would change America forever.

"Of this sum there was $2,100 left unused at the end of the year. Let me use this unspent money to erect six one-room schools for negroes in the rural section near Tuskegee," the letter asked.[19]

Booker believed in JR's philosophy that people appreciate gifts more when they are required to contribute. Much of JR's philanthropy throughout his lifetime was made in the form of matching grants. "I will give you $50,000 for the YMCA, but you also have to put in $50,000," JR might offer. Making the recipient contribute funds demonstrated that there was public support for the initiative, and it meant that the recipient was likely to take care of the resources it received.

Booker's proposition included a series of matching grants, where JR would contribute funds, but the state would also have to contribute, and so would the local Black community. Given what Booker knew about state commitment to education throughout the South, he saw the writing on the wall: the responsibility of keeping up the buildings would have to be shouldered by locals and not the state. If the community wasn't interested in raising funds, they would not be interested in keeping the building up. This meant that money would only go where the community was invested.

JR wrote back, saying, "I approve."

Y'all, please sit down, and remain seated for the rest of our journey, because I am about to tell you about something that has never happened anywhere else in the world, before or since.

Over the next nearly two decades, Julius Rosenwald, in partnership with the Tuskegee Institute and thousands of Black communities, built nearly five thousand schools in the United States. Five thousand schools. And not just schools: Houses for teachers. Buses for students. Gymnasiums. Cafeterias. Libraries.

If you came to me and said, "Hey, I built a school," I would say, "Dang, good for you! That's impressive!" If you built five schools, my mouth might hang open for a few minutes while you told me the whole story. If you built fifty schools, I would probably call my mom and share the good news with her. But five thousand schools? I almost don't even know what to do with that information. Five thousand, y'all, okay? Five thousand. Five followed by three zeroes. Do you know how many children can be educated in five followed by three zeroes schools? A lot. A lot.

Booker built an infrastructural system to make sure that there was buy-in from local communities, that they furnished the building supplies from local sources, that they could line up a teacher, that they were prepared to contribute their resources to it. He took states to task, reminding them how stupid they looked if they walked away from free money.

JR formed the Rosenwald Fund and hired people to help run it. He sent employees directly to communities, and he visited some of the schools himself. One of JR's employees wrote: "I have never seen greater human sacrifices made for the cause of education. Children without shoes on their feet gave from fifty cents to one dollar and old men and old women, whose costumes represented several years of wear, gave from one to five dollars." The employee went on: "It should be borne in mind that funds with which this project was completed came from people who represented a poor working class, men who worked at furnaces, women who washed and ironed for white people, and children who chopped cotton in the heat of the day for money to go in their snuff boxes."[20] Everyone did what they could, where they were, with the resources available to them. JR was a rich man with staff. He could well afford to fund five thousand schools. Some of the community members could give only fifty cents. JR may be out here getting maximum credit, but those small gifts mattered. That fifty cents was a sacrifice for some. The widow who pushed five dollars into the collection basket deserves just as much respect as the millionaire.

Initially, most of the schools had two rooms, built to exacting standards. Rosenwald insisted on huge windows for natural light and repeatable designs that were easy to construct and maintain. Soon, demand for schools was so great that architects had to draw up plans for seven- and eight-room facilities. Schools were built at first of wood, and later their construction, spread across fifteen states, was moved to brick.

One examination of the historic impact of the Rosenwald schools found that nearly 90 percent of Black students in Alabama were educated in Rosenwald schools from the time they were built, beginning in 1917, until schools were legally integrated—for some, not until the 1960s. Across the entire American South, more than six hundred thousand African American children attended a Rosenwald school.[21]

But the true reach was far greater than just the hundreds of thousands of children who had the opportunity to receive an education. It's easy to make the argument that the five thousand schools impacted millions, maybe even tens of millions. Not only did a child receiving an education affect their immediate family, it affected that child's children, and their grandchildren, and their communities at large. Civil rights icon John Lewis, members of the Little Rock Nine, Maya Angelou, and Medgar Evers all attended schools that were made possible by Julius Rosenwald and the widows, the children, the men working two jobs, the sharecroppers, and the infirm, who all gave to the schools.

Were the schools separate? They were. Did JR and Booker T. Washington, who died partway through the project, try to create integrated facilities? No. They were working within the confines of an existing societal structure, believing that educating students had to be realistic. Were they equal? No. Did they still change the course of history in an imperfect way? Yes.

The Washington Post interviewed several people in Maryland who attended a Rosenwald school. LaVerne Gray said of her time there, "You were expected to grow up and be a credit to your race."

Her cousin Corinthia Boone said, "Oh yes, you were expected to be somebody. Our teachers wanted us to be contributors to society."

Maya Angelou recalled that the Rosenwald school she attended was "grand."[22]

And so while the schools were not equal or integrated, many of the leaders of the civil rights movement were educated in Rosenwald schools. Without their ability to become educated, integration and equality under the law would not have occurred. Education was simply too powerful a weapon, and without the lift from JR, there is little chance that states would have allowed African Americans to wield it.

JR later established the Rosenwald Fund Fellowship, which awarded grants to talented African Americans. Winners include W. E. B. Du Bois, Ralph Bunche, James Baldwin, Marian Anderson, Langston Hughes, Maya Angelou, and John Hope Franklin. He also provided the major funding for Chicago's Museum of Science and Industry, conceived of during the time when Inez Milholland was kicking off her speaking tour for the National Woman's Party.

The Palace of Fine Arts building, left over from the World's Columbian Exhibition, was fortified and became the museum's permanent home. He declined to have it called the Rosenwald Museum—in fact, he spent years trying to get them to rename the museum after people began to call it the Rosenwald Museum.

JR refused to tie up his fortune in vaults beneath the earth, restricted in perpetual endowments. He declined to drip it out slowly, like many of his predecessors. He came by his money by chance, by virtue of proximity, and the least he could do, he believed, was use it to improve the condition of another.

A man once asked JR, "Why are you doing so much to help the Negro?"

"I am interested in America," he said. "I do not see how America can go ahead if part of its people are left behind."[23]

In another address, JR said, "We whites of America must begin to realize that Booker T. Washington was right when he said it was impossible to hold a man in the gutter without staying there with him, because if you get up, he will get up. We do not want to remain in the gutter. We, therefore, must help the Negro to rise."[24]

In his final letter to Julius before his death, Booker wrote:

My dear Mr. Rosenwald:

You do not know how grateful we are for the privilege of having some part in the expenditure of this money which is accomplishing so much good.

*   I often wish that you could have time to hear and see for yourself some of the little incidents that occur in connection with this work. I wish you could hear the expressions of approval that now come from white people—white people who a few years ago would not think of anything bearing*

upon Negro education. I wish you could hear the expressions of gratitude uttered over and over again by the most humble classes of colored people.

Let me repeat, that we count it a great privilege to have some little share in this glorious work.

I am planning to see you in Chicago sometime the first week in November and go over matters a little more in detail.

Yours very truly,

Booker T. Washington[25]

By the time Julius Rosenwald died in 1932, he had given away one billion dollars in today's money. He left strict instructions that anything left of his foundation must be disbursed within twenty-five years of his death. Echoing the words of Virginia Randolph: now, he felt, is the best time to do the next needed thing.

When Virginia Randolph, the first Jeanes teacher, saw her life's work go up in flames in 1929, it was the Julius Rosenwald Fund that gave some of the money to construct the new and bigger school out of brick.

Much of the rest was raised by her and the thriving community she had built.

☆

Go for Broke

——————

EIGHTEEN

THE INOUYES

Hawaii, 1924

The baby was born dead. When the midwife who delivered him into a slum in 1924 couldn't revive him, she pressed his father into service: "Bring ice water!" she yelled. The midwife held his lifeless blue body upside down, delivering several smacks to his backside. His mother was exhausted, but adrenaline now coursed through her veins. She sat upright. Fearful. Praying.

The new father thundered up the stairs, the bucket of icy water sloshing his ankles. The midwife dipped her fingers in and stroked the cold water across the baby's forehead and neck, whispering life into his little ear. Then, incredibly, he began to cry.

His mother sank back into the bed pillows with relief. "Daniel," she whispered, after the prophet who survived the lion's den. His was a great courage, a courage that was steadfast. Too soon, her little son would have a chance to live up to his name.

Daniel's family arrived in Hawaii from Japan in 1899, propelled by a debt they couldn't pay. A fire had broken out at the Yokoyama home of his great-grandfather, Wasaburo, damaging the neighborhood. Together, the village elders decided Wasaburo must pay four hundred dollars to make the families who lost their homes whole again. It was a sum Wasaburo had no hope of earning in Japan, but not paying the debt—a matter of honor—was not even a consideration.[1]

There remained but one hope: Wasaburo's oldest son, Asakichi, must leave the village in Japan and seek employment elsewhere. Recruiters were promising ten dollars a month for Japanese laborers to leave behind everything they knew and sail into the unknown, across the Pacific, to Hawaii.[2]

Asakichi and his wife left their two daughters in the care of his father, but they brought with them their young son, Hyotaro. They walked from their small village to Fukuoka City, where they caught a boat to Honolulu—an arduous voyage across the rolling sea. Fifteen days in cramped, contaminated quarters brought them to the bright green of the islands, the waters full of fish, the jungles full of fruit. Asakichi signed a five-year contract to work on a sugarcane plantation, hoping that his ten dollars per month in earnings would allow him to pay off his father's debt by the end of the sixty months.[3]

But no matter how many fifteen-hour days Asakichi labored under the Hawaiian sun, his paychecks were meager. Credit at the company store was easy to use, and they were required to shop there. At the end of the month, they had only one, maybe two, dollars left to send back to Japan. By the end of the five years, only one quarter of the four-hundred-dollar debt had been paid. He had no choice but to sign a five-year employment extension.

Discouraged by the slow progress they were making on the debt and desperately missing their daughters, Asakichi began to ruminate on what else he could do to earn money. One morning, unable to sleep, his thoughts drifted to something else he missed from home: a warm bath. Here in the meager company housing, little better than hastily built shacks staked into Hawaii's volcanic soil, there was no place for the luxury of a bathhouse.

He decided to build one. Soon, he was earning one penny per bath, each person getting five minutes to luxuriate in the warm water, wistfully thinking of the sights and smells of Japan and the people they missed from home. His wife was also enterprising. She missed tofu cakes, and took the profits from the baths to buy supplies so she could make and sell them. Asakichi rose at 2:00 a.m. each morning to earn extra money to pay off the debt of his father.

It took thirty years.

Their son, Hyotaro, was four when they were first assigned to a plantation on the island of Kauai. And as children are wont to do, the boy sprouted like sugarcane. Though Hyotaro wished he could attend school regularly, he learned in fits and starts, snatching a few weeks here and a few weeks there, working in the family businesses and the sugarcane fields. It took him eight years to finish elementary school. In order to pursue more schooling, he would have to leave the island, and he did: attending boarding school on the Big Island and high school in Honolulu. By the time he had completed his studies, he was twenty-five. Still, his family's debt was not satisfied.

Hyotaro met a vivacious girl named Kame, an orphan who had been raised by Methodist missionaries, and they married. One year after they vowed to be faithful and true, baby Daniel was born. Dead, but raised to life by ice water and whispered prayers.[4]

Growing up, Daniel felt he was an ugly child—he described himself as having a massive head, with his face looking like a dark prune. When his mother's adoptive parents saw him, they were allegedly so dumbstruck that all they could squeak out was, "Well, he has nice ears." When he got a bit older, he got his hair shaved off in a style that matched his father and grandfather. His mother, irate at the sight of her son, who she felt most definitely should not be bald, scooped up the shorn hair, moaning at the sight of her firstborn. She fashioned a rudimentary wig out of the hair that moments ago had sprung from his scalp, and forced Daniel to wear it until the prickles of his new growth began to poke through. Daniel said he looked like an "owl-eyed dwarf" with his head shaved.[5]

Daniel Inouye was the first of four children, and when I say his family was poor, I mean his mother would cook one hardboiled egg for breakfast and split it six ways. But Daniel said it mattered little, because everyone else he knew was also poor. It wasn't like he was the only child in his class without shoes—no one else wore them either, so he didn't feel the sting of comparison until he was old enough to meet families who had more than his own.

Schools were de facto segregated in Hawaii. In 1853, 97 percent of Hawaii's population was native. By 1923, only 16 percent of Hawaii was native, with massive influxes of foreign laborers brought from Japan, China, the Philippines, Portugal, and Korea.[6] The economy on the islands was controlled by a handful of white families who dominated the sugar and fruit industries, driven by the world's economic insatiability for what thrived in the gorgeous climate of the archipelago. Technically, the public schools were open to all and weren't segregated by race, but instead, children were weeded out by language. These "English Standard" schools had admissions requirements, and children were expected to speak near-perfect English in order to attend.[7]

The children of recent immigrants, who often lived in company housing with people who spoke their native language, could not easily adapt to some of the sounds found in English. To give their children a chance at a better education, Hyotaro and Kame switched to speaking only English at home, which was a difficult sacrifice. To shed the language that your brain naturally thinks and dreams in requires Herculean effort, especially when surrounded by mostly Japanese speakers.

In seventh grade, Daniel and a friend were wrestling, acting like normal middle school–age boys. Mid-wrestle, Daniel fell on his arm in such a way that it broke in several places—a significant compound fracture. His mother rushed him to the only doctor she knew—an ear, nose, and throat specialist who had been treating her other son for an infection. The ENT said that he was no orthopedic surgeon, but he would do his best to set Daniel's arm.[8]

When the cast came off, the arm hung crookedly, as if it belonged to someone else, and Daniel could barely move it. Not only was the arm next to useless for Daniel, it was also a source of anguish for his parents— what kind of life would their son have without the use of one arm? They started asking friends and neighbors: "Do you know of a doctor that could fix Daniel's arm?" Everyone seemed to give them a different name. Eventually, Kame brought him to the children's hospital, where Dr. Craig gave them encouraging news.

"You better start learning how to throw lefty, because soon it will be stronger than your right," the doctor winked. "It can be fixed with sur-gery," Dr. Craig told Kame, who felt great relief that something more could be done for her son. Immediately following the surgery, Daniel had far greater use of his arm. The hospital staff seemed pleased.

At Daniel's postoperative visit, Dr. Craig smiled broadly, clearly proud of the results of the procedure. As they got up to leave, Kame said, "We will not be able to pay you all at once, but we will bring you a small amount each month until the whole amount is paid. I hope you will al-low this and not worry, for we are grateful to you. And even if it takes a lifetime . . ."

"You owe me nothing," Dr. Craig said.

Kame stared, not understanding. "Nothing?"

"You will have the hospital costs, I believe that come to thirty dollars, but the operation is my gift to Dan. The payment will be that you will be a good student." He grinned at Daniel. "You going to be a left-handed pitcher?"[9]

The moment Daniel saw the incredulity and relief on his mother's face, everything changed. He felt what it was like for her to be released from a debt it would take forever to pay, the shock and gratitude washing over her from head to foot. Dan vowed to become a surgeon, and to do for someone else what Dr. Craig had done for him and his family.

Over the years, Hyotaro and Kame sent Daniel to bring baskets of garden produce, a freshly plucked chicken, and other small tokens of their appreciation to Dr. Craig. And when Dan entered the doctor's office, bearing the fruit of his parents' labor, he saw other baskets lined up. *We won't forget what you did for us*, the many tokens said. He realized exactly what kind of person the doctor was, and he wanted to be that kind of person too.

Daniel went to high school, where he learned that he loved history. "The story of America had the ring of an adventure in human progress, troubles and setbacks, and the inexorable march down to the present," he remembered of his adolescence.[10] He practiced his English, and the saxophone, and gambling with his friends. He kept homing pigeons. He took a Red Cross first-aid class and started teaching first-aid lessons all over the island.

"I was never spanked," Daniel said, "because it would never occur to me to disobey my parents."[11] When his parents said be home by 10:00 p.m., he was. No matter if he was providing the entertainment at a school dance or blowing his sax in the ROTC band, he ducked out of the festivities to make it home on time.

And one night, December 6, 1941, he left his place in the band just a bit too late. By the time he neared his house, Dan was full-on running, pumping his legs until his hand connected with the doorknob. He burst into the living room.

"You should leave earlier," his mother said, barely looking up. "Then you wouldn't have to run."[12]

That was Daniel's last night as a child. By morning, the boyish face that only needed to be shaved every third day would be gone. And in the mirror would be a man.

Daniel was up early, getting ready for church, carefully buttoning the only white shirt he owned. He clicked on the radio, as was his habit, gazing out at the blue skies. The sun had already burned off its usual haze, the great Pacific sparkling in the distance.

Vaguely, Daniel heard the voice of the radio announcer, who sounded upset. He moved in closer to the radio. "This is no test," he heard the announcer say. "Pearl Harbor is being bombed by the Japanese! I repeat, this is not a test or a maneuver! Japanese warplanes are attacking Oahu!"[13]

Blood throbbed through his temples. "Papa!" Daniel yelled. He was enveloped by a dread that left him with a deep knowing: *The world you knew is gone.* Daniel stood silent, motionless, as the announcer panicked.

"This is not a test! This is the real thing! Pearl Harbor has been hit! We can see the Japanese planes . . ."

"Come outside!" his father ordered. His voice was hard. Hyotaro and Daniel walked out the door of their small home and into the bright sunshine, into a Hawaii that would be irreparably scarred.

On the horizon, they saw black puffs of smoke in the harbor. This was no test. Practice drills used white smoke. Soon, huge plumes of gray leapt heavenward, followed by columns of fire. They could hear the muffled whistle of bombs, as they stood, helpless.

They saw movement in the sky erupt through the clouds of smoke: three planes, silver with red dots on the underside of the wings, flew immediately over their heads, and they knew: this was it.

"You fools!" his father screamed at the planes. "FOOLS!"[14] The singular pain of the country of his ancestry attacking the country of his heart twisted his face. In a world where many Americans already hated the Japanese, it was like watching a slow-motion nightmare play out before his eyes.

Except no one was asleep.

The phone inside the house rang. It was the director of the Red Cross, calling on Daniel's first-aid training. Daniel stripped off his church shirt. "Where are you going?" his mother panicked. "They'll kill you!"

Hyotaro put his hand on Kame's arm. "Let him go. He must go."

Daniel rode his bike through the now crowded street. An old Japanese man grabbed his handlebars in disbelief: "Who did it! Was it the Germans! It must have been the Germans!" He too could not face what would come next. More planes. Many ships hit. Thousands dead. He had only been seventeen for a few months, but Daniel felt the collective anguish of Hawaii's 158,000 residents of Japanese ancestry.[15]

He saw a few boys he knew and they yelled, "Where are you going?"

"Where the trouble is," Daniel replied. "Follow me."[16] It was Daniel who picked up the first civilian dead in the Pearl Harbor attack. He found an old woman, a neighbor, who had been hit by U.S. anti-aircraft shrapnel, a mistake from choosing the wrong settings before the shell was released. Another was a young woman holding a baby, both of them nearly headless, the mother missing both her legs. Her husband, who had been at work on the other side of the island, arrived, begging to see his loved ones. Daniel told him, "Sir, no. You don't want to see them," but he was overruled by a doctor.

"Sir, if you show this man the remains, he is going to go nuts," Daniel whispered privately to him. But the husband insisted, and the doctor allowed it.

Daniel showed him to a cardboard box where his wife stared, unblinking, sightless, her hand severed and placed in the corner of the box. The man ended up in an asylum.[17]

Somehow, Daniel did not faint or throw up. They opened a medical clinic and a morgue at the elementary school, and for the next five days, he stayed there, stealing thirty minutes of sleep once or twice a day.

He found one woman unable to walk, clutching stumps where her legs should have been. Buildings started on fire, and it was Daniel's job to sift through the rubble, recovering corpses and looking for survivors. He did his best to get all of a person's body parts into one box, but as he picked through the hollowed-out structures, sometimes limbs just fell off when he tried to lift them. "I did my job. But every horrid detail is etched in my memory," he said later.[18]

Red Cross volunteers were hired as part of the civil defense command, which was activated because the nation was now at war. Daniel was still in school, so they gave him the overnight shift working at the aid station, and he worked each night from 6:00 p.m. to 6:00 a.m. He grabbed breakfast at home, went to school, where he was expected to learn advanced math, and stumbled home, where he slept for two hours until his mother shook him awake in time to make it to work.

He was paid $125 per month, more money than he had ever dreamed he could earn at age seventeen. But the money meant nothing to him.[19]

———

The United States had a long history of discriminating against people of Asian descent, beginning with the Chinese Exclusion Act of 1882 that severely restricted immigration, forbidding them from becoming citizens no matter how long they lived in the country, ensuring that many professions were off-limits, and in many states, keeping them from owning property. It didn't matter how prosperous someone became, it didn't matter how hard they worked or how deeply they believed in the promise of America, if they had the wrong face, they were an "other."

Labor leaders and government officials formed an exclusion league. A club, of sorts, this one wielding not hoods and crosses but the power of government contacts and well-placed individuals. This Japanese Exclusion League, later called the Asiatic Exclusion League, pressured state and federal government leaders to create policies like the Alien Land Law, which was advertised as a way to "Save California from the Japs" and prevent them from buying land.[20]

Why? Fear is the simple and all-encompassing answer.

Fear of people who didn't look European.

Fear of people who spoke an unrecognizable language.

Fear of people whose traditional dress was different.

Fear of people who had different religious practices.

Fear of people taking their jobs.

Fear that someone else's success threatened their own.

Fear of people not being "American" enough.

Fear, the most powerful motivator of human behavior. Now imagine this set of fears as a pile of sticks arranged in a campfire ring. Pour on the gasoline of international animosity between the United States and the country of Japan. And now light the match of the Pearl Harbor attack. With a *WHOOOOSH*, the flames of hate popped skyward, the intensity of the heat burning the skin, hot ash coating the lungs.

Law-abiding Japanese immigrants woke up to find "JAP" painted on their doors. Dr. Seuss drew political cartoons depicting Japanese people holding bars of TNT, waiting for a signal from the homeland to light them on fire and blow up the United States. Soldiers were taught "how to spot a Jap" via manuals printed by the United States Army. The manuals described how Japanese people shuffle, have buck teeth, and have a wide space in between their first and second toes.[21]

Life magazine printed an article on how to distinguish between a Japanese and Chinese person. The magazine said the Japanese have "blob" noses and wear the expressions of "ruthless mystics." The Japanese were depicted in nationwide propaganda as literal snakes wearing Japanese flags or as frightening killers with pointy teeth, wielding knives in the dead of night behind the backs of white women.[22] I wish I were kidding.

In February 1942, Franklin Delano Roosevelt, having been relentlessly pressured by western state lobbyists, economic groups, military generals, and some members of Congress, signed Executive Order 9066. The order created military zones on the West Coast and authorized the military to exclude any people who were deemed to be a national security threat from those military zones.[23]

It started with curfews for people of Japanese ancestry. Soon, it blossomed into exclusion and removal orders. Those living in Military Zone One, which meant people within seventy-five miles of the Pacific coast, would be rounded up and forced from their homes.

They wanted people to go as quietly as possible, so first they came for the leaders within the Japanese American community. The pastors and civic group presidents, the successful businessmen and the revered elders. With no one to lead them, they thought, the community wouldn't be able to organize an uprising.

The federal government began to hastily construct incarceration camps, where they would send men, women, and children who had been accused of no crime. Maybe you've heard them called internment camps, but FDR initially called them concentration camps, because that's what they were doing—concentrating people into one confined place.[24] But as word of the German concentration camps spread, the U.S. government stopped using the term publicly. They changed the term to internment, but today, members of the Japanese American community largely resist this name.

"Internment" is what happens to citizens of the enemy you are fighting. But the majority of people who were sent to the camps were citizens of the United States by birth. They, by definition, could not be interned. They were imprisoned. Incarcerated without due process. While you may still hear people call them internment camps, every person I have interviewed prefers incarceration or concentration camp, because the term more accurately describes what was happening.

The camps, situated on desolate scraps of land far from the Pacific, were placed in Utah, Arizona, Wyoming, Idaho, Colorado, Arkansas, and inland California. Tar-paper barracks sat in forlorn rows, surrounded by barbed wire, guarded by men with machine guns pointed at the inmates.

NINETEEN

THE MINETAS

California, 1942

While Daniel was manning the first-aid station on Oahu in 1942, Norman Mineta was only ten years old. He loved baseball and the Boy Scouts, and his parents were deeply involved in their Methodist church.

Norm's father, Kunisaku, immigrated to the United States at age fourteen, alone. He was meant to disembark his ship in San Francisco, but he got off the boat nine hundred miles from his destination, in Seattle. Working in lumber camps and slowly making his way south, it took more than a year for him to reach the home of his uncle, where he'd meant to end up all along. When his uncle saw that he couldn't speak English, he did something wildly humiliating: enrolled him in first grade. The boy of (now) sixteen was learning with six-year-olds.[1]

Ten years after his arrival, Kunisaku, who went by Kay in the United States, was twenty-four, had regular employment, and decided it was time to get married. He wrote to a friend in Japan inquiring about a wife, and his friend sent back several pictures for his consideration. As an afterthought, his friend also sent a picture of his younger sister that they used to tease mercilessly, who was now all grown up.

"I'd be honored to marry her," Kay said, and in short order, twenty-year-old Kane embarked on her own voyage across the Pacific.[2] Teddy Roosevelt was president at the time, and he had signed a gentleman's agreement with the leader of Japan: we will only let people into the United States who are joining family members, and you will help us enforce this by refusing to issue them passports. As a result, tens of thousands of Japanese women immigrated alone as "picture brides" during this period, engaged to be married to the laborers who had previously made their way to America's shores.

Japanese immigrants categorized themselves into generations. The *Issei* were the first generation, and their children were *Nisei*, or second generation. The *Nisei* generation, to which Norm belonged, were born American citizens. Kay and Kane worked hard to integrate into American society: they bought a house in San Jose, California. Kay opened an insurance agency.

After the shock and devastation of the attack on Pearl Harbor, Kay sat his children down and said, "I don't know what's going to happen to your mother and me. But just remember: All of you are U.S. citizens and this is your home. There is nothing anyone can do to take this away from you." A few weeks later, Franklin Roosevelt signed Executive Order 9066, and six weeks after that, men with guns were at the door of Norm's home, riffling through the luggage they'd been forced to pack to make sure there were no contraband items: Flashlights. Radios. Cameras.

Posters rustled on every telephone pole and street corner, reading: "Instructions to all persons of Japanese ancestry. . . . Pursuant to the provisions of the Civilian Exclusion Order . . . all persons of Japanese ancestry, both alien and non-alien . . . will be evacuated by 12:00 noon on May 7, 1942." Anyone whose face looked Japanese would be forced to leave their home and report to a civil control station for "evacuation."[3]

Evacuation has an air of "you must leave for your own good, a hurricane is coming," doesn't it? It feels like "a wildfire threatens your home, get out now so you will be saved." In that sense, this wasn't an evacuation, then. It wasn't removing people for their own safety, it was imprisoning them so that white people would be less afraid.

Many families were forced to sell all their possessions for a pittance, never knowing when they might be back. "I'll give you five dollars for your refrigerator," unscrupulous gawkers offered. "You can't take your car with you, I'll buy it for two hundred dollars." Scholars like Lorraine Bannai say that because traditional Japanese society is collective and group identity is important, standing out was not valued.[4] To be singled out for exclusion was experienced as shame. Saddled with that weight, many families accepted prices for their belongings that were far lower than what they were worth.

The evacuation instructions said that families could only bring a few changes of clothes, some bed linens, and eating utensils. Their businesses, homes, cars, and household goods were sold for pennies on the dollar or forcibly abandoned. Kay's insurance license was suspended for no reason other than he was of Japanese ancestry. Families who had money in Japanese banks had their accounts all but frozen, leaving them unable to withdraw funds to pay for essentials.[5]

Norm's family was lucky in one respect: a white attorney named J. B. Peckham was incensed by California's long-standing policy of not allowing people of Asian descent to own land, so he created a workaround. He would purchase property in his own name, allowing the Asian family to pay *him* for the mortgage, and when a family's oldest child, a U.S. citizen by birth, turned twenty-one, he would legally transfer the property to them. On paper, Peckham appeared to be one of the wealthiest men in Santa Clara County, California. In reality, he owned the properties in name only. He gave the dream of home ownership to hundreds of families for whom it would have been otherwise out of reach.[6]

No pets were allowed where Norm's family was going, and he had to give his dog, Skippy, away, which haunted him. Would he be able to get Skippy back when they returned? How long would they even be gone? He hugged his beloved friend goodbye, told him to be a good boy, and turned over his leash to the family who was taking him. He never saw Skippy again.[7]

At the appointed hour, his parents dressed in their nicest clothes—his father in a suit, his mother in heels—and they headed to the train station. "On the day that we left," Norm later recalled, "I was wearing my Cub Scout uniform, baseball glove, and had a baseball bat. As we got on the train, the MPs took my bat. I went running to my father, crying."[8] His bat, they told him, could be used as a weapon, and wasn't allowed.

His family boarded the train to leave behind the life they had worked for. They remained calm and cooperative to demonstrate their loyalty to America—they were willing to sacrifice, if that's what it took. Norm sat opposite his mom and dad, the window shades pulled down so that people outside watching the train roll by wouldn't be afraid when it was full of Asian faces. Tears streamed down his father's face. What had he done but raise good children and run his own business? The train journey to Southern California took more than sixteen hours, and it was full of the quiet suffering of people who knew in their hearts their only crime was having been born of the wrong womb.

When the train finally stopped, Norm realized where they were: at a famous horse track, Santa Anita, the one where Seabiscuit had raced.[9] They soon saw that the grounds of the racetrack had been transformed into a facility to imprison Japanese Americans. Barracks had been erected, latrine facilities slapped together, the horse barns transformed into housing.

The MP barked at them to head to the mattress-stuffing station, where Norm got his Cub Scout uniform covered in dirt from the straw. He winced as his mother, still wearing her best high heels, demonstrated how to stuff straw into a rough cotton sack.

"You're going to have to sleep on this," his father said, coaxing the lumps from the rudimentary mattress.[10] They arrived, mattresses in tow, at their assigned barrack, which was nothing but a small room for the entire family, with a single light bulb. Cots lined the walls. There was no other furniture—no table, no chairs. This is where they were to live now; for how long was anyone's guess.

The one saving grace was that the weather was nice, which made sitting outside comfortable. Old men sat in the bleachers of the race rack, gazing at the San Gabriel Mountains in the distance. They were only a handful of miles from the mission where Maria de Lopez lived. Perhaps, if the wind was right, they could hear the bells tolling on a Sunday morning. Women worried together, collectively watching their children make up games without toys.

When night fell, Norm laid down on his crunchy, dank mattress and pulled the covers over his head. Even still, he couldn't shut out the constant sweep of the searchlight. If they were being forced to stay here for their own protection, as they were told, why were the guns pointed at *them*?

So many people were living at a racetrack that was designed to house no one that it took hours to do anything. Each mealtime, Norm's family waited for more than an hour in line to receive a plate of unfamiliar canned food. Green beans. Spam. Perhaps a scoop of potatoes. It was all flavorless and gluey.

After months living at Santa Anita racetrack, Norm's family got new orders, and they once again boarded the train for a long journey. When they arrived at the new incarceration camp, they found 740 acres of land ringed by barbed wire, their living quarters finished with tar paper. Heart Mountain housed more than fourteen thousand people in barracks, which made it larger than the nearby town of Cody, Wyoming. Signs erected in the windows of Cody businesses read, "No Japs allowed. You sons of bitches killed my son at Iwo Jima."[11]

The Heart Mountain camp operated like a small city that people of Japanese ancestry were not permitted to leave. Able-bodied adults were assigned jobs like farming, teaching, or providing medical care. Incarcerated Japanese doctors were paid $19 per month, while white nurses from the outside were paid $150 per month.[12]

Mothers gave birth to more than five hundred babies while imprisoned at Heart Mountain. Life was somber, the unknown stretching endlessly before them, waves of grief swallowed silently as children ran up and down the lanes between the barracks, stopping short of the barbed wire.

The War Relocation Authority offered children a small selection of recreation opportunities, like baseball and scouting. One of the Wyoming scoutmasters wanted his local Boy Scout troop to visit the children inside the barbed wire for activities, but the white families refused, certain their kids would be harmed or killed, either by the people who were incarcerated or by the men in the watchtowers.

"These children are Americans, who read the same handbook and say the same oath as you, we should go," Scoutmaster Glenn Livingston insisted.[13] Eventually, a Boy Scout jamboree was planned for inside the Heart Mountain camp. Dozens of young boys were paired in pup tents for the sleepover, eyeing each other warily. They spent the day tying knots, starting fires without matches, and actively playing tricks on each other. As night drew nearer and the canvas tents were erected, the boys each built a small moat around their tent in case it rained.

Norm and his tent partner dutifully shoveled out their trench, and his partner said, "There's a kid from my troop in that tent right there, and I don't really like him much. Do you care if we direct the water from our moat that way?"

Norm said, "I don't care, it's no skin off my nose."

When rain began to fall during the night, Norm's tent partner began to laugh hysterically, so much so that Norm had to whisper, "Keep it down, buddy!" The boys stuck their heads out of the tent long enough to watch the water from their moat flood the tent of the other, unliked scout, sweeping it off its stakes, toppling it over.

This struck both of them as tremendously funny, and they collapsed into their sleeping bags, burying their faces in their pillows to stifle their laughter. Now bonded over their shared peskiness, they saw each other again every time a Boy Scout activity occurred. Norm's new friend felt it was unfair that American boys should be imprisoned behind barbed wire. They wrote letters back and forth, keeping up their correspondence for years, even after Norm's family was allowed to leave the camp near the end of the war. The Minetas moved to Illinois, where Kay taught Japanese to members of the military.[14]

When Norm joined the military after college and was deployed overseas during the Korean War, he and his friend lost touch. Norm's family was one of the lucky ones—after their incarceration ended and they spent a few years in Illinois, they were able to return to their California home, which had been rented out to a college professor in their absence. Most other Japanese families didn't have the same good fortune, their lives and livelihoods forever disrupted by the stroke of a president's pen.

TWENTY

DANIEL INOUYE

Europe, 1943

When Daniel finished high school, he wanted to join the war effort. The day after the Pearl Harbor attack, the United States declared war on Japan, and men were being drafted to fight, not just in the South Pacific, but also in Europe and Africa against the Nazis. Daniel was shocked to receive a piece of mail that showed his draft status had been changed: no longer a 1A, fit and ready to serve, but 4C: an enemy alien. Japanese Americans were to be excluded from military service.

Instead of joining the army, Daniel decided to fulfill his promise to become a doctor. Japanese Americans living in Hawaii largely escaped incarceration, thanks to some local officials who stood up to U.S. military generals. One was a police captain who said, "I have complete confidence in Hawaii's Japanese Americans."[1] Plus, to move most of the population off some of the islands would be next to impossible, and they made a convincing case to higher-ups that they could just step up enforcement.

One day, Daniel heard a knock at the door. When he opened it he found three armed and uniformed men demanding his father's prized possession: a new shortwave radio. His dad had registered it as required, so he was sure they just wanted to check it out and make sure all was well. Instead, one of the officers pulled out a screwdriver. He plunged the screwdriver into the back of the radio, snapping the wiring inside. He pulled the tubes out and smashed them on the ground.

Daniel felt sick inside as his father watched them destroy his radio. "Here," his father said, grabbing an axe. "Let me help you." Daniel watched as his father smashed his own radio into tiny splinters. "Now you'll never have to worry about it, eh?" he said. "My son will clean up the mess."

Throat tight, Daniel choked out, "He gave blood twice."[2] His father was a good American. His eyes blurred at the men's cruelty. It would have been enough to disable the radio. Destroying it entirely was inhumane.

Japanese Americans, the *Nisei* generation, citizens at birth, petitioned the government repeatedly to allow them to contribute to the war effort. For over a year, the petitions fell on deaf ears. Meanwhile, Daniel kept up his pre-med studies. Finally, in March 1943, President Roosevelt agreed to form a segregated military unit of *Nisei*. Eighty percent of eligible Japanese Americans volunteered for military service. They bought more war bonds than any other group.[3] But they would only be allowed to serve in Europe—the Pacific theater was too great a security risk.

The young *Nisei*, thirty-three hundred of them, reported for duty, their oversize packs dwarfing their average five-foot-five stature. Their training in Mississippi had to be extra rigorous, because the Japanese American men would stand alone in battle, unsupported by other units. They would have their own equipment, their own mechanics, their own medics, all Japanese Americans. They, too, were forced to ride with the window shades drawn when they passed through towns, so as not to scare the white people who might be watching.

Daniel joined the 442nd Regimental Combat Team, whose motto was "Go for Broke."[4] When he left, his parents put their hands on his shoulders. "You do not dishonor this family," they said, "and you do not dishonor this country. If you must die, die with honor."[5]

He had never fired a gun before—not even a BB gun. His mother was such a devout Christian that she "didn't want anything like that in the household." So it was a surprise to Daniel that he was an excellent shot, and one of his first assigned jobs was that of sniper.

His unit shipped to Italy, and when they arrived, Daniel was stunned at what he saw: a city nearly completely destroyed by bombing. Children begging on the street for food. Men on street corners trying to entice the arriving soldiers by offering their teenage daughters up for a sexual encounter. "Two dollars, two dollars," the fathers said in broken English, pointing to their fourteen-year-olds.

Tasked with setting up the kitchen area while many of the men in his unit were off having fun, Dan noticed a dozen Italian men and women lurking near the edges of camp. Their eyes were black, their frames gaunt. "*Signor!*" one man called to him.

Dan walked across the field and asked, "What can I do for you?"

"We work, eh?" the man said. "We clean—kitchen, clothes, eh? Whatever you want." The man seemed terrified.

"How much? *Quanta lira?*" Dan asked.

"No, no *lira*," the man replied. "Is nothing to buy. You give us garbage. We work for garbage." The man gestured to the rows of garbage cans outside the kitchen tent.

Assuming the group wanted the garbage to fertilize their farms, Dan said, "Sure, go ahead, help yourself."

The men and women ran, headlong, to the trash, plunging their fists into the coffee grounds and congealed stew. They shoveled the potato peels and discarded cigarette butts into their mouths, desperate. They scooped the garbage into sacks and bandanas, until Daniel, horrified, compelled them to stop.

"You said we could," the man said. "You promised. We work."

"No, no! Listen! I'll get you food! Clean food! Put that garbage back." The group gripped their sacks tightly to their chests. "Come back at six, and there will be food for you!"[6]

From then on, a new rule was implemented: no man would take any food he didn't fully intend to eat, and any food that wasn't eaten—a piece of potato or a heel of bread—was set aside in clean containers and given to the starving Italians.

Daniel's unit was sent to France but later came back to Italy. He saw battle after battle, earning himself a wartime commission at age twenty. The war was nearly over, but troops received word that they had to fight harder now than they ever had, because any military losses the Axis powers faced would benefit the Allies in surrender negotiations.

This next part is going to seem like it is straight out of a superhero movie. You're going to think, *That can't possibly be true, come on.* But I promise, it is.

It was April 20, 1945. Word had just reached Dan's unit that FDR had passed away, and the men took all of their feelings about America losing their commander in chief and channeled it into beating the enemy. They were going to move up in FDR's honor, come hell or high water.

Their commanding officer briefed Dan on the next day's assignment: take the mountain in front of them for the Allies. Anxiety descended on the camp. They were exhausted after fighting for weeks without a break. Soldiers kissed their Saint Christopher medals. They fingered their *senninbaris*, pieces of cloth with a thousand stitches on them that were meant to protect the wearer from a thousand misfortunes. They pulled out their Buddhist charms and their talismans, mentally preparing for what lie ahead.

Daniel had his own good luck charms—two silver dollars he had won gambling—in his breast pocket. Gambling was his not-so-secret vice, and his chest bore a purple welt from where a bullet had struck one of the silver dollars and ricocheted off only a few weeks prior. The night of April 20, Dan thrust his hands in each of his many pockets, listening for the familiar jangle of the coins, waiting to feel their cool roundness graze his fingertips. But the silver dollars were nowhere to be found. Panic rose from his belly and into his chest. "Fellas, did you see my lucky silver dollars?" he asked. But over and over, they shook their heads no. Anxiety turned Dan's stomach into knots.

Daniel and his company set off at sunrise without his lucky coins. He had an ominous feeling about what they were about to walk into. Every time they encountered a group of Germans, they took them out easily, grenade toss after grenade toss landing exactly where they aimed. Dan gripped the pineapple-shaped piece of cast iron, pushed the lever into the web of his hand, pulled the pin, and let it sail, counting 1 . . . 2 . . . 3 . . . *BOOM!* The grenades exploded, embedding fragments of metal shrapnel in those unlucky enough to be nearby. Working in sync, Daniel and his men walked toward the mountain ahead, pushing the lever, pulling the pin, letting it sail, *BOOM.* They wiped out a German patrol without even slowing down—push, pull, sail, *BOOM.*

Before they knew it, the base of the mountain was before them. The slope had no cover, and at the top sat three German machine guns, Nazi soldiers staring down at the *Nisei* unit hugging the rocky soil. *Go for Broke,* they told themselves, heartbeats pounding in their ears.

Dan pulled out a grenade and found his legs being propelled by a force larger than himself, carrying him out of his prone position, running straight toward the nest of a German machine gun. A hail of bullets rained around him as he pushed the lever, pulled the pin, and let the grenade sail. He saw the *BOOM* hit the bunker, and as the men left alive staggered out, he took them out with his gun.

"My God, Dan, you're bleeding! Get down and I'll get an aid, man!"[7]

Dan looked down and watched as blood oozed from his stomach.

But he knew that if they stayed on this slope with no cover, the two remaining machine-gun nests would methodically pick them off, one by one. His legs continued moving up the hill, his men following, and before the German soldiers even noticed him, Dan sailed two grenades into their bunker.

One left, and the mountain would be theirs.

Daniel's legs were barely holding up his 115-pound frame, but he struggled forward, moving straight for the last nest. The gunner had spotted them, and Daniel's men had no choice but to crawl, belly first, up the mountain. Dan knew they needed to get close enough for his agile arm to launch a grenade, and he slowly drew closer, closer, until finally he pushed the lever, pulled the pin, and . . .

Daniel saw a German soldier stand up and squeeze the trigger of his rifle. He heard the boom, but realized this time it wasn't from his own grenade.

As if in slow motion, Dan looked to his right and saw his arm hanging from his body by a few bloody shreds. He saw his grenade, ready to launch, squeezed in the fist of the hand he no longer controlled, and he knew he only had a few seconds before it would explode and kill him.

"GET BACK!" Daniel yelled, as he used his left hand to pry open the fingers of his right, picking up the live grenade and hurling it at the man who had just destroyed his arm. The Nazi was reloading and didn't even see Daniel's grenade coming.

BOOM.

For good measure, Dan squeezed off a few rounds with his gun as his right arm flopped uselessly against his hip.

But the man who severed Dan's arm wasn't the last German in the bunker. Another took the dead gunner's place and fired several rounds at the men of the 442nd. And this time, he hit Dan in the leg, knocking him over and sending him rolling back down the hill they climbed. Dan lay there bleeding and badly wounded, his men hovering over him, debating how to evacuate him.

"Get back up the hill," Dan ordered. "No one called off the war!"[8]

The men did as they were ordered, leaving Dan alone to wait for a medic. His Red Cross training kicked in, and he tried to apply a tourniquet on his arm but realized there wasn't enough soft tissue to make it work. He fished around in what was left of his appendage until he found an artery, and he pinched it, keeping himself from bleeding to death while he waited for help.

He had to wait for nine hours. Rescue helicopters were still a thing of the future, and when he finally arrived at the hospital, he saw rows and rows of occupied beds. Nurses triaged patients as they were brought in, sorting them into three categories:

1. This soldier might be savable, but needs immediate surgery.
2. You're not that serious, you're going to have to wait.
3. God loves you.

Dan knew what *God loves you* meant. He saw the nurses and doctor confer and then nod to a chaplain waiting nearby. The religious man approached his stretcher and kneeled down. "God loves you, son," he said.

"Oh yes, I know that," Daniel told the chaplain. "I love him, too, but I'm not ready to see him."

The chaplain stared at him, studying his face. "You're serious, aren't you?" the chaplain asked.

"Absolutely. I am not ready to go yet," Daniel answered.[9] The chaplain ran to get the doctor, pleading Daniel's case. The medical staff returned and whisked him away for surgery, which they had to perform without any anesthesia. Daniel had already had too much morphine en route, and they didn't think he could have anesthesia and survive. The rest of his arm was amputated. During the surgery, the doctors discovered that the bullet in his stomach had missed his spine by the merest of margins.

Dan required seventeen units of blood, and each time the doctors would bring the bottle to his bedside, as was the custom, and show him the label. They wanted soldiers to see who had sacrificed for them, to experience the solidarity that came from giving each other blood. Dan saw the name Thomas Jefferson Smith, and realized the blood he was receiving came not from the men of the 442nd, but from the all-Black 92nd, serving nearby. As he lay on the bed, drifting in and out of a woozy unconsciousness, he saw names like Woodrow Wilson Peterson and wished he could hop up and personally thank each man who was giving a part of what gave them life so that he could live.[10]

During surgery, the doctors fixed his arm and his abdominal wound, but no one noticed the fact that he'd been shot in the leg. Several days after his initial surgery, Dan was getting examined by the doctor, who found he was healing well. He mentioned that his leg was hurting and that he didn't think anyone thought to look at his other extremities. Within ten minutes, they were cutting off his pants, and the next thing he knew, his leg was ensconced in a huge cast.

While Dan recuperated in the hospital, he befriended another soldier who had been seriously injured, a man named Bob Dole, who would later go on to be a senator and the Republican nominee for president. The two became lifelong friends, bonded by the horrors of war. Both had dreamed of being doctors. Both lived out other dreams.

Two weeks after Dan lost his arm, the war ended. He still had two years of rehabilitation ahead of him, but thanks to the G.I. Bill, he finished college and went to law school, determined to do something to give back the way he had promised Dr. Craig.

The 442nd, the all-*Nisei* military unit that had fought to be able to fight, became the most decorated military unit of its size in history. They had ten unit-wide citations and 3,915 individual citations. Seven hundred men from their unit died, and 3,600 more—men like Dan—were wounded in combat.[11]

Daniel finally returned to Hawaii, East Coast law degree in his left hand. He got involved in politics. Hawaii was not yet a state, but it had a territorial government, which Dan was eager to serve in. Unlike most residents of Hawaii, Dan decided to join the Democratic Party instead of the Republicans. He ignored the advice of people who said he'd never get elected as a Democrat and insisted that the reason he wanted to be a Democrat was that he thought that the Republicans wanted to protect property—what we have—but the Democrats wanted to protect people—who we are.[12]

He resented that in the 1950s, people associated Democrats with communists. "I gave this arm to fight fascists," Dan said. Gesturing to his one good arm, he shot back, "If my country wants the other one to fight communists, they can have it."[13]

Daniel met a pretty girl, Margaret, and proposed on their second date. She said yes.

Daniel Inouye became successful in politics. He was elected to Congress, and when Hawaii became a state, he was one of the very first senators to represent the fiftieth state. When he got to Washington, D.C., he remembered his friend Bob Dole, who had grand political aspirations before he did. He sent a telegram that read "Bob. I am here. Where are you?"[14]

Congress was not just a cushy job for Dan: he did things of consequence. If you watched the Watergate hearings, maybe you saw him on TV. But he didn't just draft legislation. He made friends. A lot of them.

TWENTY-ONE

NORMAN MINETA

1950s

When the incarceration camps closed, the people who had been imprisoned for years were actively discouraged from congregating in groups. Fan out, they were told. Don't all move back to the West Coast. Try to blend in. Many families decided they would do anything to keep this from happening to them again, so they were going to be 110 percent American. "In the long run, we are going to prove our loyalty to this country," his father, Kay, told him.[1]

Norm returned from his military service and tried to rent an apartment. He saw an ad for a place that seemed perfect and telephoned the landlord, who said, "Sure, come on over and look at it."

When he arrived, the landlord took one look at him and said, "Oh, it's already been rented." With a sinking feeling that this was about prejudice and not rental status, Norm walked around the corner to a pay phone and called the landlord's number, pretending to be a different person. "Yes, it's available," he was told.[2] Turns out, prejudice wasn't eradicated when the Japanese surrendered at the end of the war.

He joined his father's insurance business, but Norm's true love was politics. He built enough connections in San Jose to get appointed to the city council when a spot became available, and eventually Norm won election to the mayor's office. His win became international news, and represented a giant step for mankind: voters had elected an Asian American mayor of a major city.[3]

Early in his first term as mayor, an assistant brought Norm a letter. It appeared personal, and when Norm opened it, he found it was a note congratulating him on being elected mayor. The sender had read a newspaper article and recognized Norm immediately.

It was his friend from the pup tent. "Hey Norm," the letter read. "Remember that fat kid from Cody?"[4]

Norm stared at the letter. He certainly did remember that fat kid from Cody. It was Alan Simpson. And after Norm and Alan had spent time as Boy Scouts in a pup tent, Alan brought shame to his family name. His father was in politics, and Alan was a proper juvenile delinquent who set fire to federal buildings. He and his friends stole bullets from stores and stood opposite one another with guns, shooting at rocks near the others' heads. They terrorized their Wyoming town, blowing holes in mailboxes with their .22 calibers, killing cows, and shooting up road construction equipment.

Alan was caught and put on federal probation, the judge telling him that he had to make restitution with his own money, which forced him to get a job. One night, as Alan was exiting a pool hall, he saw someone he knew who had been in a knife fight. "What happened to you?" Alan asked, concerned.

The man told him he had used a racial slur and had gotten jumped for it. "Man, that's dumb," Alan remarked. As it turned out, his acquaintance didn't like being called dumb, and he attacked Alan, which led to the police being called for the brawl on the street. When the officer arrived, Alan hit the officer too.[5]

The officer struck Alan with his club and hauled him to jail. Jail was a wakeup call, and Alan vowed to set his feet on the straight and narrow. He served overseas in the military, his six-foot-seven frame towering above the rest of his army buddies. When he returned, his sharp jaw, piercing eyes, and quick wit made him the perfect hire for anyone seeking an attorney in Cody, Wyoming. He started a family, marrying the sweetheart who had refused to bail him out of jail when he got arrested.

Having a father who served as governor and senator made him politically astute, and Alan kept up with the happenings of his community and the world, never one to shy away from voicing his opinion with a cheerfully barbed tongue. One morning, a cup of coffee and the local paper in hand, a smile spread across Alan's distinctive long face. He dashed off a letter to his old buddy Norman Mineta.

When Norm ran for Congress and won, Alan Simpson wasn't far behind. The friendship formed inside the barbed wire of Heart Mountain, Wyoming, picked up where it left off. When Alan and Norm met again, they immediately started laughing, greeting each other with the hugs and kisses that come from the hearts of only the truest of friends.

They couldn't have been more opposite: Alan was cowboy stock: large, pale, and steely. Norm was the son of an immigrant, with a thick shock of black hair. He barely came to Alan's shoulder. When you watch interviews of them together, they either spend all their time laughing or trying to make each other cry.

"You know," Alan joked, "the word *politics* is interesting. It comes from the Greek. *Poly* meaning many, and *ticks* meaning blood sucking insects." Norm bursts into laughter. "Today, we don't talk of Scouts, we have organ recitals," Alan said. "How's your heart? How's your liver? You know, we recite our organs."[6] Norm is laughing before Alan even gets to the punch line.

But Alan can't help but extoll Norm's virtues. "It's been a wonderful, rich ride of true friendship, which is a beautiful thing"[7] and "I really respect and admire him. And love him. He is a wonderful, wonderful individual."[8] These are words you don't expect from a juvenile delinquent cowboy from Wyoming.

"There are a lot of issues where I've had an opposite view," Norm said. "I'm a liberal Democrat. He's a conservative. He's a good Republican. So it's not that we had agreement on everything. . . . We had fights in committees or subcommittees, and then we'd slap each other on the back and say, 'Come on, let's go have dinner. Let's go have a drink.' I don't know how to describe it. We just see each other and begin to laugh."[9]

Norm Mineta and Daniel Inouye were proud to be among the first Asian Americans in Congress. Together with other Japanese American congressional leaders, they proposed legislation that would make amends for the atrocities the government leveled at Japanese Americans during World War II. The bill, called the Civil Liberties Act of 1988, gave a payment of $20,000 to every survivor who had been incarcerated in America's incarceration camps. They said, "It's not about the money, it's about honor."[10]

It seemed an impossible ask: $1.2 billion in reparations for the remaining sixty thousand survivors. The bill had over one hundred cosponsors, including Alan Simpson, Joe Biden, Al Gore, Orrin Hatch, Bob Dole, Ted Kennedy, and Dan Quayle. As a sponsor, Alan said: "He was an American citizen, and they stuck him behind barbed wire. That's a hell of a thing to do."[11]

Norm went to bat for HR 442, named after the 442nd Regimental Combat Team. It came up for debate in 1987, on the two hundredth anniversary of the Constitution. He said, "Though this bill is a deeply personal one for a small number, this legislation touches all of us, because it touches the very core of our nation. Does our Constitution indeed protect all of us, regardless of race or culture? We lost our homes, we lost our businesses, we lost our farms, but worst of all, we lost our most basic human rights. Our own government had branded us with the unwarranted stigma of disloyalty which clings to us still to this day."[12]

The bill passed. When President Reagan signed it into law, he said: "My fellow Americans, we gather here today to right a grave wrong. More than forty years ago, shortly after the bombing of Pearl Harbor, one hundred twenty thousand persons of Japanese ancestry living in the United States were forcibly removed from their homes and placed in makeshift internment camps. This action was taken without trial, without jury. It was based solely on race, for these one hundred twenty thousand were Americans of Japanese descent. . . . We must recognize that the internment of Japanese-Americans was . . . a mistake. For here, we admit a wrong; here, we reaffirm our commitment as a nation to equal justice under the law."[13]

Norm served ten terms in Congress. After he left to work in the private sector, President Clinton called and asked him to be the Secretary of Commerce. He accepted, becoming the first Asian American cabinet member in U.S. history.

When George W. Bush was inaugurated in January 2001, he asked Norm to stay in his cabinet, this time as Secretary of Transportation. It's only the fourth time in history that a cabinet member has served presidents of opposite political parties. "I tried to depoliticize my cabinet. I didn't want people in there serving the Republican Party, I wanted people in there serving their country. There is no better servant for America than Norm Mineta," Bush recalled.[14]

There was only one objection to his nomination at his confirmation hearing: a senator who said she couldn't understand why it had taken so long for someone to nominate Norman Mineta for a cabinet position. He was confirmed 98–0.[15]

Norm watched in horror when planes struck the World Trade Center on September 11, 2001. He was summoned to a secure bunker in Washington, D.C., with Vice President Dick Cheney, and they sat in front of a radar screen that refreshed every seven seconds.

They watched as a plane bound for the Pentagon was fifty miles away. Then twenty. Then ten. They heard the report of an explosion. Fuming with righteous anger, Norm phoned the head of the FAA and told him to ground every plane in the air immediately. No similar order had been given before, or since.

The head of the FAA said he would give the order, but would leave some room for pilot discretion. "F*** PILOT DISCRETION. GET THOSE G**D*** PLANES ON THE GROUND!" Norm shouted at him.[16] All told, 4,546 civilian aircraft were grounded, a feat that took more than 2.5 hours. Many pilots weren't even told what was going on, just that there was a security incident. Pilots who did know largely didn't tell their passengers.[17]

As soon as Canada heard that the FAA had grounded all flights, they implemented Operation Yellow Ribbon, shutting down nearly all of its own air travel, to allow room for incoming international flights that were bound for the United States, and to allow U.S. planes a safe place to land if they needed it. Many incoming international flights were past the point of no return, meaning they had to continue on to their destination, as they didn't have enough fuel to turn around and go back. As many as forty-five thousand people were diverted to Canada on September 11.[18]

Norm quickly saw United States sentiment begin to turn on people who wore traditional Muslim dress, or who had names that sounded like they might have Middle Eastern heritage. He thought back to that moment, at age ten, when his baseball bat and puppy were taken from him and his family was imprisoned without due process because of the sound of their name and the appearance of their faces. He refused to do that to anyone else.

So he sent a letter to all U.S. airlines saying they were forbidden from using racial profiling or subjecting Muslim or Middle Eastern passengers to extra scrutiny. He said it was the "right and constitutional thing" based on his own experience as someone who had lost the most basic human rights during his childhood incarceration.

Norm influenced presidential policy post-9/11. Bush said that "one of the important things about Norm's experience is that it reminds us that sometimes we lose our soul as a nation. That the notion of all equal under God sometimes disappears. And 9/11 certainly challenged that premise. I didn't want our country to do to others what had happened to Norm."[19]

When he died in 2012, Daniel was nearly ninety, and was one of the longest serving senators in U.S. history. Then–Vice President Joe Biden spoke at his funeral, after having served with him in the Senate for decades.

Biden said, "I'm here to tell you that his physical courage was matched by his moral courage. I don't know of anybody else I can say that of. He was, in my thirty-six years in the Senate, more trusted by his colleagues than any man or woman I ever served with. No one ever doubted that Danny Inouye had such integrity at his core that he would meet any obligation thrust upon him with absolute steadiness and objectivity. With the exception of my father, there are few people I have ever looked at and said, 'I wish I could be more like that man.'"[20]

Daniel Inouye was President Obama's senator when Obama was growing up in Hawaii. Obama said, "For him, freedom and dignity were not abstractions. They were values that he had bled for. Ideas he had sacrificed for. He taught so many of us, including a young boy growing up in Hawaii, that America has a place for all of us. May God bless Daniel Inouye. And may God grant us more souls like his."[21]

When Daniel had finished lying in state in the Capitol and being eulogized in the National Cathedral, his casket traveled home to Hawaii, where hundreds gathered. Senator Jon Tester played taps. A bagpipe corps played "Danny Boy."

As I watched his funeral(s), which you can find on YouTube, I cried for a man I had never met. I saw the members of the honor guard fire their guns. I watched nineteen cannons salute him, and listened to the roar of four jets flying over the assembled crowd of family, friends, and members of the 442nd Regimental Combat Team. One of them remarked, "He was a giant among men. A hero among heroes."

Two years later, in 2014, the United States Navy commissioned a destroyer to be named in his honor. It was to be built about as far away from Hawaii as one could go in the United States: Bath Iron Works, on the Kennebec River, in Maine.

The *Daniel Inouye* left Maine in 2021, bound for its home port. In November, it sailed into Pearl Harbor, 59 feet wide and 509.5 feet long. Soldiers in white stood at attention on the decks. It received its commission on December 8, 2021, eighty years and one day from the time a seventeen-year-old went to bed a boy and woke up a man.[22]

When Daniel Inouye left home for the first time to undergo his rigorous military training, his leader was a man he greatly admired, but who was later killed in battle. He impressed on his unit, the 442nd, something that Dan carried with him the rest of his days. "Those that survive," he told the *Nisei* unit, "will have the chance to make a world where every man is a free man, and the equal of his neighbor."[23]

So Dan went for it. He went for broke.

In a letter dated the day of his death, Inouye wrote to the governor of Hawaii, saying, "People have asked me how I want to be remembered and I say very simply that I represented the people honestly and to the best of my abilities. I think I did okay." His last word was "Aloha."[24]

Norm and Alan helped form the Mineta-Simpson Institute at Heart Mountain, which has a retreat space and funding dedicated for communication about the atrocities of Japanese incarceration. There are pictures of them seated near each other, Mineta dwarfed by Simpson. They are always in states of uproarious laughter, their faces consumed with glee.

Norm died in 2022. Before he passed, he said, "The word *compromise* today is a bad word. People think of it as a weakness, rather than a strength to get something done."[25] Alan Simpson, as of this writing, is ninety-two years old.

What will history remember with kindness? The leader with the most cunning tweets? The one with the most self-aggrandizing speeches and the biggest audiences? No, it's not the cynics who emerge the heroes, but the people who spent their lives in service to others. It's those that fight for justice for someone whose reflection they don't see in the mirror.

☆

Momentum

———

TWENTY-TWO

CLAUDETTE COLVIN

Alabama, 1950s

Here's a lie you might have learned in school: Rosa Parks was a tired seamstress who wanted to rest her feet, so she declined to move seats on the bus.

Here's another one: Rosa Parks ignited the civil rights movement by chance.

The real thing Rosa was tired of that day in December was giving in. And while Rosa was a very important catalyst, she certainly was not the first person to challenge bigotry on the buses of Montgomery, Alabama.

Nine months before Rosa's fateful encounter in December 1955, fifteen-year-old Claudette Colvin boarded a bus with her friends. There was only a half day of school that day, and Colvin sat near several of her classmates. Their excitement at being let out early was palpable. She sat in the section reserved for Black passengers, but before she knew it, the white spaces on the bus were filled. The bus repeated its familiar pattern, pulling away from the curb, accelerating, pulling toward the curb, stopping, doors opening.

At this stop, a white woman walked up the steps, scanning the front section, reserved for people like her. Seeing that it was full, she walked toward Claudette. "Move back," the woman insisted, not just to Claudette but to every Black passenger in the row. To the white woman looking for a seat, occupying a space with other Black passengers meant that she viewed herself as equal to them. Which she most certainly did not.

Watching from the large mirrors near his seat, the white bus driver barked at the teenagers to give up their seats, and all of Claudette's classmates obeyed. But she could not. *Don't do it, Claudette*, she told herself. *You're not doing anything wrong by sitting in the seat you paid for.* The woman huffed. "MOVE BACK," she insisted. Claudette could feel the animosity radiating off the woman who loomed above her. *Don't you get up*, she heard in her mind. The other Black passengers who moved back had made three empty seats for the white woman, but she still refused to sit down until Claudette was gone.

"I might have considered it if the woman were elderly," Claudette said later. But she wasn't.

"Get up!" the driver barked at her. *I'm done doing that*, she thought. But instead of arguing, Claudette sat silently, resolutely. Had she known the work of Lin-Manuel Miranda, she might have thought of the lyric, "History has its eyes on you," but instead what she felt were the guiding forces of her community of ancestors, those women who came before her, who showed her what to do now.

"History kept me stuck to my seat," she recalled. "I felt the hand of Harriet Tubman pushing down on one shoulder, and Sojourner Truth pushing down on the other."[1] In this moment, getting up felt like giving up. And Claudette? She was done with that.

Claudette was a bright, inquisitive child who wore glasses and peppered the adults around her with questions. "Where did their dog go after it died?" "Why don't stars fall out of the sky?" And, as Claudette recalled it, one of the most pressing questions of her childhood was, "How did white people come to dominate the South?"[2] Adults often told her that Black people were cursed.

Claudette was like, "Immediately no." She just knew that it couldn't be true. She told the minister of her church that she didn't want to serve a God who cursed people.

Mary Anne and Q. P. Colvin had adopted Claudette and her sister, Delphine, from a relative. They moved the girls to a working-class neighborhood of Montgomery, and Claudette found herself hemmed in on all sides by the realities of segregation and racism. At clothing stores, she and her sister were never allowed to try on shoes, being forced instead to use paper outlines of their feet to approximate their size. White shop clerks refused to sell them the Easter bonnets that the girls wanted, instead trying to force them into styles that were less "uppity." *Why can't I wear what I want?* Claudette's bright mind wondered. There just didn't seem to be a reason that made sense.

As a girl, Claudette needed to have her vision examined, and when they arrived at the scheduled time, the receptionist took one look at the color of their skin and canceled the appointment. White people wouldn't want to sit as equals in the singular waiting room. And in order to keep the system of white supremacy humming like a well-oiled machine, it was important that everyone participate in it. "You can come back at the end of the day," the receptionist told them. "After the last white patient has left."

Claudette was on the cusp of adolescence when her little sister died of polio. Delphine had been the one constant in her life, and Claudette didn't know how she was supposed to continue just . . . going to school? Getting dressed every day? How? Claudette was gutted. The smallest provocation set her off. She wondered how she was supposed to start high school two weeks after her sister's funeral, how she was supposed to look right and act right when nothing in her world was right.

But school did start, and it became Claudette's refuge. Her English teacher, Geraldine Nesbitt, seemed to understand how important it was that her curriculum connect her students to the broader world. Rather than being forced to read dusty, musty novels of which there were too few anyway, Nesbitt used things like the Constitution and Magna Carta as texts. They read the Bible as literature. She brought in great speeches from history, like Patrick Henry's "Give me liberty or give me death!" written two hundred years prior in Virginia Randolph's native Richmond, and asked students to analyze how it might apply to their lives.

The grief from her sister's death didn't grow lighter over time. But Claudette grew stronger, and each day, it became a little easier to carry it. Then the world changed again. One of her classmates pulled her aside in the hallway. "Did you hear about Jeremiah?" they asked. Jeremiah Reeves, a senior at her school, had been arrested. Reeves was a drummer—a popular, good-looking boy who had a job delivering groceries. He had been caught in a romantic embrace with a white woman on his route, part of an ongoing affair the two had been having. When they were found together, the white woman immediately declared that he had raped her.

Rage spilled out of the officers that day as they hauled Reeves to jail and strapped him into the electric chair. "We know what you did. Confess," they spat, as they stood poised, ready to switch on the chair.[3]

Reeves was distraught, terrified that the police would turn the electric chair on unless he told them what they wanted to hear. Even though he knew the relationship was consensual, after a night of torture spent strapped into the electric chair, he admitted to the rape. The police then forced him to admit to every other rape that had been reported that entire summer before they unhooked him from the confines of the instrument of death. Reeves felt his choices in that moment were to confess and try to sort it out later, or to be immediately electrocuted. Reeves chose the former. He was only sixteen.

Jeremiah Reeves quickly recanted his confession. Students at Booker T. Washington High were shocked and horrified. Whispers of the brutality of his torture at the hands of the police spread like wildfire. At his trial, an all-white jury sentenced him to death within thirty minutes, despite death not typically being a sentence for rape. The United States Supreme Court granted him a new trial, because they found it was wrong that the jury had not been allowed to hear evidence of his torture in jail.

Another all-white jury was convened for a new trial. Reeves was convicted again in under an hour, and the state of Alabama imprisoned him until he was old enough to kill. Reeves walked to the electric chair, the same one that had been used to extract his confession under duress, when he was twenty-two years old.[4]

Rage bubbled in Claudette's chest. Nothing about this was okay, and she was being asked to pretend that it was.

A few days after Reeves's execution, on Easter Sunday in 1958, Martin Luther King led a group of mourners in prayer on the grounds of the Alabama state capitol. "Truth may be crucified and justice buried," he thundered. "But one day they will rise again. We must live and face death if necessary with that hope."[5]

Claudette recalled, "My mother and grandmother told me never to go anywhere with a white man no matter what. I grew up hearing horror story after horror story about Black girls who were raped by white men, and how they never got justice either. When a white man raped a Black girl—something that happened all the time—it was just his word against hers, and no one would ever believe her. The white man always got off. . . . That changed me. That put a lot of anger in me. I stayed angry about Jeremiah Reeves for a long time."[6]

Overwhelmed by the injustice of the Jim Crow South, Claudette began to imagine a life's mission for herself, one modeled after her personal hero, Harriet Tubman. To Claudette, Tubman was the epitome of courage—a pistol-wearing woman who never lost a passenger on the Underground Railroad. Claudette wasn't going to become like other members of the Black middle-class in the South, who were overwhelmingly teachers and preachers. She was going to become a lawyer. She was going to *do something*.

"I was tired of adults complaining about how badly they were treated and not doing anything about it. I'd had enough of just feeling angry about Jeremiah Reeves. I was tired of *hoping* for justice. When my moment came, I was ready," she said years later.[7]

On that early spring day, streets crowded with oblivious children freed from the confines of school, the bus driver yelled at Claudette. "Why are you still sitting here? You've got to get up!" *I'm done playing this game,* Claudette thought. *I'm not going to pretend it's okay anymore.* When she sat, unmoving, the bus driver flagged down an officer, who boarded the bus.

"You have to get up now," the officer insisted. *No,* Claudette thought. *No, I do not.*

The students at the back of the bus buzzed with energy as this scene unfolded, while the white passengers in the front craned their necks to see the person who was refusing to participate in the carefully crafted caste system. "Get her off the bus," one person in the front might have called. "I have an appointment to get to."

"Get up and move," the officer repeated. "You have to get up."

One of Claudette's classmates, a girl named Margaret, yelled from the back of the bus, "She ain't got to do nothing but stay Black and die!"

Over and over, the whites in authority repeated their demands that Claudette relinquish what she had paid for. But she would not budge. She sat calmly, tears now rolling down her cheeks, repeating, "I have constitutional rights. It's my constitutional right to sit here as much as that lady. I paid my fare; it's my constitutional right."[8] She was doing it for Harriet and Sojourner, for Delphine and Jeremiah. She was doing it for herself.

When the transportation officer realized she wasn't going anywhere, he informed the bus driver that he'd done all he could, but he didn't have arrest power. So the bus driver moved the bus a few blocks up the street and flagged down some Montgomery police officers.

One officer looked at Claudette and said, "I've had trouble with that thing before."[9]

Thing? Claudette thought. *THING?*

"Are you going to get up?" one of them barked at Claudette.

"No, sir. It's my constitutional right to sit here," Claudette said. The officers grabbed her arms and yanked, and Claudette's books went flying. She went limp as a baby, because she knew what would happen if she tried to fight back. One of the officers kicked her repeatedly as they dragged her up the aisle and out of the bus.

Claudette swallowed her fury. She wanted to kick and scream at those officers; she wanted them to listen, just listen for one second, to understand what they were doing to her. To everyone. To Montgomery. To America. Instead, she bore their assault, knowing that anything she did would be blown out of proportion and used against her. "It just killed me to leave that bus. I hated to give that white woman my seat when so many Black people were standing. I was crying hard," she remembered.[10]

Claudette was handcuffed and put in the back of a police car. She pressed her knees tightly together. *Yea, though I walk through the valley of the shadow of death*, she thought. *I will fear no evil.* One of the officers wedged himself in the back seat next to her, speaking about her to the driver as though she weren't sitting right there. Psalm 23, which she had memorized in Sunday school, now filled her mind. *Thy rod and thy staff they comfort me.*

"N****r b***h!" The officer's voice dripped with contempt. "What do you think her bra size is?"[11]

Thou preparest a table before me in the presence of mine enemies, Claudette hoped.

They drove her, not to the juvenile facility where they would normally take a fifteen-year-old, but to the adult jail, where more officers called her names no one should ever call a child. She was thrown into a cell, and the lock clanged shut with a sickening thud.

In the middle of the cell, Claudette dropped to her knees and sobbed, praying the prayer of the terrified and desperate.

Claudette's mother didn't have a car, so she called their minister to drive her to the jail to bail her daughter out. They found her, overwrought, terrified that she would be trapped there forever like Jeremiah Reeves. "Are you all right?" her mom soothed, too worried to be mad. Claudette might have walked out of jail that day, but she didn't wake up from the ensuing nightmare. The Colvins were now a target. They knew that it would occur to some Klan member that they should firebomb their house—or worse. No one on their street slept that night. Her father sat facing the door, unblinking, shotgun in hand.

Their family minister said to her, "Everyone prays for freedom. We've all been praying and praying. But you're different—you want your answer the next morning. And I think you just brought the revolution to Montgomery."[12] Claudette didn't have some master plan in her mind—she was a teenager. But what she did know is that she was done pretending. She was done pretending all of *this*—picture Claudette sweeping her arm toward society at large—was fine. Because it wasn't fine, and what she just had to endure on that bus, in that police car, and in that jail was evidence of that.

In 1955 Montgomery, some leaders of the civil rights movement believed this was their moment, the revolution they'd been waiting for. A boycott of the bus system, which was primarily patronized by the African American community, had been discussed for months, but leaders were afraid that the wrong person, someone whose background was questionable in some way, would stall their efforts if they became the face of the movement.

The Colvins got in touch with two civil rights workers in Montgomery, E. D. Nixon and Fred Gray. Gray was a recent law school graduate, who as of this writing is still practicing law in his nineties. Fred Gray was determined to destroy everything segregation touched, and that included the Montgomery bus system. But when Gray met with Claudette and her family, he urged them to seriously consider the repercussions of publicly fighting the charges the police had levied against her: assaulting a police officer, disturbing the peace, and violating segregation laws.[13]

But the Colvins didn't need time to think—they were ready to move forward.

If not now, when? If not them, then who?

The first time Claudette met Rosa Parks was not long before her assault trial, when she began to attend NAACP meetings for young people. When Parks first laid eyes on Colvin, whose name was all over the papers, she said, "You're Claudette Colvin? Oh my god, I was looking for some big old burly overgrown teenager who sassed white people out . . . but no, they pulled a little girl off the bus."[14]

Rosa helped raise money for Claudette's legal defense, baking homemade cookies and selling them after church services on sunny Sunday mornings. She and Claudette became close, and Claudette sat near her, watching as Rosa altered wedding dresses with her tiny, perfect stitches.

———

Claudette went to trial in March 1955. Fred Gray called more than a dozen witnesses who had been on the bus, all of whom attested to the same facts: Claudette did not fight back, she didn't assault any officers, and she was sitting in the section for Black riders. The police, on the other hand, testified under oath that Claudette hit and kicked and scratched them, and they solicited letters from other white bus riders, who said that the officers were perfect gentlemen and didn't so much as lay an unkind finger on the unruly Claudette.[15]

It didn't take long for the judge to consider the testimony of whites and weigh it against the testimony of Blacks, and to find Claudette guilty of all the charges. He declared her a ward of the state, sentenced her to probation, and sent her home with her parents. Spectators in the courtroom brushed away their own tears, listening to the anguished sobs of the teenage girl who had just been wrongfully convicted.

Before Claudette's case could be appealed, two of the charges—disturbing the peace and violating the city's segregation laws—were dropped. One has to ask themselves why they would drop the charges for which it seemed so easy to gain a conviction? The most obvious answer was strategy. Prosecutors knew that Claudette's lawyers planned to file a federal lawsuit challenging Montgomery's bus segregation laws. By dropping the charges, they closed off the legal avenue Claudette's lawyers needed for the challenge. Claudette's assault conviction, however? That was upheld.

———

Clifford Durr was a southern man, born and bred. One of his grandfathers owned a plantation, the other was a cotton broker. Both of them served in the Confederate Army during the Civil War. Clifford was married to Virginia Foster Durr, whose sister was the wife of Supreme Court justice Hugo Black. One of Virginia's grandfathers was in the KKK, and the other was an enslaver.[16]

You might think it odd, then, that Clifford and Virginia ultimately became civil rights activists. And you'd be right; it certainly was odd that people of the Durrs' background and pedigree would lead them to be, not on the board of an all-white Concerned Citizens League, but instead under constant surveillance by the FBI for their "subversive" work on behalf of the Black community in Montgomery and across the South. Virginia had attended Wellesley, where Katharine Bates taught years before, and credited her time there as transformational. She befriended Rosa Parks.

Clifford Durr was an attorney who worked defending people who refused to sign loyalty oaths to the government, and Fred Gray had tapped him to help appeal Claudette's case to the Supreme Court. But when the doors on that potential case closed, it freed up Durr's schedule. And it was Clifford Durr who took a phone call in December 1955 from his wife's good friend, Rosa Parks. She had just been arrested for refusing to give up her seat.

Several months before Rosa was arrested, Virginia Durr saw how down-trodden and tired she seemed, and she arranged for her to receive a full scholarship to the Highlander Folk School.[17] Highlander was the brain-child of Myles Horton, a white Tennessean who wanted to help the poor communities of Appalachia and the South develop leadership skills they could use. Highlander offered residential workshops in Monteagle, Ten-nessee, that were a week or two long.

The workshop Rosa attended was about how to go about integrating schools and other public accommodations in light of the Supreme Court's recent *Brown v. Board* decision. Rosa was painfully shy, and for the first few days at the workshop, she barely spoke. But it marked the first time in Rosa's life that she "had lived in an atmosphere of complete equality with the members of the other race."[18] Highlander had total racial inte-gration, which the vast majority of attendees had never experienced.

When civil rights leader John Lewis attended a Highlander work-shop, he said, "This was the first time in my life that I saw Black people and white people not just sitting down together at long tables for shared meals, but also cleaning up together afterward, doing the dishes together, gathering together late into the night in deep discussion and sleeping in the same cabin dormitories."[19]

"From the beginning," sociologist Aldon Morris writes, "Highlander was a rarity. In the midst of worker oppression, racism, and lynchings, Highlander unflinchingly communicated to the world that it was an is-land of decency that would never betray its humanitarian vision."[20]

When Rosa left Highlander after her workshop, her mood was notably changed. Virginia Durr remarked, "When she came back she was so happy and felt so liberated and then as time went on she said the discrimination got worse and worse to bear after having for the first time in her life, been free of it at Highlander. I am sure that had a lot to do with her daring to risk arrest as she is naturally a very quiet and retiring person."[21]

And here, my friend, is where I get to introduce you to someone you should know. Because without Rosa's time at Highlander, it's not at all clear that she would have refused to give up her seat on the bus that December day. And Rosa's time at Highlander would have been nothing without Septima Clark.

TWENTY-THREE

SEPTIMA CLARK

Charleston, South Carolina, 1898

Septima Poinsette Clark was the daughter of a formerly enslaved man and a laundress. She was raised in Charleston, and her mother refused to allow her children to become "domestics," a job that involved doing domestic chores, like childcare, cleaning, and laundry for white families. Domestic work was easy to get, but it also made people extremely vulnerable to abuse and fraud. If women working as domestics were raped, assaulted, or not paid as promised, they had no recourse in the legal system that was set up to benefit whites. Victoria, Septima's mother, wanted more for her children. So Septima became a teacher, one of the best tickets to the Black middle class at the time.

As an aside, I kept coming back to Septima's maiden name, Poinsette. Like, *poinsettia*, I wondered? The Christmas flower? And in fact, yes, exactly like the Christmas flower. Peter, Septima's father, had been enslaved at the home of Joel Poinsett, and Poinsett was friends with Andrew Jackson. Poinsett was named secretary of war under Jackson's successor, Martin Van Buren.[1]

Joel Poinsett was Septima's biological grandfather. He was an amateur botanist whose home had unique and glorious gardens, and when he was appointed the first U.S. minister to Mexico, he found that a native plant with large red flowers bloomed at Christmastime. Mexicans called it Flower of the Holy Night, but when Poinsett brought it to South Carolina, it became known as the poinsettia.[2]

As secretary of war, Poinsett oversaw the Indian Removal Act and the Trail of Tears, which dispossessed Native Americans of millions of acres of their ancestral land and forced them to move west of the Mississippi to "Indian Territory."

So it's remarkable that Peter Poinsette—up until the mid-1800s, many names did not have standardized spellings—grew to be a kind, gentle man who was quick to help anyone who needed him. Septima's mother was feisty and stubborn, and Septima was raised to be a combination of both of her parents. "Strengthen each other's weaknesses," Septima's father always told her. "See that there is something fine and noble in everyone."[3]

When Septima was coming of age, Black teachers were not allowed in Charleston public schools. And I don't just mean Black teachers couldn't teach in the white schools, I mean they couldn't teach at all, in any schools. Like many Black teachers, Septima was required to accept a position in a poor rural school outside the district that served only Black students.

In 1916, South Carolina had no school taxes and no laws mandating school attendance. According to historian Katherine Mellon Charron, South Carolina schools, on average, spent $48.59 per year educating a white student and $.95 educating a Black student. Only 5 percent of Black South Carolinians entered high school, and even though there were eighteen thousand more Black students than white, schools that served Black students made up only 9 percent of school properties.[4]

Black teachers often had fifty to one hundred students in a single-room school, and the school year was only three to four months long.

Coleman Blease, on his first day as governor of South Carolina, proclaimed, "I am opposed to white people's taxes being used to educate
Negroes. . . . In my opinion, when the people of this country began to try
to educate the Negro, they made a serious and grave mistake, and I fear
the worst result is yet to come So why continue?"[5]

Septima's first job was on Johns Island, one of the many barrier islands
that dot the coast of South Carolina and Georgia. Black residents that
lived on Johns and other islands had largely been cut off from the main-
land since the 1700s, when they were enslaved there as rice farmers. Over
time, they developed their own culture and language, called Gullah or
Gullah Geechee. Gullah was a mixture of Portuguese, English, Spanish,
and West African vocabulary, put into a West African accent and gram-
matical structures.[6] Most outsiders couldn't understand it, but Septima
found that she could get by well enough, and what she needed to learn,
she did.

Septima witnessed firsthand the abject poverty of Johns Island in
1916. Mothers were forced to work to provide for their children, and
babies were often left at the edges of rice fields unattended, a "sugar tit"
in their mouths. Mothers mixed together sugar and lard in a cloth and
put it in the mouths of their little ones to keep them quiet. But babies
would be swarmed by flies and mosquitoes, and the humid, swampy climate led to huge numbers of contagious illnesses. Infant mortality was
staggering.[7]

Septima's first classroom at Promise Land school was a log structure
with no glass in the windows, so shutters were used instead. The shutters
made the inside of the single room dark, and children were forced to sit
on backless benches. There were chalkboards, but no chalk. There were a
handful of outdated books, but none of them matched. She was paid
thirty-five dollars a month, while her white counterparts made eighty-
five dollars teaching three students and had all the supplies they needed.[8]

Septima was eventually able to teach in Charleston, after the NAACP became involved and threatened to sue the district if they continued to refuse to hire Black teachers for Black schools.

She married a man named Nerie Clark and had a baby girl that she named after her mother, Victoria. When baby Victoria was three weeks old, it was discovered that she had an undetected birth defect, and she died.[9]

Distraught at the loss of the daughter she deeply loved, Septima contemplated suicide. What was the point of carrying on, if carrying on meant leaving her baby girl behind? She walked down the dock overlooking the sea, pondering whether to throw herself in. Her family didn't approve of her marriage to Nerie. She was a disappointment to them in every way, she was sure of it. Before she had a chance to act, Septima saw her little brother riding his bike toward her. Their mother had sent him out to look for her, worried that she might be thinking of doing something she couldn't take back. "Mama wants you to come home," he told her. She loved her little brother too much to make him watch her death, so she pushed her contemplations aside and followed him back to their mother's house.

A few years later, Septima had another child, Nerie Jr., and then discovered something that was impossible to fully comprehend: her husband was unfaithful. And not just a cheat, but a master of deceit. When he wasn't with Septima, she believed he was off working. But while he was away at work, he was also spending time with his secret second family, able to chalk up his extended absences to his job as a sailor. And then, shortly after Septima's discovery, he died. Septima spent the rest of her life as a single mother, struggling to make a way for her child. For Septima, this often meant being forced to leave Nerie Jr. in the care of Nerie Sr.'s family for months at a time so she could work.[10]

It's difficult to imagine how Septima must have felt in this moment:

her baby girl was dead, she had married a man her mother did not approve of, she discovered her husband was a philanderer and liar, and then he died, forcing her to leave her son in the care of her dead husband's parents. Septima had no choice but to believe in the importance of her work and to rely on her faith. "Faith I must have and will keep to lean heavily on," she said.[11]

Throughout her long career, Septima believed that God had spared her life on many occasions: once, when her brother saved her from suicide. Other times, she survived a plane accident, a bus wreck, and a train crash. Another, police officers caught a group of boys on their way to firebomb her house. "I'll never know how a sheriff caught up with three white boys, all teenagers, coming to bomb the house I slept in just in time to take away the dynamite. I said to myself, 'God kept me that night, so I'll put my body in His care each night thereafter,' and I did."[12]

She continued her work with the NAACP, which helped highlight the tragedy of adult illiteracy. Many men who were drafted into the army couldn't even write well enough to sign their names for payroll. At the time, printing was not an acceptable way to write one's name for banking purposes—you needed to learn cursive. She helped the men who would soon be shipping out learn to sign their names and read well enough to understand directional signs and where a bus said it was headed. Education wasn't only liberation, she came to realize; education was self-sufficiency. It was independence. It reduced your vulnerability, because it was much harder to cheat someone who could read and do basic sums. It was connection, allowing you to read and send letters to your loved ones. It was faith, because it let you read your scriptures.

Septima taught adults to read in a way that did not make them feel judged or like they were stupid. "A good teacher meets her learners where they are," she said.[13] She created a curriculum that wasn't reliant on the Dick and Jane readers of the day, which she felt humiliated adults with their babyish stories. Instead, they learned to read information that was important to their lives: geographical and demographic data, the names of the surrounding cities and towns, who the mayor was, and who represented them in Washington, D.C.

By the 1950s, Septima had been teaching for decades. "Why are Black teachers paid the same amount as white teachers elsewhere, but not here?" she wondered. She again worked with the NAACP to file a lawsuit that aimed to equalize teacher salaries based on equal certification. They were successful, and Septima's salary went from $780 a year to $4,000 a year.[14]

One of the things Septima found most upsetting was that even though Black men and women had the right to vote, they often couldn't. Literacy tests prevented them from being able to access the polls. You might be under the impression that a literacy test is just asking somebody to read some passages to make sure that they can comprehend English. You might think that they are objective tests. And sadly, you would be wrong. Scoring was highly subjective, and was always done by white southerners.

To test how effective literacy tests were at keeping African Americans from voting in the Jim Crow South, a law professor at Duke University, William Van Alstyne, conducted an experiment in the 1960s. He sent the questions found on Alabama's voter literacy tests to all of the professors who were currently teaching Constitutional Law in American law schools.[15]

The professors were told to answer all of the questions without the aid of anything else. No books, no phoning a friend, nothing. Ninety-six law professors sent back their answers. Seventy percent of the answers that were returned were incorrect. These are generally people with the highest degrees in American law, and they answered the majority of the questions incorrectly. Consider, then, the incredible barrier that these tests represented for the average person trying to access the polls with minimal literacy skills.

Then, and now, one of the most effective ways to stop cultural change is to create a moral panic around it. Moral panics have been around since this country's inception, with the Salem witch trials being among the first widely publicized (and deadly) panics. Since then, moral panics have been used as a tool to subvert and dismantle movements that the dominant caste views as a threat. And this included civil rights.

Sociology professors Erich Goode and Ben-Yehuda Nachman have identified the five stages of moral panic, which they say are "culturally and politically constructed, a product of the human imagination."[16]

1. **Concern:** Something occurs that gives someone a sense of alarm.
2. **Hostility:** A group or subculture is then looked on with disdain or aggression as a result of the concern.
3. **Consensus:** The dominant group builds agreement that the group or subculture is the cause of the concern, and that they are justified in their hostility toward them.
4. **Disproportionality:** The threat of harm posed by the group or subculture is then exaggerated for effect.
5. **Volatility:** The moral panic erupts, and/or dies down when it is replaced with another moral panic.

In the 1940s and '50s, the quickest way to sink an activity you didn't like was to include it in the broad moral panic surrounding communism, which we now call the Red Scare. Civil rights? Communism. The NAACP? Communism. Highlander Folk School? Communism. Martin Luther King? Communist. Myles Horton? Communist. Clifford Durr? Communist. Eleanor Roosevelt? Communist.

Civil rights leader Dorothy Cotton remembered that there was a "large billboard on a major highway with Mrs. Eleanor Roosevelt's photograph, and that of Dr. Martin Luther King, with a caption indicating that they were 'at that communist school' in Tennessee."[17]

Determined to capitalize on the threat of a communist infiltration, South Carolina made it illegal for any government employees to be a member of the NAACP. Septima wasn't having any of that nonsense. (Dorothy Cotton later reported that, at Myles Horton's funeral in 1990, the fact that civil rights work was viewed as communism was joked about. "They wouldn't know communism from rheumatism," Horton's friends laughed.)[18] When employees were required to fill out a form listing all of their group memberships and attesting that they were not in the "communist" NAACP, Septima refused to hide her membership. She knew it was likely that she would be terminated, but she was unwilling to live a lie.

And she was terminated by the Charleston Public Schools. Which only gave her more time to devote to her activism. She didn't have time to sit around being angry, not when there was so much to be done. "You know the measure of a person is how much they develop in their life," she said. "Some people slow down in their growth after they become adults. But you never know when a person's going to leap forward or change around completely—I've seen growth like most people don't think possible. I can even work with my enemies because I know from experience that they might have a change of heart any minute."[19]

If I were a preacher or motivational speaker, I would have exclaimed Septima's words in a fever pitch, and then I would drop my voice to barely above a whisper, repeating in staccato what you just heard for emphasis. "I.can.even.work.with.my.enemies.because.I.know.from.experience. that . . ." My voice would swoop back up, projecting to the back of the room: "THEY MIGHT HAVE A CHANGE OF HEART ANY MINUTE! At any minute!" My arms would move wildly, underscoring what it is we should all walk out of the room knowing: "How can our enemies have a change of heart if we don't work with them? How can they be convinced that they're on the wrong path if we cut them out of our lives? How can we possibly hope to influence someone with whom we have no relationship?"

And then, I would get close to the microphone, my body still. "They can't," I would whisper. "They CAN'T. Your enemy won't change because you refuse to sit with them at a dinner table! We have but one hope, one hope," I would repeat. "The hope that change is always possible if we refuse to give up on people!" My speech/sermon would probably go on to give other examples of people who saw extraordinary change only after they persevered in the face of extraordinary adversity.

And then at the end, I would come back to Septima's message. I would repeat the hope that she did not feel, but that she chose. I would remind the audience that Septima was fired from her job. She was denied equal pay and job opportunities. I would remind them that her students were learning in the dark with no books. I would say that her baby died and her husband was a liar and that she nearly perished, over and over and over, that people tried to kill her, but still, she refused to give up on her enemies. "WHY?" I would ask. "WHY? Because she knew that her enemies might have a change of heart at any minute. Any minute. But only if she stayed in the game. Only if she refused to give up hope." And then I would hope that the audience would leave my talk encouraged by the idea that their labors are not in vain. That despite current evidence to the contrary, their enemies were capable of change. But only if they refused to quit. Only if they chose to hope.

Septima, who had already attended a workshop at Highlander, began teaching there after she was fired from Charleston Public Schools. Rosa Parks was one of her students, and Parks later took what she learned at Highlander and became the face of a movement. Septima went on to develop an educational program that you've probably never heard of. But it became a cornerstone of the civil rights movement.

What we need, Septima argued, was Citizenship School. Classes for adults who couldn't read that would teach them literacy AND how to access the polls. How to order from the Sears catalog AND how to write a letter to your congressman. The first Citizenship School, a collaboration between Septima, Myles Horton, Septima's cousin Bernice Robinson, and Esau Jenkins, a political organizer, was set up on Johns Island, where Septima had taught so long ago.[20]

Every location they planned to use for the two-hour-long, twice-a-week classes ended up canceling the class, because, communism. Even churches that were sympathetic to their cause worried that they would be firebombed or targeted by the state. Eventually, Esau was able to obtain a grant for a building, and at the front, he put a small store. Hidden in the back of the store, behind a wall of freezers and produce, was a classroom they could use. Because the shop was a Black-owned business, it was unlikely any white people would even step foot inside, much less discover the secret classroom.

Bernice Robinson was tapped to be the teacher because she was a hairdresser. When Septima and Esau asked her to consider it, she kept saying things like, "Wait, why would I do that? I'm a hairdresser, not a teacher" or "I don't know how to teach adults how to read."[21] Bernice Robinson is one of many people throughout history who felt completely ill-equipped to step forward into their calling, but who just moved forward anyway.

The Gullah people of the island were suspicious of outsiders. They knew Septima because she had gained their trust, and Bernice was her relative. But really, there was a bigger reason that Bernice was chosen. As a hairdresser, Bernice knew how to listen. She talked with people for hours every day, heard their problems, and made them feel important. Those were the soft skills many other people lacked.

On the first day of classes, Bernice told her students, "I'm not going to be the teacher. We're going to learn together. You're going to teach me something, and maybe there are a few things I might be able to teach you, but I don't consider myself a teacher, I just feel that I'm here to learn with you. We'll learn things together."[22] She helped the class make a list of what they wanted to learn about, and Bernice began to devise lessons. Septima helped her come up with a system of using a large piece of cardboard with someone's name written on it, so they could trace their name over and over to practice signing it in cursive. As word spread, even more Johns Island residents showed up for the classes, despite the fact that they had already begun.

Groups of teenage girls were brought by their parents, and Bernice kept them busy by giving them crocheting and sewing projects to do while they listened. Soon, the classroom was not just packed, but another thirty-five people stood in the store, craning their necks, trying to listen to the instruction. At the end of her first Citizenship School, every one of Bernice's fourteen official students received their voter registration certificates.[23]

One of Bernice's students was a sixty-five-year-old woman who could not read or write a single word. At the end of the Citizenship School, Bernice wrote all of her students' names on the board. Bernice said, "I will never forget the emotion that I felt when she got up, took the ruler out of my hand and said, 'There's my name, A-N-N-A, Anna. There's my last name, V-A-S-T-I-N-E.' Goose pimples came out all over me."[24]

Within a few years, more than thirty-seven Citizenship Schools sprung up on the Sea Islands of South Carolina. Students of the Citizenship Schools went on to do things like begin low-income housing projects, credit unions, a nursing home, and other key infrastructure within their communities. In four years, Black voter registration in communities with Citizenship Schools was up 300 percent.[25] All because Septima continued to choose to hope.

As the Citizenship School program expanded across the South, Highlander insisted that all classes had to be taught by African Americans. By

1968, Citizenship Schools had helped move tens of thousands of Black voters onto the voter rolls, and most of the leaders of the civil rights movement had been trained by Septima, Bernice, or other Highlander teachers.

And this momentum, this ever-rising tide of Black voters? The people intent on preserving white supremacy and the status quo of the South just couldn't handle it. They stepped up the moral panic rhetoric. The FBI and the state of Tennessee created reports that were picked up by news stations around the country that painted Highlander as a hotbed of communism. They revoked their tax-exempt status. The state of Tennessee took away their school charter, and the concept of Citizenship School had to be transferred to the Southern Christian Leadership Conference, the organization headed by Martin Luther King.

And then the government set their sights on the leader that was making such a difference: Septima herself. She was a known teetotaler, but the police arrived at the door one night and arrested Septima for breaking alcohol laws. They had found what they believed to be illegal whiskey at the home of Myles Horton, but it didn't belong to Septima. They threw Septima, who was now a grandmother, into the back of a squad car while her young granddaughter wailed, "WHERE ARE YOU TAKING MY GRANDMOMMIE?"[26] The idea that a Black woman was at the helm of a group training the next generation of activists was an idea that some people would have done anything to stop.

TWENTY-FOUR

AMERICA

1950s

During the Cold War, the period in which Claudette's story unfolds, government officials and historians tap-danced as fast as they could to distance the United States from the Nazis, downplaying exactly how much inspiration the United States' racial segregation laws provided to the Third Reich. But the evidence is copious. Hitler emulated America's westward expansion in his annexation of territory in Europe, and its treatment of Native Americans in his programs to remove Jews from places he felt should be occupied by Aryans. According to historian James Q. Whitman, "The Nazis took a sustained, significant, and sometimes even eager interest in the American example in race law"—racial segregation laws like the ones present all over the South.[1] In other words, the Nazis looked to our racial discrimination policies and liked what they saw.

And here was Claudette, in 1955, more than ten years after Hitler shot himself in a bunker. The United States had become the world's greatest superpower because of our war production, economic prowess, and victory against Germany and Japan, but we were still arresting and assaulting Black children for sitting on a bus. Strapping them into electric chairs to pressure them to confess to crimes they did not commit.

The Supreme Court had issued their initial opinion in *Brown v. Board of Education* the year prior, and a follow-up opinion, *Brown v. Board of Education II*, earlier in 1955. The dominant narrative surrounding *Brown v. Board of Education* is that it integrated schools. Separate but equal was unacceptable. The Supreme Court said it, the schools did it. Black students were equal to white students.

This is, at best, a gross misrepresentation of the facts. And at worst, it's an intentional lie meant to cover up years of continued flagrant flouting of the US Constitution by states that refused to integrate.

Did segregated schools rush to integrate? Did they create comprehensive plans to make sure that all children had equal educational opportunities? The simple answer is absolutely not.

The Little Rock Nine—Ernest Green, Elizabeth Eckford, Jefferson Thomas, Terrence Roberts, Carlotta Walls, Minnijean Brown, Gloria Ray, Thelma Mothershed, and Melba Pattillo—the students who publicly attempted to integrate Central High School in 1957, were very prominent, visible members of this quest for school equality and integration.

But to get to Little Rock, we need to travel through Topeka, and we need to stop by the home of minister Oliver Brown in 1950. Oliver's young daughter, Linda, was ready to be enrolled in school.

Oliver held Linda's hand as they walked down the street of their mixed neighborhood to the elementary school that many of her friends attended. "Sit here," he told Linda, leaving her in the waiting area while he entered the principal's office, closing the door behind him.[2]

Linda could hear the voices inside the principal's office getting louder. Her father reappeared, his face hard. He grabbed her firmly by the hand and marched her out of the school. Linda didn't know what had happened, but she knew it wasn't good.

He had just tried to enroll his daughter in the closest elementary school to their home, a school for white children, and was denied. The district said she would need to attend the more distant school for Black children. It's not that Oliver Brown didn't think Linda could learn at the all-Black school; it's that he didn't think she should have to.

Oliver Brown would become the lead plaintiff in the landmark *Brown v. Board* Supreme Court case, by nature of his last name being first alphabetically. *Brown v. Board of Education* was actually a number of cases joined together, lawsuits from multiple states and Washington, D.C., all suing over the doctrine of "separate but equal" rendered under *Plessy v. Ferguson,* which had told people like Clara Brown that she wasn't a citizen of the country she was born in.

Attorney Thurgood Marshall argued the case in front of the Supreme Court in 1952, and before the Supreme Court could release their opinion, the chief justice died. Eisenhower appointed a new chief justice, the governor of California, Earl Warren. Warren decided to order that the case be reheard so he could listen to the oral arguments.

Earl Warren was born in the late 1800s to Scandinavian immigrants who had moved to California, and he embarked on a fifty-year career in public service, working as a prosecutor and later serving as the only person to be elected to three terms as governor of California. In fact, Warren did something that's basically unheard of in American government: he won both the Republican gubernatorial primary and the Democratic gubernatorial primary. Warren's version of good government was one that was efficient, transparent, and nonpartisan.

As a prosecutor, Warren and his team tackled corruption head-on, vigorously racking up conviction after conviction, to the tune of thousands of people being sentenced for bribery, bootlegging, prostitution, and fraud.

Perhaps Warren's most famous prosecution, however, was Alameda

County sheriff Burton Becker. Becker was openly a "Klailiff," or vice president of a KKK chapter. He ran for sheriff on a platform of Christian values, vowing to clean things up when it came to crime. Becker was easily elected, given that his opponent was implicated in the grisly murder of a dismembered woman found floating in an estuary.

Warren had his eye on Becker, and during one of their meetings issued a stern warning to him to clean up his act. Becker was defiant, urging Warren to "take care of his own business, and I'll take care of mine."[3]

While the KKK openly supported Prohibition, Becker was engaged in one of the largest graft operations in the country. Liquor still operators paid off Becker's deputies. But if they refused to pay up, Becker would raid them, making the public think he was cracking down on crime. An informant kept him abreast of any impending federal enforcement actions. A series of low-level criminals testified before a grand jury that they had been paid off by Becker, and Becker was finally sent to San Quentin prison.

In May 1922, some fifteen hundred Klansmen gathered in the hills above Oakland, California. The next day, the *San Francisco Chronicle* read: "Standing with bared heads before the fiery cross of the Invisible Empire, 500 novices were initiated into the Knights of the Ku Klux Klan in Oakland Friday night. An American flag snapped in the breeze, and on the flag-draped altar was a Bible, a sword, and a goblet of water. The group of novices was surrounded by a phalanx of white-robed members of the Klan. Kneeling, they recited the oath, and were sprinkled with water from the goblet. Many of the novices are said to have fainted during the ceremony."[4]

Warren was having none of it.

Earl Warren was elected attorney general in 1938 and governor in 1942, and he held these positions during World War II, when California assisted the federal government in incarcerating more than one hundred twenty thousand Japanese Americans. Even when the incarceration camps closed in January 1945, he argued against releasing the people imprisoned there, saying, "If the Japs are released, no one will be able to tell a saboteur from any other Jap. . . . We don't want to have a second Pearl Harbor in California. We don't propose to have the Japs back in California during this war if there is any lawful means of preventing it."[5]

These racist and xenophobic viewpoints would later haunt Warren.

Warren rose to national significance when he ran for vice president on the Republican ticket with Thomas Dewey, and later, in the 1950s, he threw his support behind Dwight Eisenhower. In exchange for his support, Eisenhower promised Warren the first seat available on the Supreme Court, a decision Eisenhower would live to regret.

There was already a former member of the KKK on the Supreme Court, Justice Hugo Black, previously a senator from Alabama, and the brother-in-law of Virginia Durr. Black tried hard to distance himself from the Klan after being sworn in, going out of his way to hire Catholics, Jews, and African Americans for court jobs and taking the extraordinary step of publicizing these hires. He wanted to send a clear message that his days of prejudice were behind him. Still, Black authored the Supreme Court *Korematsu* opinion that said the incarceration of Japanese Americans was constitutional.

In 1953, the chief justice of the Supreme Court, Fred Vinson, had a massive heart attack and died in office. Eisenhower made good on his promise and offered the position of chief justice to Earl Warren. Eisenhower viewed Warren as a man much like himself: a man whose popularity transcended party. A pragmatist who cared about people. A man who had dedicated his life to public service.

While Earl Warren had never been a judge, he had significantly more prosecutorial experience than nearly any judge before or since. In fact, five of the nine Supreme Court justices in 1954 had never had any meaningful experience as a judge. Justice Felix Frankfurter had been a law professor, William Douglas came from the Securities and Exchange Commission, Robert Jackson had been an attorney general, and Hugo Black had briefly been a night court judge early in his career. This broad array of experiences created a certain type of intellectual diversity on the court. By contrast, today's Supreme Court justices are mostly professional judges.

It was later the Warren court that gave us *Miranda v. Arizona* and *Gideon v. Wainwright,* establishing the constitutional right to remain silent and the right to an attorney.[6]

When Thurgood Marshall argued *Brown v. Board of Education* a second time, Warren and Marshall already knew of each other. Marshall had advocated for the end of school segregation in California, under a suit filed by the family of nine-year-old Sylvia Mendez, who objected to being forced to attend a school for Mexicans. As governor, Warren later signed a bill into law ending public school segregation.[7]

Warren knew that whatever opinion the court issued in *Brown* would be controversial. And he wanted to send a strong, unanimous message. He knew that any amount of dissent on the court would empower segregationists to disregard their decision.

As it turned out, Justice Jackson was in the hospital at the time the court was getting ready to release their written opinion. Warren brought him the drafted opinion, which he agreed to sign, and the next day, when the court was scheduled to read their opinion aloud from the bench, Jackson checked himself out of the hospital in order to attend the hearing.

"Oyez! Oyez! Oyez!" the bailiff called, announcing that the court was in session. Chief Justice Warren began to read. The tension in the room grew, each word Warren spoke bringing him closer to what the crowd wanted to know: *Can separate be equal?*

"We come to the question presented," Warren read. "Does segregation of children in public schools solely on the basis of race, even though the physical facilities and other tangible factors may be equal, deprive the children of the minority group of equal educational opportunities?" Warren paused, aware of the gravity of what he was about to say.

This was the moment that Linda's dad was waiting for. This was the question that would change America.

"We unanimously believe that it does," Warren answered.[8]

A wave of emotion swept the normally silent Supreme Court chamber. Warren later said that he could barely hear it, but he *felt* it in ways that defied description.

We unanimously believe. Unanimous was better than Thurgood Marshall could have hoped for. The Brown family read about the decision afterward. "We lived in the calm of the hurricane's eye, gazing at the storm around us, and wondering how it would all end. I don't think my father ever got discouraged," Linda Brown recalled as an adult.[9]

The news of the decision made some people jubilant, the result of many years of hard work, persistence, and sacrifice. It made other people irate. School integration was an affront to their religious and moral beliefs.

For centuries, many white Christians believed that that God made the races different, and that it was only natural that some should be subservient to others. They used scriptures like Luke 12:47 to justify their beliefs: "He that knoweth his master's will and doeth it not, shall be beaten with many stripes."

After *Brown* came down, protesters on the steps of the Supreme Court held signs that read things like "Race mixing is communism," "Stop the race mixing march of the antichrist," and "Communists infiltrated our churches. Now it integrates our schools. II Peter 2:12."

(I looked up II Peter 2:12 in the King James Bible, likely the translation the protester holding the sign in 1954 used. It reads: "But these, as natural brute beasts, made to be taken and destroyed, speak evil of the things that they understand not; and shall utterly perish in their own corruption." The protester was likening Black children to animals.)

Listen, y'all don't need to write to me saying, "That's not true Christianity." I'm not asking you to believe it is. But these were not fringe beliefs in many of the evangelical churches in the South. This was how most white Christians at that time and in that place interpreted the scriptures. It was what they heard from their pulpits, and what they wanted taught in schools. White supremacy and white Christian identity are inextricably linked in American history. Facts don't require our personal approval for them to be facts.

After the first *Brown* decision, the court ordered a second hearing. The first opinion that was released in *Brown* went over the *why* of this issue—*why* it was important to integrate schools, because separate cannot be equal. The second hearing focused on the *how*. *How* were schools around the country going to integrate? The Supreme Court recognized that different regions of the country were going to require different approaches. In *Brown II*, the Supreme Court ordered schools to integrate "with all deliberate speed."

What does the phrase *with all deliberate speed* mean to you? You might hear it and think *quickly and deliberately speed things along*, right? *Be speedy about your integration. Deliberately be speedy.* That's absolutely what I thought, and what I was taught as a high school student.

But that's not what *with all deliberate speed* meant to segregationists. *Deliberate* in this context meant *slowly and carefully*. To them, "With all deliberate speed" meant integrate schools at a snail's pace. As they were creating plans for the legally required school integration, civil rights activists and lawyers made various proposals, which were rejected time after time. One lawyer, exasperated, basically asked school officials, "Well, what do you think would be a reasonable timeframe?" The other lawyers came back with: "2020." This was in 1955. Segregationists proposed integrating schools in 2020. That's what *with all deliberate speed* meant to them.

But to some segregationists, there was no distant future in which integration would occur, because they decided to close schools entirely. Led by Virginia senator Harry Byrd, some states engaged in a movement they deemed "Massive Resistance." They started by passing state laws that penalized schools that integrated, removed their funding, and closed public schools that dared a desegregation attempt. Some states gave out private school tuition vouchers so white parents who opposed integration could send their child to a private religious school. They established "pupil placement boards" that had the power to force students to attend the school the board decided upon.

And they were just getting started.

TWENTY-FIVE

TEENAGERS IN THE AMERICAN SOUTH

1950s

Arkansas governor Orval Faubus was at the helm of a state that did not want to integrate, and he soon found himself at the center of a national firestorm of his own creation. Faubus became a symbol of either what was right or what was wrong with America, depending on your perspective. Even though *Brown v. Brown of Education II* was decided in 1955, by 1957, Arkansas had failed to integrate its schools. Determined to make headway on school integration, the NAACP had been working hard to select and prepare nine students to integrate Central High School in Little Rock by that September.

The parents of Carlotta Walls, the youngest of the Little Rock Nine, bought her a new dress for school integration day, a dress that now belongs to the Smithsonian. Her mother told her, "Be prepared to go through the door, whether there is a crack in the door, or the door is flung wide open."[1] Carlotta nodded, not knowing for sure what she might face at the school.

One of the most enduring images of that morning was of Elizabeth Eckford, carrying a notebook and wearing sunglasses, trying to enter Central High School alone. Her family didn't have a phone, so when the

other students made plans to carpool and arrive together, she wasn't no-
tified. She arrived on the city bus and was immediately surrounded by an
angry mob of armed guards and segregationists.

"I stood looking at the school—it looked so big!" she remembered.
"Just then, the guards let some white students through. The crowd was
quiet. I guess they were waiting to see what was going to happen. When
I was able to steady my knees, I walked up to the guard who had let the
white students in. He didn't move. When I tried to squeeze past him, he
raised his bayonet and then the other guards moved in and they raised
their bayonets. They glared at me with a mean look, and I was very
frightened and didn't know what to do. I turned around and the crowd
came toward me. They moved closer and closer. Somebody started yelling 'drag her over this tree, let's take care of that n****r!'"[2] These were
ordinary white Arkansans whose vitriol was such that they were suggesting that a child seeking an education deserved to be lynched.

Orval Faubus called out the Arkansas National Guard to prevent the
students from entering, all the while making wild accusations claiming
he was being persecuted by the federal government. The next day, President Eisenhower sent a telegram to Orval Faubus. It said, in part, "When
I became President, I took an oath to support and defend the Constitution of the United States. The only assurance I can give you is that the
Federal Constitution will be upheld by me by every legal means at my
command."[3]

Faubus continued to send the National Guard to prevent integration,
claiming that it was for everyone's safety and refusing to comply with
court orders requiring that the Nine be admitted to school.

Eisenhower was not known to have a quick temper. But he was a career military man, and he did not appreciate Faubus's insubordination.
He summoned Faubus to come see him at his vacation home in Rhode
Island, where he calmly explained that he was at the top of the command
structure, and that Faubus was duty bound to follow the laws and his

direct orders. After the meeting, Eisenhower issued an official statement confirming that Faubus stated his intention was to respect the decisions of the United States District Court and to give his full cooperation in carrying out his responsibilities in respect to these decisions. Faubus also issued an official statement indicating his agreement. Eisenhower's presidential diary said that he understood that moving forward, Faubus knew what his assignment was, and would follow the law.[4]

One guess what happened next. Just one.

Congratulations, you win our fabulous prize package! Faubus did *not* follow through and integrate schools. Another court hearing occurred, during which all of the lawyers representing Faubus got up and walked out. "Now begins the crucifixion," Faubus seethed. "There will be no cross-examination, no evidence presented for the other side."[5]

The writing was on the wall: Eisenhower was going to have to use his authority to force compliance.

Once they were turned away from the school, the Little Rock Nine and their families were harassed everywhere they went. Multiple parents were fired, including from government jobs, because their children were integrating schools in Little Rock. Integration was the word on everyone's lips—demonstrations and riots erupted from white segregationists who felt their moral and religious beliefs, their way of life, and their power, was under attack.

On September 23, 1957, two things happened: nine children felt the fear and did it anyway, and Dwight Eisenhower said "Enough."

Faubus had withdrawn the Arkansas National Guard, which created a security disturbance so large that it overwhelmed local police. The mayor of Little Rock, Woodrow Mann, urgently telegrammed Eisenhower. He said that the mobs that were gathering in Little Rock were "agitated, aroused, and assembled by a concerted plan of action." Mann told Eisenhower that the violent uprisings were preplanned, and that Faubus was in on it.[6]

Eisenhower issued a proclamation. It said, "Whereas, the obstruction of justice constitutes a denial of the equal protection of the laws secured by the Constitution of the United States and impedes the course of justice under those laws . . ."[7] But what it meant was: "If y'all don't stop this immediately, I'm going to do what I need to do."

Mann sent another telegram the following day, saying essentially, "PLEASE SEND FEDERAL TROOPS TO LITTLE ROCK, IT IS REALLY BAD."[8] Eisenhower, man of the military, placed the Arkansas National Guard under federal control. And then, thinking ahead, he realized there was a good chance that the Arkansas National Guard wouldn't be loyal to his command. Eisenhower decided to send federal troops.

So, just to make it crystal clear: the president of the United States, a man in charge of the entire U.S. invasion at Normandy, realized that some Americans, including members of the military, had such an intense commitment to white supremacy they were likely to disobey his lawful, direct order. Just like they had been disobeying the orders of federal courts. Orders to allow Black children to receive the same education as their white peers.

Eisenhower called up the 101st Army Airborne Division to go to Little Rock, and within hours they were in the air, winging their way to Arkansas. The commander told his men to remember that no matter their personal feelings, they had to obey their commander in chief, and there would be no sloppy soldiers on the streets. Uniforms needed to be starched and pressed, and everyone had to maintain the highest level of professionalism.

The morning of September 25, 1957, dawned, and again, the Nine got ready for school, impeccably grooming themselves, steeling their nerves against the fact that what they represented was so hated that the president had to send a thousand soldiers to their school to quell the violence.

The first order of business was to get the children into the school safely. And then they had to keep it that way.

Some soldiers remained outside the building, while others were assigned to the Little Rock Nine inside the building. More than three years after *Brown* was decided, and three weeks since the school year had begun, the Little Rock Nine integrated Central High School. Despite the presence of troops, which gradually diminished over several months, the Nine endured physical and emotional violence at school.

Some of them were pushed down the stairs, one was locked in a bathroom stall and had burning pieces of paper thrown on her to try and catch her clothes and hair on fire. Another had acid thrown in her face. Faubus gave press conferences where he solemnly held up newspapers with headlines that shouted GUNS FORCE INTEGRATION. He decried the "iron fist in free America," and said that the raw federal power Eisenhower was exerting was inappropriate.[9]

As the year wore on, the federal troops were drawn down as the local law enforcement's capacity to handle the situation increased. Not all of the Nine remained at the school. One had to leave because of harassment, another because their parents couldn't find work due to their role in the integration plan.

Eisenhower addressed the nation, calling the segregationists "demagogic extremists." He said, "During the past several years, many communities in our Southern States have instituted public school plans for gradual progress in the enrollment and attendance of school children of all races in order to bring themselves into compliance with the law of the land. Thus, they demonstrated to the world that we are a nation in which laws, not men, are supreme. I regret to say that this truth, the cornerstone of our liberties, was not observed in this instance."

He continued, "Our enemies are gloating over this incident and using it everywhere to misrepresent our whole nation. We are portrayed as a violator of those standards of conduct which the peoples of the world united to proclaim in the Charter of the United Nations. There, they affirmed 'faith in fundamental human rights' and 'in the dignity and worth of the human person' and they did so 'without distinction as to race, sex, language, or religion.'"[10]

The United States has a slow history, but a solid one, of adding to the liberties of its citizens over time. By 1957, you can see evidence of this evolution: the president of the United States, a man who grew up with segregation, was heralding the UN Charter's commitment to human rights that affirmed the dignity and worth of all people. But secretly, he resented Earl Warren for putting him in this position to begin with.

Faubus smoldered. At the end of the school year, he could stand it no more, and decided to take matters into his own hands. A sign appeared outside the high school with the lie: THIS SCHOOL CLOSED BY ORDER OF THE FEDERAL GOVERNMENT.[11]

The high schools in Little Rock would be closed altogether the following school year. Rather than having troops at the school every day, Faubus decided that they just wouldn't have school. Closing school for everyone was better than sharing the white schools with Black children, he reasoned. (Except football—that was allowed.)

Other private religious schools for whites only popped up—locals called them "segregation academies." Many of the United States' private religious schools in the South were founded during this time, for exactly this purpose: providing a haven for white parents to protect their children from students of other races. (For real, though . . . if your southern religious school was founded in the 1950s, chances are extremely high it was a segregation academy. They may have failed to mention that in the brochure.)

The "Mothers' League" was also instrumental and active in working against school integration. They educated voters on which school-board members supported their segregationist beliefs and which didn't. Their fliers read: "Do you want negroes in our schools? If you do not, then go to the polls this coming Monday and VOTE. PLEASE VOTE RIGHT!!!! Join hands with us in this fight—send your contributions to THE MOTHERS' LEAGUE."[12]

Closing the schools only further deepened the racial and socioeconomic divide, as the overwhelming majority of white students were able to obtain other schooling. They could go to private school, drive to suburban schools, or stay with relatives elsewhere. The number of Black students who were able to obtain some kind of education was about half that of white students.

Toward the end of the school year, the Little Rock school board purged dozens of teachers from their midst who were deemed too sympathetic to the NAACP.[13]

Today, it's shocking for us to even think about a governor closing a school for a year, their prejudice so deep that they refuse to entertain the idea of Blacks and whites sharing a common space. But in Prince Edward County, Virginia, it was even worse.

Farmville, Virginia, had two high schools: a school for Black children and a school for white children. The white school had a gymnasium, a cafeteria, an infirmary, and other resources. Moton High School, reserved for Black students, had none of these things. A building designed for 180 students held 450. Two or three classes were always being held in the auditorium at one time. Some classes were held in tar-paper shacks and school buses.[14]

Members of the Black community in Farmville and the local NAACP chapter worked hard to get a new school built, but the powers that be refused to allocate land or money to make it happen.

This was frustrating to everyone, but most especially to a sixteen-year-old girl named Barbara Johns. Barbara voiced her frustration to one of her teachers: How was it that the school she attended did not even have a single microscope to use in biology class?

Barbara's uncle was Vernon Johns, a well-known pastor and advocate for Black civil rights. In fact, he was pastor at the Dexter Avenue Baptist Church before Martin Luther King Jr. took over, and was so well-known at the time that King introduced himself as Johns's successor. As time passed and King's fame grew, Johns the Baptist, as some called him, was relegated to the role of the man who came before Martin Luther King. Perhaps it was Vernon's influence, but when Barbara's teacher listened to her complaint and encouraged her to do something about it, the idea took root in Barbara's young mind. *Why not me?* Barbara asked herself.

She pondered how she, a literal teenager, could fix the situation. An idea finally occurred to her: *We could go on strike.* She began to plan exactly how to carry out a school strike, and on the appointed morning, she had notes delivered to every teacher's classroom. The notes said: "Come immediately to the auditorium for an emergency meeting."[15] Once they were in the meeting, they said the Pledge of Allegiance, and then Barbara asked all the teachers to leave.

It's hard for me to imagine teachers being like, "Okay, sure, we'll leave you here unsupervised," but maybe they were with Barbara in solidarity.

Barbara rallied the students to go on strike with her until they got what they wanted, which was a new school building. The students decided to contact the NAACP for help with their efforts. The NAACP later said that the students were so intent and they handled themselves so well that they would help if the students' parents were also on board. But, the organization told them, the strike couldn't be just about better facilities. It needed to be about equality and integration. A month later, the NAACP filed a lawsuit.[16]

Prince Edward County schools denied the NAACP's request to integrate, but they suddenly found the money to build a new high school. After it opened in 1953, many white residents were puzzled as to why the NAACP didn't drop their lawsuit. After the case became part of the *Brown v. Board of Education* cohort that made its way to the Supreme Court, Virginia senator Harry Byrd said it was "the most serious blow that has yet been struck against the rights of the states in a matter vitally affecting their authority and welfare. . . . In Virginia now we are facing a crisis of the first magnitude."[17] To be clear, the "crisis" Byrd believed they were facing was that white and Black children might be ordered to share schools.

White citizens' councils sprang up around the country, opposed to the integration of schools. Eventually, more than eighty thousand people belonged to one of these groups, who were actively working to keep races separate.[18]

After *Brown v. Board II*, one white group, the Defenders of State Sovereignty and Individual Liberty, held a meeting in Prince Edward County. More than thirteen hundred people showed up. The group presented their plan: if a court ordered them to integrate, they would simply close the schools.[19]

Senator Byrd and other southern members of Congress signed on to "The Southern Manifesto," which said, in part: "This unwarranted exercise of power by the Court . . . is destroying the amicable relations between the white and Negro races that have been created through ninety years of patient effort by the good people of both races. It has planted hatred and suspicion where there has been heretofore friendship and understanding." It went on to say, "We commend the motives of those States which have declared the intention to resist forced integration by any lawful means."[20]

The Virginia General Assembly then passed a set of laws known as the Stanley Plan, which gave the governor the power to close any schools that integrated and remove their state funding.[21] But Virginia lost a series of court battles, and slowly, schools around the state began integration. Not Prince Edward County, though. Prince Edward County, a mere seventy-five miles from where Virginia Randolph was living out her retirement, decided to form private schools that were only available to white students and to give white parents tuition vouchers so their children could attend. No such provisions were made for Black students.

School closures didn't just affect school-age children, they affected the entire family. Some parents had to enroll their children in the state welfare system so they could be placed with foster families in other parts of the state to be able to attend school. Some children lived with teachers like Virginia Randolph. Several women began grassroots learning centers in homes and churches. They wouldn't make them full-fledged schools, because they feared that if they created private schools, it would impact their lawsuit. One student's father rented an empty, dilapidated house across county lines to establish the fact that he lived there, so he could drive his children there and they could be picked up by the school bus.

Prince Edward County closed its public schools for five years.

The school closures lasted until the 1960s, when Attorney General Robert Kennedy got involved. "We may observe with much sadness and irony that, outside of Africa, south of the Sahara, where education is still a difficult challenge, the only places on earth known not to provide free public education are Communist China, North Vietnam, Sarawak, Singapore, British Honduras—and Prince Edward County, Virginia," he said.[22]

In 1963, Prince Edward County schools had still not integrated, nine years after *Brown v. Board of Education.*

TWENTY-SIX

MONTGOMERY, ALABAMA

1955

The civil rights movement was about far more than integrating buses. It was about far more than voting rights. It was about far more than Jim Crow laws. It was also about violence against Black women at the hands of white men.

Women like Recy Taylor were also the catalysts for the modern civil rights movement. Recy was a married mother walking home from a church event in September 1944 when a car of white men pulled over and forced her into their vehicle. They drove off into the woods, and six of them raped her. Then they dropped Recy Taylor off, blindfolded, on the side of the highway.

When Recy staggered into her house, bruised and broken, she told her husband and the sheriff what had happened to her. The sheriff knew immediately who was to blame, as there was only one vehicle in the tiny town of Abbeville, Alabama, that matched the description.

The day after the rape, Recy Taylor's house was firebombed. *How dare she report us*, the rapists thought. *She needs to shut up.* Two all-white grand juries refused to charge any of the six men with a crime. The NAACP sent

their best investigator, a woman named Rosa Parks. She went to Abbeville to get to the bottom of things, which led to two months of protests.[1]

You'd be mistaken if you believe that Black women did not speak up.
You'd be mistaken if you thought that Black women did not risk their
personal safety to work for justice. You'd be mistaken if you thought
these facts were never going to see the light of day again, swept under the
rug of today's moral panic, the moral panic of learning about the real,
true, beautiful, infuriating, horrific, meaningful history of the United
States and calling it by some other boogeyman name like Critical Race
Theory (it's not) or labeling it a divisive concept (it's only divisive if lies
and cover-ups benefit you in some way).

What is done in darkness must come to light. Seeds of resistance,
seeds of momentum, were planted not just in the hearts of men and
women all over the South, they were planted in the hearts of their children
and their relatives.

In 2011, the Alabama legislature formally apologized for never prose-
cuting anyone for Recy Taylor's rape. At the time, Recy Taylor was ninety-
two years old.[2]

Rosa, as a longtime activist and investigator, was one of thousands of
Black women, men, and children who organized and resisted and planned
and did not give up.

When Rosa Parks stepped on the bus on Thursday, December 1, 1955,
she recognized the driver. He was the driver who, years before, had humiliated her. James Blake was an overt bigot, and often made Black riders deposit their fare, exit the bus, and then reenter the bus through the
back door—they weren't even allowed to pass through the white section
of the vehicle.[3]

Back in 1943, Rosa had boarded a bus and was quickly sandwiched in
by more people who boarded behind her. Blake demanded that she get
off the bus and go in the back door, but she couldn't leave. He got up to

grab her sleeve to try to force her off. Rosa dropped her purse, and then used the moment she picked it up to quickly sit down in a whites-only seat.

Enraged, Blake forced her off the bus and drove away without her, taking her money and leaving her without a ride. Rosa vowed never to ride any bus driven by him again. But by the time she had deposited her fare that day in December 1955, it was too late. She had not recognized him in time.

The story of Rosa's refusal to stand up unfolded much like Claudette's. She was sitting in a section reserved for Black riders, behind the white section. When the white section filled, James Blake demanded that all of the Black riders in Rosa's row get up and move. At first, none of them did. Then Blake became belligerent, yelling, "Let me have those seats!" Everyone in the row got up except for Rosa, the ember of anger toward Blake growing into a hot flame inside her chest.

"No," Rosa said. "I got on first and paid the same fare, and it isn't right for me to have to stand so someone else who got on later could sit down."

"I'm going to have you arrested," Blake seethed.

"You may do that," she told him.[4]

Everything Rosa had done and seen had led to this moment. It wasn't that she was tired from Christmas shopping or a long day at work. It was decades of organizing, of investigating rapes, of baking cookies to sell for someone's legal defense. It was witnessing violence against people she knew and loved, it was a lifetime of feeling threatened and humiliated.

Nothing had been wasted. Not one moment, not one sacrifice. Everything she lived through was now being used.

She was arrested and famously photographed after being taken to the police station. Her friend's husband, attorney Clifford Durr, came to her aid.

Rosa wasn't alone in her efforts that December. Jo Ann Robinson (no known relation to Bernice) had a job teaching at Alabama State. She was a member of the Women's Political Council, which was a political activism group for Black women. She was so important and integral to the civil rights movement that Martin Luther King mentioned her by name in his memoir. He said, "Apparently indefatigable, she, perhaps more than any other person, was involved in every level of protest."[5]

Every level of protest. And few people even know her name.

When Claudette Colvin was arrested, Jo Ann was outraged, recalling a time when she was new to town and sat in a white section of a bus inadvertently, uneducated on the rules of the caste system. *How dare they*, she thought. *How dare they treat a little girl that way.* Jo Ann began collecting accounts of other people, most of them Black women, who had been abused by white male bus drivers.[6] Soon, her file was fat with papers, and she began writing letters to the city council and the mayor.[7] The mayor of Montgomery was named—get this—William "Tacky" Gayle. And he was Tacky as heck too.

Jo Ann attended Claudette Colvin's trial, and when Rosa Parks was arrested, Jo Ann stayed up all night using the mimeograph machines at Alabama State to make thirty-five thousands leaflets.[8] If you're not familiar with a mimeograph machine, it's a precursor to a copy machine, and you make reproductions by rotating the handle. So to make thirty-five thousands leaflets, she didn't just press a button and come back later when the copies were done—she literally stayed up turning a handle all night long.

Jo Ann sent messages to organizers to come pick up the leaflets in the morning and distribute them all over town. One of the organizers who helped leaflet Montgomery was Claudette Colvin's favorite teacher, Geraldine Nesbitt. The leaflets read, "This is for Monday December 5th, 1955. . . . Another negro woman has been arrested and thrown into jail because she refused to get up out of her seat on the bus for a white person to sit down. Negroes have rights too. . . . If we do not do something to stop these arrests, they will continue. Next time it may be you or your daughter or mother."[9]

Jo Ann drove more leaflets around the city to spread the word far and wide. By the end of Friday, December 2, nearly the entire Black community of Montgomery had agreed to a plan. The plan was cemented by Black religious leaders from the pulpit on Sunday. The following day, Monday, December 5, 1955, as many Black Montgomerians as were able would not take the bus. They would instead walk, ride bikes, call in sick, and organize carpools. They agreed to reconvene Monday evening after a one-day boycott to see how it went and if they should continue. Between thirty and fifty thousand Black residents said "enough is enough," and refused to step foot on the bus that day.

The one-day bus boycott was so successful that the leaders agreed to make it last longer, and within a few days they had organized the MIA, the Montgomery Improvement Association, with Martin Luther King Jr. playing a prominent role.

Schedules of ride shares were created. Organizers asked cab drivers to charge Black residents the same fare as the bus, which was ten cents. Cab drivers agreed.

Montgomery city officials couldn't just let people exit the system of white supremacy and create a new societal structure. So they passed an ordinance saying that cab drivers had to charge no less than forty-five cents, and any driver who didn't comply would be fined.[10] The MIA held meetings with city leaders, and the city refused their demands. So the boycott continued. Because 70 percent of the city's bus riders were Black, the city urgently doubled fares to make up for the lost revenue.[11]

People participating in ride-sharing were constantly harassed and ticketed in an attempt to dissuade them from continuing. Black people with cars, like Martin Luther King, were arrested, and some were jailed based on the assumption that they were all involved in the boycott and that it violated city rules.

But the boycott was just getting started, and at the end of January

1956, Martin Luther King Jr.'s home was firebombed. He wasn't home, and fortunately, the rest of his family wasn't injured.[12]

Jo Ann Robinson's car had acid poured all over it. Her front window shattered when a huge rock was thrown through it. Both of these acts of vandalism were carried out by police officers in uniform in broad daylight.[13] But still, she refused to quit.

As the calendar flipped to February 1956, attorney Fred Gray had been hard at work on a federal lawsuit contesting Montgomery's policies of racial segregation on buses. He put together a group of women, all of whom had refused over the past year to abandon their bus seat for the sake of white deference. The plaintiffs were teenager Mary Louise Smith, elderly Susie McDonald, motherly Aurelia Browder, and the now sixteen and pregnant Claudette Colvin. One woman dropped out of the lawsuit because of death threats and the fact that her employer said she would be fired if she proceeded.

At a ball game, Claudette Colvin had met a man who she estimated to be at least ten years older than her. He took an interest in her, encouraged her passion for civil rights and societal change, and for once, made her feel like she wasn't being stupid or difficult for caring about things like the Constitution.

And then this man took advantage of her. Claudette had no idea what was going on, because she had received absolutely no education on the topic, at home or in school. So when she wound up pregnant, she wasn't even sure what had made it happen. This man, whom Claudette has always refused to name, was married, so there was no hope of him marrying her to care for their child.

Claudette's actual boyfriend, wanting to do the right thing, came over to her house to propose. She desperately wanted to say yes, to make this problem disappear, but in the end, she chickened out.

Pregnant girls were kicked out of Booker T. Washington High, so

Claudette decided to hide her pregnancy as long as possible, then go back to Birmingham to stay with her biological mother for a while to give birth. But Claudette was a small girl and couldn't hide her pregnancy for long. A teacher soon figured it out and told the principal, who called Claudette, a good student, down to the office for expulsion.

She tried staying with her biological mom for a few weeks but ultimately moved back to Montgomery, figuring she could just get her GED someday. Her adoptive mother told her, "If God is for you, the devil can't do you any harm," and Claudette clung to that promise.[14]

When her baby, Raymond, was born in March 1956, he came out with blond hair and blue eyes. Now Claudette had yet another reason to be a pariah: people assumed her baby's father was a white man.

As the federal lawsuit Fred Gray filed propelled forward, Claudette laid awake at night staring at Raymond sleeping in his bassinet. She had never abandoned the idea that she was meant for more and that the time to act was now.

The morning of the trial, she pumped her milk so she wouldn't leak through her dress in the courtroom. Her mom had to work that day, as she was the sole breadwinner, but before she left, she prayed for Claudette. "Courage," she whispered, squeezing her daughter's hand.[15]

Baby Raymond stayed with a family friend while Claudette sat in the courtroom listening to the testimony of the other women who had refused to give up their seats on the bus. Fred Gray had saved her as the last witness. Her story of arrest and conviction was the most dramatic, and Claudette was the most determined.

As she recounted how she had been kicked and objectified by the police, the sound of muffled sniffs and the labored breathing of crying filled the courtroom. On cross-examination, the city's attorney tried to trap Claudette into saying that she had been swindled by the silver-tongued Martin Luther King, who put her up to all of this. But Claudette was too smart for him.

"Why did you stop riding the buses?" the attorney asked, hoping she would talk about how the Montgomery Improvement Association had told them to.

She stared him in the eye and confidently said, "Because we were treated wrong, dirty, and nasty."[16]

The city tried to argue that segregation was necessary to maintain law and order. Without it, there would be violence, they said.

One of the three judges on the federal panel asked the city attorney, "Can you command one man to surrender his constitutional rights to prevent another man from committing a crime?"[17] The attorney had no way to answer that.

Meanwhile, the bus boycott continued. Take a moment to think about how willing you would be to commit to doing something that was a significant inconvenience to you for many months. Most people fail at New Year's resolutions within a couple of weeks. The Montgomery bus boycott was a massive push against the forces of resistance that wanted, more than anything else, for things to stay the same. It required the daily choice by tens of thousands of people to take part in something bigger than themselves for a cause greater than themselves.

The three-judge panel came back: segregation on Montgomery buses was a violation of the Fourteenth Amendment's Equal Protection Clause. One of the judges later said, "The boycott case was a simple case of legal and human rights being denied."[18]

Claudette heard about the outcome in the news. No one from the legal team or any of the civil rights activists called her. No one offered her any help with the baby. No one brought her a baby gift or threw her a shower. She felt like she had been used for her compelling story. She was forced to get a job, but found it difficult to hold a restaurant position down because people kept recognizing her and it spooked her employers.

Not surprisingly, old Tacky Gayle didn't like the outcome of the case and ordered the city to keep fighting. The case was appealed to the

Supreme Court, the Warren court, who agreed to hear it, and in November 1956 the Supreme Court released their opinion in *Browder v. Gayle*. They said that segregation on Montgomery buses was unconstitutional. The headline of the *Alabama Journal* read, BUS SEGREGATION IS KNOCKED OUT.[19]

On December 20, 1956, the bus boycott officially ended. After nearly thirteen months of refusing to ride the bus, Black riders returned. After their prolonged, significant, and collective effort, along with a concerted desire to create change, the small and mighty ordinary Americans had done it.

Except: snipers began firing on integrated buses. Right after Christmas, a woman who was eight months pregnant was shot in both of her legs. Violence broke out around the city, and the bus system was shut down for several weeks. Four churches and the homes of two ministers were firebombed. All of them had openly supported the integration of buses. Reverend Ralph Abernathy, whose church and home were both firebombed, announced: "Despite the wreckage and the broken windows, we will gather as usual at our church, and offer special prayers for those who would desecrate the house of God."[20]

Two white KKK members were indicted for the bombings. They confessed. And color me unsurprised: the all-white jury acquitted them anyway.[21] The boycott was over, but the civil rights movement was just getting started.

Years later, in the 1980s, *The Washington Post* tracked down bus driver James Blake and went to his house. He said he was just doing his job when he called the police in 1955 and had Rosa arrested, but my hope for a redemption story went out the window when he began to use the N-word to the *Post* reporter.[22]

Earl Warren was "conscience stricken" about what he had participated in when he ordered people like Norman Mineta's family to leave their homes and move to incarceration camps.[23] So he spent the rest of his career trying to ensure all citizens were equal in the eyes of the law. He tried to do what was just, despite his past mistakes.

Septima Clark, who in 1975 had a gray, chin-length bob and cat-eye glasses, who once had not even been permitted to work in a Charleston classroom, was elected to the Charleston School Board. When the district created a new curriculum for civics, she noticed the books contained exactly zero Black children, so she protested. "I wanted to know who the Black children would have to look up to in that book. There was nothing in there that would help Black children to feel that they had a right to the tree of life, and I know how important that is."[24]

She wrote, "To me, social justice is not a matter of money, but of will, not a problem for the economist as much a task for the patriot."[25]

Septima Poinsette Clark retired to a home for the elderly on Johns Island, built by one of her former Citizenship School students, and passed away in 1987. "I never feel discouraged," Septima said near the end of her life. "I know that each step is a stepping-stone in the right direction."[26]

In 2019, the Highlander Research and Education Center, the facility that held all of Highlander's records, burned down. Nearby were symbols of white nationalism.

That same year, Montgomery unveiled a new statue of Rosa Parks, along with markers for Claudette Colvin, Aurelia Browder, Susie Mc-Donald, and Mary Louise Smith—women who, along with Jo Ann Robinson, Recy Taylor, Septima Clark, and thousands of others, refused to stand up so the rest of us could rise.

Claudette Colvin, the brave fifteen-year-old who refused to give up her seat, asked to have her criminal record expunged. Her request was finally granted in December 2021. She said in an interview when the request went through that she wanted her grandkids to "know that their grandmother stood up for something. Against the injustice in America. The laws will change, and a lot of people, not only myself, paid the price and made sacrifices. We are not where we're supposed to be, but don't take the freedom that we do have for granted."[27]

The civil rights movement would be nowhere without the courage of people with the least amount of political, social, and economic power. Those whose very lives breathed oxygen into justice and freedom, whose cumulative actions worked to unfasten the padlocks of centuries of oppression. None of them could do it all, but they all could do something.

These are the small and the mighty. And we can be too.

CONCLUSION

———

A nd here, my friend, is where our journey ends. For now, but not forever.

When I interview authors on my podcast, *Here's Where It Gets Interesting*, I often ask them, "When the reader finishes the last page and closes the book, what is it that you hope they know?"

And it seems only fair that I answer my own question.

I'd want you to know that often, the small are truly the mighty. That their stories may be eclipsed by a dominant sun, but that doesn't mean they aren't ours to discover, auroras in the predawn hours of morning. We should get up early. We should look for them. We should let the complicated truth of their lives wash over us and orient our spirits toward hope.

I'd want you to know that great Americans aren't only people who existed long ago, their faces captured on a frame of black-and-white film. Great Americans live. Whatever year you are reading this in, know that you are surrounded by a cloud of witnesses, people who see you and depend on your efforts. Our ancestors made a way in the wilderness for us, descendants they didn't even know, but whose existence was assured.

They built benches upon which we can rest, so that we will not be discouraged in doing good, just as those who have come before us were not discouraged in doing good.

Upon this path are the signs that point the way to liberty and justice for all. Some of the signs are but a child's drawing affixed low on the branch of a tree. Others are written in the neat cursive of a teacher, placed prominently for everyone to notice. Some look like signs of protest, hand-lettering drawn on a placard. Some are simply an arrow, pointing straight ahead. *This way*, they say. *This way* down the path they forged through adversity, through the great unknown, through resistance, illness, trials, and tribulation.

I'd want you to know that the weight of the world does not rest on your shoulders alone. Our unique skills, talents, and abilities are meant to be used in ways that only we can.

Alexander Hamilton, Gouverneur Morris, and Katharine Lee Bates were incredible writers, and their words made America.

Clara Brown and Rebecca Mitchell had the audacity to continue to hope, despite all evidence to the contrary, and the perseverance never to quit even when people told them they should.

Inez Milholland and Maria de Lopez used their speaking and organizational skills to help create meaningful change.

Claudette Colvin and Rosa Parks were willing to stand up to injustice, even though it might have looked like they were remaining seated.

Anna Jeanes and Julius Rosenwald knew that a lasting legacy didn't have to mean your name on the side of a building, but that it came from improving the condition of others.

Daniel Inouye and Norman Mineta knew the power of consensus building, and what an apology can do.

Septima Clark and Virginia Randolph knew that education is liberation. And an educated population is very difficult to oppress.

I—and the small and mighty people in this book—want you to know that being a great American isn't dependent on fame or fortune. It doesn't require your name to be recorded in the annals of history or to appear on a ballot.

I'd want you to know that the American experiment is full of ill-equipped people, people with the "wrong" faces and the "wrong" life circumstances, who just went for it. They just tried something no one had done before. They were willing to let other people watch them fail. They just did the next right thing.

I'd want you to know that you should keep going. That often the biggest breakthroughs happen after the darkest nights.

I'd want you to know that despite all the things Gouverneur Morris got wrong—like the unfortunate whalebone—there was something he got very, very right. America at her best is just. She is peaceful. She is good. And she is free. And it is us, the small and the mighty, who make America great.

Not again, but always.

I'd want you to know that there will come a moment in your life, a moment when you will be asked to choose: will I retreat, or will I move forward with courage? You'll realize, just like the people in the pages of this book, that every experience you've had, every setback and heartbreak, every triumph and joy, will all be used. The character that you've been cultivating will be called upon, and when that moment comes, whenever it is, I hope you'll rise to it.

I'd want you to know that for some of you, that moment is today.

I'd want you to know that we are the ones we've been waiting for.

The small. And the mighty.

ACKNOWLEDGMENTS

This book was years in the making. No one could have guessed where I was headed when this voyage departed the shore, most especially me. To all of you who waited patiently while I researched, wrote, revised, honed, and rewrote this manuscript, thank you. I hope the wait has been worth it.

Writing an acknowledgments section feels like writing an Oscar acceptance speech. You want to thank everyone you've ever known so that they all know how much they mean to you. But no pressure, no pressure.

To Chris, who is a model of selflessness and service. To Cullen, Eleanor, Margaret, and Louisa, of whom I am so proud, and who I hope will be proud of me. To my mom, Julie, who has patiently listened to history facts she surely does not care about for twenty-nine long years. To Carolyn, who greatly regrets not letting me pressure her into spending hours on synchronized swimming routines, and to Sara, who gets things done like no one I've ever met and will jazz scat while doing it.

This is for Lexi, who has the best attitude on planet Earth, and for my entire team at SME, who, in the words of Grace Banker, just "managed,

managed, managed" while I devoted much of my time to working on this manuscript.

This is for Adam Grant and Richard Pine, to whom I owe my deepest thanks.

It's for Helen Healey-Cunningham and Katherine Howe, who challenged my ideas and helped shape this book into something meaningful.

It's for Heather Jackson and Kari Anton, who helped me make friends with some of the characters on the pages you just read.

This is for Adrienne, who sends me the best memes and who always laughs at mine. And for James, who is small and mighty.

This is for Carlos Whittaker, who just kept saying "You got this" whenever I needed him to, for Nicole Walters, who is the cheerleader you hope will always be at the game, and for Lauren Kachinske, who is willing to kick me in the butt. This is for Mary Wagner, one of my oldest and dearest, who did me an incredible favor.

This is for Hilary Rushford, Layla Palmer, Jenna Fischer, Angela Kinsey, Kendra Adachi, Abi Ayres, Dani Coke Balfour, Brittany Ratelle, Shanté Cofield, Ashley Spivey, Laura Pinkston, Jessica Malaty Rivera, Brittany Richman, Andrea Reeve, Kristina Kuzmic, Emily Freeman, Mary Marantz, Annie Downs, Becky Kennedy, Emily Calandrelli, Mosheh Oinounou, Melissa Urban, Nora McInerny, Kathleen Ashmore, MeiLi Coon, Tim Whittaker, and V Spehar, who make my life better each and every day just for being themselves.

This is for Jermaine Fowler, JeMar Tisby, and Jasmine Holmes, with my sincerest thanks.

This is for Governerds everywhere, far and wide. It is my great privilege to know you and to be a part of the movement you are propelling.

And finally, to the Governerd Book Club, I like you and I love you.

NOTES

Introduction

1. "From Alexander Hamilton to Elizabeth Hamilton, [4 July 1804]," Founders Online, National Archives, https://founders.archives.gov/documents/Hamilton/01-26-02-0001-0248.
2. "The Funeral, [14 July 1804]," Founders Online, National Archives, https://founders.archives.gov/documents/Hamilton/01-26-02-0001-0271.
3. "The Funeral, [14 July 1804]."
4. Max Farrand, ed., *The Records of the Federal Convention of 1787: A Century of Lawmaking for a New Nation: U.S. Congressional Documents and Debates, 1774–1875*, vol. 3 (New Haven, CT: Yale University Press, 1911), 92, https://oll.libertyfund.org/titles/farrand-the-records-of-the-federal-convention-of-1787-3vols.
5. Henry Bain, "Errors in the Constitution—Typographical and Congressional," *Prologue Magazine* 44, no. 2 (Fall 2012), https://www.archives.gov/publications/prologue/2012/fall/const-errors.html.
6. "James Madison to Jared Sparks, 8 April 1831," Founders Online, National Archives, https://founders.archives.gov/documents/Madison/99-02-02-2323.

One: Clara Brown, Kentucky, 1830s

1. Because Clara was illiterate, she never wrote her own version of events, instead recounting them many times to family and friends. This dialogue is reconstructed from oral histories of Clara's life.
2. Karen A. Johnson, "Undaunted Courage and Faith: The Lives of Three Black Women in the West and Hawaii in the Early 19th Century," *Journal of African American History*, 91, no. 1 (Winter 2006).

3. Kathleen Bruyn, *"Aunt" Clara Brown: Story of a Black Pioneer* (Boulder, CO: Pruett Publishing Company, 1970), 3.

4. Linda Lowery, *One More Valley, One More Hill: The Story of Aunt Clara Brown* (New York: Random House, 2002), 17–18.

5. Jeanne Varnell, *Women of Consequence: The Colorado Women's Hall of Fame* (Boulder, CO: Johnson Books, 1999), 1.

6. Reconstructed from oral histories.

7. Johnson, "Undaunted Courage and Faith."

8. Gayle Corbett Shirley, *More Than Petticoats: Remarkable Colorado Women* (Guilford, CT: Globe Pequot Press, 2012), 4.

9. Varnell, *Women of Consequence*, 1.

10. Bruyn, *"Aunt" Clara Brown*, 13.

11. Mary Ellen Snodgrass, *Settlers of the America West* (Jefferson, NC: McFarland & Company, Inc., 2015), 25.

12. Erin McCawley Renn, "German Food: Customs and Traditions in the Missouri Ozarks," *OzarksWatch* III, no. 3 (Winter 1990): 16, https://thelibrary.org/lochist /periodicals/ozarkswatch/ow303f.htm.

13. Renn, "German Food," 16.

14. Reconstructed from oral histories.

15. Snodgrass, *Settlers of the America West*, 25.

Two: Bleeding Kansas, 1850s

1. *Dred Scott v. Sanford* (1857), https://www.archives.gov/milestone-documents/dred -scott-v-sandford.

2. John Russell Bartlett, ed., *Records of the Colony of Rhode Island and Providence Plantations, in New England*, vol. 4 (Providence: A. C. Greene & Brothers, 1865), 191.

3. Harriott Horry Ravenel, *Eliza Pinckney* (New York: Charles Scribner's Sons, 1896), 32–33.

4. David Shuck, "When Levi's Was 'The Only Kind Made by White Labor,'" Heddels, July 1, 2021, https://www.heddels.com/2021/07/levis-kind-made-white -labor/.

5. Jaclyn Diaz and Jonathan Franklin, "A Pair of Levi's That Sold For $76K Reflects Anti-Chinese Sentiment of 19th Century," National Public Radio, October 14, 2022.

6. Joanne B. Freeman, *The Field of Blood* (Farrar, Straus and Giroux, 2018).

7. S. P. Chase, Charles Sumner, J. R. Giddings, Edward Wade, Gerritt Smith, Alexander De Witt, "Appeal of the Independent Democrats in Congress to the People of the United States, Shall Slavery Be Permitted in Nebraska?," Washington, January 19, 1854.

8. The Kansas-Nebraska Act, May 30, 1854, U.S. Senate, https://www.senate
    .gov/artandhistory/history/minute/Kansas_Nebraska_Act.htm.

9. *"Jane Pierce, Recalling Her Deceased Child, Is Haunted by Happier Times*, August 2,
    1853," Shapell.org., https://www.shapell.org/manuscript/franklin-jane-pierce
    -first-lady-death-of-son-ben-pierce/.

10. Franklin Pierce, Inaugural Address, March 4, 1853, printed with Pierce's emen-
    dations, https://www.loc.gov/item/pin1901/.

11. Jean H. Baker, *James Buchanan* (New York: Henry Holt and Company,
    2004), 25.

12. Bleeding Kansas: A Stain on Kansas History, Fort Scott National Historic Site,
    https://www.nps.gov/articles/bleedingks.htm.

13. Dale E. Watts, "How Bloody Was Bleeding Kansas? Political Killings in Kansas
    Territory, 1854–1861," *Kansas History: A Journal of the Central Plains* 18, no. 2
    (Summer 1995): 116–29.

14. David Donald, *Charles Sumner and the Coming of the Civil War* (New York:
    Knopf, 1960), 287.

15. The Caning of Senator Charles Sumner, May 22, 1856, U.S. Senate, https://
    www.senate.gov/artandhistory/history/minute/The_Caning_of_Senator_Charles
    _Sumner.htm.

Three: Clara Brown, Colorado, 1870s

1. Linda Lowery, *One More Valley, One More Hill: The Story of Aunt Clara Brown*
    (New York: Random House, 2002), 61.

2. Lawrence B. de Graaf, "Race, Sex, and Region: Black Women in the American
    West, 1850–1920," *Pacific Historical Review* 49, no. 2 (May 1980): 285–313.

3. Aunt Clara Brown, *Savannah Courier*, January 7, 1886, 1.

4. Lowery, *One More Valley, One More Hill*, 93.

5. Kathleen Bruyn, *"Aunt" Clara Brown: Story of a Black Pioneer* (Boulder, CO:
    Pruett Publishing Company, 1970), 13.

6. William Loren Katz, *The Black West* (New York: Simon & Schuster, 1996), 78.

7. "Aunt Clara Brown," *Columbia Herald-Statesman*, November 6, 1885, 2.

8. Lowery, *One More Valley, One More Hill*, 135.

9. "The Kansas Sufferers," *Weekly Register-Call*, vol. 18, no. 9, September 26,
    1879, 3.

10. Lowery, *One More Valley, One More Hill*, 166–68.

11. *Genealogical Index to the Records of the Society of Colorado Pioneers*, Colorado Ge-
    nealogical Society, 1990, 12.

12. William Loren Katz, *Black Woman of the Old West* (New York: Atheneum
    Books, 1995), 25.

13. Lowery, *One More Valley, One More Hill*, 193.

14. "Happy Reunion of Mother and Daughter After Years of Separation," *Leaven-worth Times*, March 4, 1882, 4.
15. Lowery, *One More Valley, One More Hill*, 201.
16. Gayle Corbett Shirley, *More Than Petticoats: Remarkable Colorado Women* (Guilford, CT: Globe Pequot Press, 2012), 8.
17. Lowery, *One More Valley, One More Hill*, 204.
18. "UNC Expert Interviewed in Documentary About Ex-Slave Clara Brown," University of Northern Colorado, *True North*, December 27, 2016, www.unco.edu/news/articles/georgejunne-clarabrown.aspx.
19. Lowery, *One More Valley, One More Hill*, 203.

Four: Virginia Randolph, Virginia, 1890

1. Lance G. E. Jones, *The Jeanes Teacher in the United States, 1908–1933* (Durham: University of North Carolina Press, 1937), 37.
2. Jones, *The Jeanes Teacher in the United States*, 21–22.
3. Historic Richmond Colored Normal School, Maggie L. Walker National Historic Site, National Park Service, https://www.nps.gov/places/historic-richmond-colored-normal-school.htm.
4. "Miss Randolph Dies, Was Pioneer Educator," *Richmond Times-Dispatch*, March 17, 1958, 22.
5. H. J. Eckenrode, *The Randolphs: The Story of a Virginia Family* (Indianapolis: Bobbs-Merrill, 1946).
6. Jones, *The Jeanes Teacher in the United States*, 26–27.
7. *Richmond Dispatch*, July 24, 1900, 8.
8. *Richmond Dispatch*, July 24, 1900, 8.
9. McCormick Semmes, "Milestones in the Life of Virginia Randolph," *Richmond Times-Dispatch*, June 8, 1947, 6.
10. Robert A. Margo, *Race and Schooling in the South, 1880–1950: An Economic History* (Chicago: University of Chicago Press, 1990), 21–22.
11. Jones, *The Jeanes Teacher in the United States*, 40.
12. Jones, *The Jeanes Teacher in the United States*, 35.
13. Harry Kollatz Jr., "Miss Randolph: Celebrated Henrico Educator Virginia Randolph Didn't Just Teach Lessons, She Lived Them," *Richmond Magazine*, March 23, 2018.

Five: Henrico County, Virginia, 1907

1. Mildred Williams et al., *The Jeanes Story: A Chapter in the History of American Education, 1908–1968* (Jackson, MS: Jackson State University, 1979), 196–98.
2. Louis R. Harlan and Raymond W. Smock, eds., *The Booker T. Washington Papers, Vol. 7: 1903–1904* (Champaign: University of Illinois Press, 1977), 235.

3. W. E. B. Du Bois, *Black Reconstruction in America* (New York: Atheneum, 1992), 30.
4. Lance G. E. Jones, *The Jeanes Teacher in the United States, 1908–1933* (Durham: University of North Carolina Press, 1937), 41, 45, 65.
5. Jones, *The Jeanes Teacher in the United States*, 25.
6. McCormick Semmes, "Milestones in the Life of Virginia Randolph," *Richmond Times-Dispatch*, June 8, 1947, 6.
7. Semmes, "Milestones in the Life of Virginia Randolph," 6.
8. Historical Timeline of the Mountain Road School, Virginia Randolph Museum, https://henrico.us/locations/virginia-randolph-museum-plaque/.
9. "Building of Colored School Is Destroyed," *Richmond Times-Dispatch*, February 12, 1929, 6.
10. Jones, *Jeanes Teacher in the United States*, 31.
11. Julian Houseman, "Virginia Randolph Lauded for Her Educational Feat," *Richmond News-Leader*, May 16, 1940, 2.
12. 1930 United States Federal Census, Henrico County, Richmond City, Enumeration District 116-24, sheet 1A, census taker Mrs. Anna P. Prescott, rows 27–41, 8 adopted daughters, 6 adopted sons.
13. "Virginia Estelle Randolph: Pioneer Educator," Henrico County Government, YouTube, video, https://www.youtube.com/watch?v=zbRC-zitl7s, 25:12.
14. Semmes, "Milestones in the Life of Virginia Randolph," 6.
15. Dr. Samuel Chiles Mitchell, "A Richmond Woman's Work Is Described," *Richmond Times-Dispatch*, May 29, 1938, 5.
16. Mitchell, "A Richmond Woman's Work Is Described," 5.
17. Jones, *Jeanes Teacher in the United States*, 141.
18. Houseman, "Virginia Randolph Lauded for Her Educational Feat," 2.
19. "Virginia Estelle Randolph: Pioneer Educator," Henrico County Government, YouTube, video, https://www.youtube.com/watch?v=zbRC-zitl7s, 2:11.
20. Mitchell, "A Richmond Woman's Work Is Described," 33.

Six: Katharine Lee Bates, Cape Cod, 1859

1. Melinda Ponder, *Katharine Lee Bates: From Sea to Shining Sea* (Chicago: Windy City Publishers, 2017), 1–2.
2. Dorothy Burgess, *Dream and Deed: The Story of Katharine Lee Bates* (Norman: University of Oklahoma Press, 1952), 147.
3. Burgess, *Dream and Deed*, 3.
4. Katharine Lee Bates, "The Falmouth Bell," in *America the Beautiful and Other Poems* (New York: Thomas Y. Crowell, 1911), 39–41.
5. Paula D. Hunt, "Sybil Ludington, the Female Paul Revere: The Making of a Revolutionary War Heroine," *New England Quarterly* 88, no. 2 (June 2015): 187–222.

6. Esther Forbes, *Paul Revere & the World He Lived In* (Boston: Houghton Mifflin Company, 1942), 3–5, 12.

7. Arthur Howard Nichols, *Early Bells of Paul Revere* (Boston: [s.n.], 1904), "reprinted from New-Eng. historical and genealogical register, for April, 1904," 3–9.

8. "Paul Revere Bell Rings Daily in Falmouth," CapeCod.com, December 13, 2018, https://www.capecod.com/lifestyle/paul-revere-bell-rings-daily-in-falmouth/.

9. Ponder, *Katharine Lee Bates*, 5; from Arthur Lee Bates, *A Few Recollections*, handwritten family memoir, 1937, 123, courtesy of Elizabeth Olmstead.

10. Ponder, *Katharine Lee Bates*, 16; from Diary, August 15, 1866.

11. Ponder, *Katharine Lee Bates*, 16; from Diary, August 15, 1866.

12. Burgess, *Dream and Deed*, 20.

13. Florence Morse Kingsley, *The Life of Henry Fowle Durant: Founder of Wellesley College* (New York: Century Co., 1924), 200–201.

14. Kingsley, *The Life of Henry Fowle Durant*, 206.

15. Katharine Lee Bates, "The Wellesley Vision," *Wellesley College Magazine* XXIV, no. 7 (April 1916): 17.

16. Kingsley, *The Life of Henry Fowle Durant*, 238–39.

17. Ponder, *Katharine Lee Bates*, 43.

18. Ponder, *Katharine Lee Bates*, 46.

19. "The American Heroine," *Boston Evening Transcript*, July 21, 1879, 4. This is a letter to the editor of the *Transcript*, signed KLB.

20. Ponder, *Katharine Lee Bates*, 79.

21. Kingsley, *The Life of Henry Fowle Durant*, 246.

22. M. C. Hazard, ed., Congregational Sunday-School and Publishing Society, Letter to Katharine Lee Bates, January 15, 1889.

Seven: Katharine Lee Bates, England, 1880s

1. Dorothy Burgess, *Dream and Deed: The Story of Katharine Lee Bates* (Norman: University of Oklahoma Press, 1952), 56.

2. Patricia Ann Palmieri, *In Adamless Eden: The Community of Women Faculty at Wellesley* (New Haven, CT: Yale University Press, 1995), 101.

3. Kenneth Turino and Susan Ferentinos, "Entering the Mainstream, Interpreting GLBT History," *History News* 67, no. 4 (Autumn 2012): 24.

4. Judith Schwarz, "Yellow Clover: Katharine Lee Bates and Katharine Coman," *Frontiers: A Journal of Women Studies*, 4, no. 1 (University of Nebraska Press: Spring 1979): 63.

Eight: Katharine Lee Bates, Chicago, 1890s

1. Phil Patton, "Sell the Cookstove if Necessary, but Come to the Fair," *Smithsonian* 24, no. 3 (1993): 38–51. Cited in Anna R. Paddon and Sally Turner, "Afri-

can Americans and the World's Columbian Exposition," *Illinois Historical Journal* 88, no. 1 (Spring 1995): 19–36.

2. John R. Russell, "Francis Bellamy's Pledge," *University of Rochester Library Bulletin* XIII, no. 1 (Autumn 1957).

3. President Grover Cleveland, Address at the Opening of the World's Columbian Exposition (Chicago World's Fair), May 1, 1893, https://www.presidency.ucsb .edu/documents/address-the-opening-the-worlds-columbian-exposition -chicago-worlds-fair.

4. *Addresses and Reports of Mrs. Potter Palmer, President of the Board of Lady Managers, World's Columbian Commission,* Rand McNally, and Co., 1894, 137.

5. Lynn Sherr, *America the Beautiful: The Stirring True Story Behind Our Nation's Favorite Song,* (Cambridge: Public Affairs, 2001), 133.

6. Beth Cooney, "A Stirring Story Behind 'America the Beautiful,'" *Los Angeles Times,* November 9, 2001.

7. Sherr, *America the Beautiful,* 58.

8. Sherr, *America the Beautiful,* 48.

9. Sherr, *America the Beautiful,* 52.

10. Ellen Leopold, "My Soul Is Among Lions: Katharine Lee Bates's Account of the Illness and Death of Katharine Coman," *Legacy* 23, no. 1 (2006): 61.

11. Judith Schwarz, "Yellow Clover: Katharine Lee Bates and Katharine Coman," *Frontiers: A Journal of Women Studies,* 4, no. 1 (University of Nebraska Press: Spring 1979): 65.

12. Melinda Ponder, *Katharine Lee Bates: From Sea to Shining Sea* (Chicago: Windy City Publishers, 2017), xvi–xvii.

13. Sherr, *America the Beautiful,* 88.

14. "Jessye Norman, Legendary Opera Soprano," Grammy Award for Lifetime Achievement, Washington, D.C., July 22, 2012, https://achievement.org/achiever /jessye-norman/#interview.

15. Dorothy Burgess, *Dream and Deed: The Story of Katharine Lee Bates* (Norman: University of Oklahoma Press, 1952), 176.

16. Patricia Ann Palmieri, *In Adamless Eden: The Community of Women Faculty at Wellesley* (New Haven, CT: Yale University Press, 1995), 139.

17. Leopold, "My Soul Is Among Lions," 63.

18. Burgess, *Dream and Deed,* 177.

19. Burgess, *Dream and Deed,* 106.

20. Burgess, *Dream and Deed,* 227.

Nine: Inez Milholland, New York, 1910

1. Linda J. Lumsden, *Inez: The Life and Times of Inez Milholland* (Bloomington: Indiana University Press, 2004), 4.

2. *The Vassarian,* vol. 21, Vassar College, Poughkeepsie, NY, 1909, 53.

3. Phyllis Eckhaus, "Restless Women: The Pioneering Alumnae of New York University School of Law," *N.Y.U. Law Review* 66 (1996).

4. Paula Giddings, "Missing in Action: Ida B. Wells, the NAACP, and the Historical Record," *Meridians* 1, no. 2 (Spring 2001): 1–17.

5. "The Gibson Girl's America: Drawings by Charles Dana Gibson," Library of Congress, https://www.loc.gov/exhibits/gibson-girls-america/the-gibson-girl -as-the-new-woman.html.

6. Lumsden, *Inez*, 66.

7. Lumsden, *Inez*, 74.

8. Lumsden, *Inez*, 71.

9. Lumsden, *Inez*, 146.

10. Sidney R. Bland, "New Life in an Old Movement: Alice Paul and the Great Suffrage Parade of 1913 in Washington, D.C.," *Records of the Columbia Historical Society* (Washington, D.C.: DC History Center, 1971/1972), 657–78.

11. "Woman Suffrage Parade," Washington, D.C., ca. 1913, photograph by Harris & Ewing, https://www.loc.gov/item/2013648101/.

12. "Five Thousand Women March at Capital," *San Francisco Examiner*, March 4, 1913, 1.

13. Bland, "New Life in an Old Movement," 657–78.

14. "Insult to Womanhood," *Baltimore Sun*, March 6, 1913, 1, 7.

15. "New York Women Bitter in Denunciation of Police," *Baltimore Sun*, March 6, 1913, 1.

16. *Report of the Committee on the District of Columbia United States Senate Pursuant to S. Res. 499. March 4, 1913, Directing Said Committee to Investigate the Conduct of the District Police and Police Department of the District of Columbia in Connection with the Woman's Suffrage Parade on March 3, 1913*, submitted by Mr. Jones, May 29, 1913, XIII.

Ten: Maria de Lopez, California, 1911

1. "Suffrage in Spanish," *Los Angeles Times*, October 9, 1911, 8.

2. Eileen V. Wallis, *Earning Power: Women and Work in Los Angeles, 1880–1930* (Reno: University of Nevada Press, 2010), 25.

3. Wallis, *Earning Power*, 25–26.

4. Kay Withers, "Chippewa Claims All of Italy," *Baltimore Sun*, September 25, 1973, 3.

5. Eileen V. Wallis, "'Keeping Alive the Old Tradition': Spanish-Mexican Club Women in Southern California, 1880–1940," *Southern California Quarterly* 91, no. 2 (University of California Press, 2009): 133–54.

6. Women's Suffrage Party, "Enclosure: Fliers supporting women's suffrage," n. d., https://www.loc.gov/item/rbcmiller004037/.

7. Maria de E. G. Lopez, "Equal Suffrage of Most Vital Moment," *Los Angeles Herald*, August 20, 1911, 4.

8. "Former L. A. Teacher to Drive French Ambulance," *Los Angeles Herald*, May 26, 1917, 3.

9. "From Schools to Trenches," *Los Angeles Times*, May 26, 1917, 11.

10. David S. McKinsey, Joel P. McKinsey, and Maithe Enriquez, "Part I: The 1918 Influenza in Missouri: Centennial Remembrance of the Crisis," *Missouri Medicine* 115, no. 3 (May–June 2018): 183–88.

11. Neal Gabler, *Walt Disney: The Triumph of the American Imagination* (New York: Knopf Doubleday Publishing Group, 2007), 78.

12. Jack Klink, *At Home and Over There: American Women Physicians in WWI* (Schaumberg, IL: American Medical Women's Association and Raw Science Foundation, November 6, 2017), https://www.amwa-doc.org/wwi-film/.

13. "L. A. Girl Cited for Bravery," *Los Angeles Herald*, October 26, 1918, 1.

Eleven: Rebecca Brown Mitchell, Idaho, 1856

1. Rebecca Brown Mitchell, "Glimpses from the Life of Rebecca Brown Mitchell," Brigham Young University-Idaho Special Collections, 2.

2. Mitchell, "Glimpses," 2.

3. "Mrs. Rebecca Mitchell," *Wilsonville Review*, October 30, 1908, 1.

4. Mitchell, "Glimpses," 2.

5. Mitchell, "Glimpses," 3.

6. Mitchell, "Glimpses," 3.

7. Mitchell, "Glimpses," 3.

8. Mitchell, "Glimpses," 3.

9. "History of School System," Bonneville County Heritage Association, http://bonnevilleheritage.org/MJFCODPg.php?pag=chap10.

10. "Population of Idaho Falls, Idaho Falls—City of Destiny, Chapter 19," Bonneville County Heritage Association, http://bonnevilleheritage.org/MJFCODPg.php?pag=chap19.

11. Mitchell, "Glimpses," 4.

12. Mitchell, "Glimpses," 4.

13. Mitchell, "Glimpses," 4.

14. Mitchell, "Glimpses," 5.

15. Mitchell, "Glimpses," 5.

16. Mitchell, "Glimpses," 5.

17. Mitchell, "Glimpses," 5.

18. Mitchell, "Glimpses," 5.

19. Mitchell, "Glimpses," 5.

20. Mitchell, "Glimpses," 6.

21. "Idaho Women Rejoice," *Shoshone Journal*, December 18, 1896, 2.

22. *Green v. State Bd. of Canvassers*, 5 Idaho 130, 47 P. 259 (1896).

23. Rebecca Scofield and Katherine G. Aiken, "Balancing Act: Idaho's Campaign for Women's Suffrage," *Western Legal History* 30, no. 1–2 (2019): 43.

24. Mitchell, "Glimpses," 6.

25. Mitchell, "Glimpses," 6.

26. "First of Her Sex for the Post," *Chicago Tribune*, July 4, 1897, 16.

27. Mitchell, "Glimpses," 7.

28. Mitchell, "Glimpses," 7.

29. "Mrs. Rebecca Mitchell," 1.

30. Dymae J. Jones and Sara E. Crow, "Round Table Resolutions," *Idaho Republican*, December 25, 1908, 1.

Twelve: Inez Milholland, the West, 1916

1. Kimberly Jensen, "'Neither Head nor Tail to the Campaign': Esther Pohl Lovejoy and the Oregon Woman Suffrage Victory of 1912," *Oregon Historical Quarterly* 108, no. 3 (Oregon Historical Society, Fall 2007): 364.

2. "Mabel Vernon," Archives of Women's Political Communication, Iowa State University Catt Center, https://awpc.cattcenter.iastate.edu/directory/mabel-vernon/.

3. "Wilson Puts Railroad Issues Squarely Before Congress Asking Action," *Arizona Daily Star*, December 6, 1916, 1.

4. "Wilson Puts Railroad Issues Squarely Before Congress Asking Action," 2.

5. Linda G. Ford, *Iron Jawed Angels: The Suffrage Militancy of the National Woman's Party, 1912–1920* (Lanham, MD: University Press of America, 1991).

6. "National Woman Party Launched," *Deseret Evening News*, June 6, 1916, 8.

7. Linda J. Lumsden, *Inez: The Life and Times of Inez Milholland* (Bloomington: Indiana University Press, 2004), 152.

8. Lumsden, *Inez*, 153.

9. "Suffrage Leader Gives Dramatic Campaign Speech," *Evening Capital News*, October 10, 1916, 3.

10. "Oust Wilson, Women Urge," *Idaho Statesman*, October 10, 1916, 1.

11. "Suffrage Leader Gives Dramatic Campaign Speech," 3.

12. "Suffrage Leader Gives Dramatic Campaign Speech," 3.

13. Lumsden, *Inez*, 156.

14. "Repudiate Party That Ignores Women's Claims," *Butte Daily Post*, October 16, 1916, 1.

15. Lumsden, *Inez*, 159.

16. Robert P. J. Cooney Jr., *Remembering Inez, The Last Campaign of Inez Milholland, Suffrage Martyr, Selections from The Suffragist 1916* (Santa Cruz, CA: American Graphic Press, 2015), 41.

17. "Faints at Her Highest Point, *Los Angeles Times*, October 24, 1916, 15.
18. Lumsden, *Inez*, 159.
19. Lumsden, *Inez*, 167.
20. Lumsden, *Inez*, 168.
21. "Honor Mrs. Boissevain," *Washington Post*, December 26, 1916, 3.
22. "Honor Mrs. Boissevain," 3.
23. Cooney, *Remembering Inez*, 74.
24. Cooney, *Remembering Inez*, 70.

Thirteen: France, 1916

1. Jill Frahm, "The Hello Girls: Women Telephone Operators with the American Expeditionary Forces during World War I," *Journal of the Gilded Age and Progressive Era* 3, no. 3 (July 2004): 274.
2. Beth A. Behn, "Woodrow Wilson's Conversion Experience: The President and the Federal Woman Suffrage Amendment" (PhD diss., University of Massachusetts Amherst, February 2012), 1.
3. Kasia Pilat, "Overlooked No More: Grace Banker, Whose 'Hello Girls' Decoded Calls in World War I," *New York Times*, May 15, 2019.
4. Elizabeth Cobbs, "Fighting on Two Fronts: World War One, Women's Suffrage, and John Pershing's 'Hello Girls,'" *South Central Review* 34, no. 3 (2017): 41.
5. Elizabeth Cobbs, *The Hello Girls: America's First Women Soldiers* (Cambridge, MA: Harvard University Press, 2017), 104–5.
6. Cobbs, *Hello Girls*, 77–78.
7. Cobbs, "Fighting on Two Fronts," 40.
8. *Telephone Engineer, 1918–07*, vol. 20, no. 1, Questex, LLC, 49.
9. Cobbs, *Hello Girls*, 154.
10. War Department Technical Manual TM 11–410, *The Homing Pigeon*, War Department, January 1945, Section V: Training, Training for Messenger Service.
11. Livia Gershon, "How Pigeons Helped Fight World War I," *JSTOR Daily*, July 26, 2021, https://daily.jstor.org/how-pigeons-helped-fight-world-war-i/.
12. Frank A. Blazich Jr., "Feathers of Honor," *Army History, U.S. Army Center of Military History*, no. 117 (Fall 2020): 32–51.
13. Irving Werstein, *The Lost Battalion* (New York: Norton, 1966), 138.
14. Werstein, *Lost Battalion*, 142.
15. "Epic in the Argonne: The Story of the Lost Battalion," United States World War I Centennial Commission, https://www.worldwar1centennial.org/index.php/233-lost-battalion.html.
16. "Cher Ami, Soldier Bird, Comes Home," *New York Herald*, April 17, 1919, 8.
17. "The Lost Battalion and Overseas Jazzophiends," *Elmira Star-Gazette*, March 3, 1920, 2.

18. Alexis N. Hill, "Hello Girls—Women Telephone Operators during WWI," *The Unwritten Record*, National Archives, March 30, 2021, https://unwritten -record.blogs.archives.gov/2021/03/30/hello-girls-women-telephone -operators-during-wwi/.

19. Woodrow Wilson, Address to the Senate on the Nineteenth Amendment, September 30, 1918, https://www.presidency.ucsb.edu/documents/address-the-senate -the-nineteenth-amendment.

Fourteen: Anna Thomas Jeanes, Philadelphia, 1822

1. Portrait of Anna T. Jeanes painted posthumously by Esther Heacock, https:// www.friendsjournal.org/the-legacy-and-philanthropy-of-anna-thomas-jeanes/.

2. Kay Sackett Fitzgerald and Eleanor Reinhardt, "The Legacy and Philanthropy of Anna Thomas Jeanes," Friends Journal, March 1, 2020.

3. Alissa Falcone, "The Forgotten Founders of Drexel Institutions," *Drexel News*, January 5, 2017.

4. S. Raymond Roberts, *Report of the Conchological Section, Proceedings of the Academy of Natural Sciences of Philadelphia* 32 (1880): 415.

5. W. S. W. Ruschenberger, "A Sketch of the Life of Joseph Leidy, M.D., LL.D.," *Proceedings of the American Philosophical Society* 30, no. 138 (1892): 175.

6. Eugene Solomon, *God?* (N.p.: Xlibris Corporation, 2010), 233.

7. Randall M. Miller and William Pencak, *Pennsylvania: A History of the Commonwealth* (University Park: Pennsylvania State University Press, 2002), 64.

8. Howard Malcolm Jenkins, *Religious Views of the Society of Friends, A Paper for the World's College of Religions at Chicago*, September 19, 1893, 15.

9. Andrew R. Murphy, *William Penn: A Life* (Oxford: Oxford University Press, 2019), 184.

10. *The United Friend*, Philadelphia, September 1894, 64.

11. *Quaker Faith and Practice*, 5th ed., "Corporate Responsibility," chapter 23, 11.

12. Home for Destitute Colored Children (Philadelphia, PA), *Seventeenth Annual Report of the Home for Destitute Colored Children, 1872, Located at Maylandsville, on the Darby Road* (Philadelphia: Kildare Printer, 1872).

13. "Caring for the Little Ones," *Philadelphia Inquirer*, September 24, 1883, 3.

14. "The Western Floods," *Philadelphia Inquirer*, February 22, 1883, 4.

15. "Cost $60,000 to Silence a Piano," *York Dispatch* (Pennsylvania), June 22, 1901, 2.

16. "Swain's Decision Pleases Students," *Philadelphia Inquirer*, December 4, 1907, 16.

Fifteen: William James Edwards, Alabama, 1869

1. William James Edwards, *Twenty-Five Years in the Black Belt* (Cornhill, 1918), 3–4.

2. Edwards, *Twenty-Five Years in the Black Belt*, 9–10.

3. Edwards, *Twenty-Five Years in the Black Belt*, 10–11.

4. Donald P. Stone, *Fallen Prince: William James Edwards, Black Education and the Quest for Afro-American Nationality* (Snow Hill, AL: Snow Hill Press, 1990), 50–51, 60, 123.

5. Edwards, *Twenty-Five Years in the Black Belt*, 32.

6. Stone, *Fallen Prince*, 126.

7. Edwards, *Twenty-Five Years in the Black Belt*, 32.

8. Stone, *Fallen Prince*, 127.

9. Letter from Booker T. Washington to William Howard Taft, from the Tuskegee Institute, May 29, 1907, *The Booker T. Washington Papers, Volume 9, 1906–1908*, eds. Louis R. Harland and Raymond W. Smock (Champaign, IL: University of Illinois Press, 1980), 281.

10. J. H. Dillard, *Fourteen Years of the Jeanes Fund*, 1909–1923, *South Atlantic Quarterly* XXII, no. 3 (July 1923): 195.

11. Linda B. Pincham, "A League of Willing Workers: The Impact of Northern Philanthropy, Virginia Estelle Randolph and the Jeanes Teachers in Early Twentieth-Century Virginia," *Journal of Negro Education* 74, no. 2 (Spring 2005): 117.

12. Benjamin Brawley, *Doctor Dillard of the Jeanes Fund* (Freeport, NY: Books for Libraries Press, 1971), 57–58.

13. Pincham, "A League of Willing Workers," 117.

14. Lance G. E. Jones, *The Jeanes Teacher in the United States, 1908–1933* (Durham: University of North Carolina Press, 1937), 62.

15. Mildred Williams et al., *The Jeanes Story: A Chapter in the History of American Education, 1908–1968* (Jackson, MS: Jackson State University, 1979), 196–98.

16. Jackson Davis, *Jeanes Visiting Teachers* (New York: Carnegie Corp. of New York, 1936), 13–18.

17. Brawley, *Doctor Dillard of the Jeanes Fund*, 7.

18. Williams, *The Jeanes Story*, 81.

19. Williams, *The Jeanes Story*, 86.

Sixteen: Julius Rosenwald, Illinois, 1862

1. Peter M. Ascoli, *Julius Rosenwald: The Man Who Built Sears, Roebuck and Advanced the Cause of Black Education in the American South* (Bloomington: Indiana University Press, 2015), 2.

2. "Julius Rosenwald," Lincoln Home, National Historic Site, https://www.nps .gov/liho/learn/historyculture/julius-rosenwald.htm, updated October 8, 2023.

3. "New Book Tells How Sears, Roebuck Grew," *Minneapolis Star Tribune*, May 14, 1950, 37.

4. Stephanie Deutsch, *You Need a Schoolhouse: Booker T. Washington, Julius Rosenwald, and the Building of Schools for the Segregated South* (Evanston, IL: Northwestern University Press, 2011), 47–48.

5. Janice R. Quick, "Write Us in Your Own Way, A Tombstone from the Sears, Roebuck Catalog," *Ramsey County History: A Publication of the Ramsey County Historical Society* 45, no. 4 (Winter 2011): 20.
6. Lawrence P. Bachmann, "Julius Rosenwald," *American Jewish Historical Quarterly* 66, no. 1 (Special Bicentennial Issue: American Jewish Business Enterprise, Johns Hopkins University Press, September 1976), 90.
7. Bachmann, "Julius Rosenwald," 90.
8. Deutsch, *You Need a Schoolhouse*, 49–50.
9. Dora Mekouar, "How Sears Catalog Fought White Supremacists," *VOA News*, Voice of America, October 3, 2019.
10. Ascoli, *Julius Rosenwald*, 38–40.
11. Ascoli, *Julius Rosenwald*, 48.

Seventeen: Booker T. Washington, Virginia, 1856

1. Booker T. Washington, *Up from Slavery: An Autobiography* (1900), 1, Internet Archive, https://archive.org/details/in.ernet.dli.2015.268643/mode/2up.
2. Washington, *Up from Slavery*, 7.
3. Washington, *Up from Slavery*, 26.
4. Veronica A. Davis, *Hampton University* (Charleston, SC: Arcadia Publishing, 2014), 13; S. C. Armstrong, *Education for Life* (Hampton, VA: Press of the Hampton Normal and Agricultural Institute; 1913), 16–17.
5. Washington, *Up from Slavery*, 54.
6. John H. Denison, "Samuel Chapman Armstrong," *The Atlantic*, January 1894.
7. James D. Anderson, *The Education of Blacks in the South* (Durham: University of North Carolina Press), 1988, location 808, Kindle.
8. Anderson, *The Education of Blacks in the South*, location 707, Kindle.
9. Peter M. Ascoli, *Julius Rosenwald: The Man Who Built Sears, Roebuck and Advanced the Cause of Black Education in the American South* (Bloomington: Indiana University Press, 2015), 87.
10. "White Man Assaults Booker Washington," *New York Times*, March 20, 1911, 1.
11. Stephanie Deutsch, *You Need a Schoolhouse: Booker T. Washington, Julius Rosenwald, and the Building of Schools for the Segregated South* (Evanston, IL: Northwestern University Press, 2011), 96.
12. Deutsch, *You Need a Schoolhouse*, 98.
13. Deutsch, *You Need a Schoolhouse*, 99.
14. Deutsch, *You Need a Schoolhouse*, 106.
15. Deutsch, *You Need a Schoolhouse*, 107.
16. Deutsch, *You Need a Schoolhouse*, 107.
17. Deutsch, *You Need a Schoolhouse*, 114.
18. Ascoli, *Julius Rosenwald*, 123–24.

19. T. H. Alexander, "Rosenwald, Friend of Negro Education, Sees Steady Business Growth in South," *The Tennessean*, October 2, 1927, 45.

20. Anderson, *The Education of Blacks in the South*, 162.

21. Michael J. Solender, "Inside the Rosenwald Schools," *Smithsonian*, March 30, 2021.

22. Karen Heller, "The Enlightening Legacy of the Rosenwald Schools," *Washington Post*, August 30, 2015.

23. Hasia R. Diner, *Julius Rosenwald: Repairing the World* (New Haven, CT: Yale University Press, 2017), 217–18.

24. William Allison Sweeney, *History of the American Negro in the Great World War* (New York: Negro Universities Press, 1969), 278.

25. Ascoli, *Julius Rosenwald*, 152.

Eighteen: The Inouyes, Hawaii, 1924

1. Daniel K. Inouye and Lawrence Elliott, *Journey to Washington* (Englewood Cliffs, NJ: Prentice-Hall, 1967), 2–3.

2. Inouye and Elliott, *Journey to Washington*, 4–5.

3. Inouye and Elliott, *Journey to Washington*, 5.

4. Inouye and Elliott, *Journey to Washington*, 14.

5. Inouye and Elliott, *Journey to Washington*, 28.

6. "Hawaii: Life in a Plantation Society," Library of Congress, https://www.loc.gov/classroom-materials/immigration/japanese/hawaii-life-in-a-plantation-society/.

7. Inouye and Elliott, *Journey to Washington*, 43–44.

8. Inouye and Elliott, *Journey to Washington*, 49.

9. Inouye and Elliott, *Journey to Washington*, 50.

10. Inouye and Elliott, *Journey to Washington*, 45.

11. Inouye and Elliott, *Journey to Washington*, 23.

12. Inouye and Elliott, *Journey to Washington*, 52.

13. Inouye and Elliott, *Journey to Washington*, 54–55.

14. Inouye and Elliott, *Journey to Washington*, 55.

15. "Personal Justice Denied," chapter 11, 261, National Archives, https://www.archives.gov/research/japanese-americans/justice-denied.

16. Inouye and Elliott, *Journey to Washington*, 59.

17. "Daniel Inouye and Norman Mineta: In Defense of Liberty," *What It Takes* (podcast), American Academy of Achievement, May 9, 2022.

18. "Daniel Inouye and Norman Mineta: In Defense of Liberty."

19. Inouye and Elliott, *Journey to Washington*, 61.

20. James Rawls and Walton Bean, *California: An Interpretive History* (New York: McGraw-Hill, 2012), 276.

21. "Anti-Japanese Propaganda," Hampton Roads Naval Museum, 4, https://www
.history.navy.mil/content/dam/museums/hrnm/Education/EducationWeb
siteRebuild/AntiJapanesePropaganda/AntiJapanesePropagandaInfoSheet
/Anti-Japanese%20Propaganda%20info.pdf.

22. "How to Tell Japs from the Chinese," *Life*, December 22, 1941, 81–82, https://
inside.sfuhs.org/dept/history/US_History_reader/Chapter11/howtotell.htm.

23. Executive Order 9066, February 19, 1942; General Records of the United States
Government; Record Group 11; National Archives.

24. Greg Robinson, *By Order of the President* (Cambridge, MA: Harvard University
Press, 2009), 261.

Nineteen: The Minetas, California, 1942

1. Andrea Warren, *Enemy Child* (New York: Holiday House, 2019), 14–16.

2. Warren, *Enemy Child*, 19.

3. "Civilian Exclusion Order: Instructions to All Persons of Japanese Ancestry,"
National Museum of American History, https://americanhistory.si.edu/collec
tions/nmah_1694663.

4. "Lorraine Bannai Interview," Densho Digital Archive, Densho Visual History
Collection, Interviewers: Margaret Chon and Alice Ito, Seattle, Washington,
March 23 and 24, 2000, Densho ID: denshovh-blorraine-01-0035, https://ddr
.densho.org/media/ddr-densho-1000/ddr-densho-1000-113-35-transcript
-15b6a71059.htm.

5. Warren, *Enemy Child*, 39.

6. Ken Ringle, "The Patriot: Norman Mineta Was Interned by His Country, but
Still He Loved It. Then He Changed It," *Washington Post*, August 20, 2000.

7. Warren, *Enemy Child*, 50.

8. Warren, *Enemy Child*, 52–53.

9. Warren, *Enemy Child*, 59–61.

10. Warren, *Enemy Child*, 61.

11. Esmeralda Bermudez, "A Japanese Internment Camp Revisited," *Los Angeles
Times*, August 21, 2011.

12. Heart Mountain World War II Japanese American Confinement Site, "Life in
the Camp," Medical Care, https://www.heartmountain.org/history/life-in-the
-camp/.

13. Mike Mackey, ed., "Remembering Heart Mountain: Essays on Japanese American Internment in Wyoming" (Powell, WY: Western History Publications,
1988), 183.

14. Julie Beck, "Two Boy Scouts Met in an Internment Camp, and Grew Up to
Work in Congress," *The Atlantic*, May 17, 2019.

Twenty: Daniel Inouye, Europe, 1943

1. Daniel K. Inouye and Lawrence Elliott, *Journey to Washington* (Englewood Cliffs, NJ: Prentice-Hall, 1967), 64.
2. Inouye and Elliott, *Journey to Washington*, 66–67.
3. Inouye and Elliott, *Journey to Washington*, 64.
4. Inouye and Elliott, *Journey to Washington*, 74.
5. "Daniel Inouye and Norman Mineta: In Defense of Liberty," *What It Takes* (podcast), American Academy of Achievement, May 9, 2022.
6. Inouye and Elliott, *Journey to Washington*, 104–5.
7. Inouye and Elliott, *Journey to Washington*, 151.
8. Inouye and Elliott, *Journey to Washington*, 153.
9. "Daniel Inouye and Norman Mineta: In Defense of Liberty," *What It Takes*.
10. Inouye and Elliott, *Journey to Washington*, 157.
11. "Going for Broke: The 442nd Regimental Combat Team," National World War II Museum, New Orleans, September 24, 2020.
12. Inouye and Elliott, *Journey to Washington*, 209.
13. Inouye and Elliott, *Journey to Washington*, 249.
14. Daniel Inouye, Dedication of Plaque Honoring Senator Bob Dole, C-SPAN .org, April 12, 2011, https://www.c-span.org/video/?298986-1/dedication-plaque -honoring-senator-bob-dole, 17:08–17:15.

Twenty-One: Norman Mineta, 1950s

1. "Norman Mineta and His Legacy: An American Story," PBS, May 20, 2019.
2. "Norman Mineta and His Legacy."
3. "Men and Events," *Los Angeles Times*, April 18, 1971, 61.
4. Ken Ringle, "The Patriot: Norman Mineta Was Interned by His Country, but Still He Loved It. Then He Changed It," *Washington Post*, August 20, 2000.
5. Nos. 08-7412 and 08-762, In the Supreme Court of the United States, *Terrance Jamar Graham, Petitioner, v. Florida*, Respondent. *Joe Harris Sullivan, Petitioner, v. Florida*, Respondent. Brief of Former Juvenile Offenders Charles S. Dutton, Former Sen. Alan K. Simpson, R. Dwayne Betts, Luis Rodriguez, Terry K. Ray, T. J. Parsell, and Ishmael Beah as Amici Curiae in Support of Petitioners, July 23, 2009, 12–13.
6. "Norman Mineta, Alan Simpson Became Lifelong Friends at Japanese Internment Camp," documentary, KPIX CBS News Bay Area, June 15, 2022.
7. Julie Beck, "Two Boy Scouts Met in an Internment Camp, and Grew Up to Work in Congress," *The Atlantic*, May 17, 2019.
8. "Norman Mineta and Alan Simpson, an Epic Political and Personal Bond, Forged Behind Barbed Wire," video interview, *Washington Post*, August 18, 2017.

9. "Norman Mineta, Alan Simpson Became Lifelong Friends at Japanese Internment Camp."

10. President Ronald Reagan, "Remarks on Signing the Bill Providing Restitution for the Wartime Internment of Japanese-American Civilians," Ronald Reagan Presidential Library and Museum, August 10, 1988.

11. "Norman Mineta and His Legacy."

12. "Norman Mineta and His Legacy."

13. Reagan, "Remarks on Signing the Bill Providing Restitution for the Wartime Internment of Japanese-American Civilians."

14. "Norman Mineta and His Legacy."

15. "Norman Mineta and His Legacy."

16. Pat Morrison, "Norman Mineta on Internment, 9/11 and a Life Spent in the Vortex of American Politics," *Los Angeles Times*, May 8, 2019.

17. "September 11, 2001: Attack on America," Statement by Norman Y. Mineta Before the Senate Appropriations Subcommittee on Transportation, September 20, 2001.

18. "Remarks Following Discussions with Prime Minister Jean Chretien of Canada," George W. Bush, September 24, 2001.

19. "Norman Mineta and His Legacy."

20. Joseph R. Biden, "Funeral Service of Daniel Inouye," YouTube, video, December 21, 2012, https://www.youtube.com/watch?v=Ho1Wh18gXu0, 10:33–10:50.

21. Barack H. Obama, "Funeral Service of Daniel Inouye," YouTube, video, December 21, 2012, https://www.youtube.com/watch?v=Ho1Wh18gXu0, 35:04–35:28.

22. Xavier Vavasseur, "U.S. Navy Commissions Its 69th Arleigh Burke-class Destroyer," *Naval News*, December 9, 2021, https://www.navalnews.com/naval-news/2021/12/u-s-navy-commissions-its-69th-arleigh-burke-class-destroyer/.

23. Daniel K. Inouye and Lawrence Elliott, *Journey to Washington* (Englewood Cliffs, NJ: Prentice-Hall, 1967), 97.

24. "Statement on the Passing of Senator Daniel K. Inouye," press release, December 17, 2012, https://www.higp.hawaii.edu/spacegrant/old/Statement_on_the_Passing_of_Senator_Inouye.pdf.

25. "Norman Mineta and His Legacy."

Twenty-Two: Claudette Colvin, Alabama, 1950s

1. "The Other Rosa Parks: Now 73, Claudette Colvin Was First to Refuse Giving Up Seat on Montgomery Bus," interview, Democracy Now!, March 29, 2013, https://www.democracynow.org/2013/3/29/the_other_rosa_parks_now_73#:~:text=In%20March%201955%2C%20she%20was,way%20to%20the%20Supreme%20Court.

2. Phillip M. Hoose, *Claudette Colvin: Twice Toward Justice* (New York: Farrar, Straus & Giroux, 2014), 11.

3. Hoose, *Claudette Colvin*, 23.

4. "Alabama Executes Jeremiah Reeves After Police Torture Him into False Confession," Equal Justice Initiative, March 28, 1958, https://calendar.eji.org/racial-injustice/mar/28.

5. Dr. Martin Luther King Jr., "Statement Delivered at the Prayer Pilgrimage Protesting the Electrocution of Jeremiah Reeves," The Martin Luther King, Jr. Research and Education Institute, Stanford University, April 6, 1958, https://kinginstitute.stanford.edu/king-papers/documents/statement-delivered-prayer-pilgrimage-protesting-electrocution-jeremiah-reeves.

6. Hoose, *Claudette Colvin*, 26.

7. Hoose, *Claudette Colvin*, 29.

8. Hoose, *Claudette Colvin*, 34.

9. Hoose, *Claudette Colvin*, 34.

10. Hoose, *Claudette Colvin*, 35.

11. Phillip Tucker Thomas, *Claudette Colvin: Forgotten Mother of the Civil Rights Movement* (N.p.: PublishNation LLC, 2020).

12. Hoose, *Claudette Colvin*, 37.

13. Thomas, *Claudette Colvin*, location 1285, Kindle.

14. Hoose, *Claudette Colvin*, 45.

15. "Negro Girl Found Guilty of Segregation Violation," *Alabama Journal*, March 19, 1955, 13.

16. John A. Salmond, The Conscience of a Lawyer: Clifford J. Durr and American Civil Liberties, 1899–1975 (Tuscaloosa: University of Alabama Press, 1990), 2.

17. Rosa Parks, *Rosa Parks: My Story* (New York: Puffin Books, 1999), 101.

18. "Highlander Folk School's Key Role in Civil Rights," *Union Review*, February 20, 2020.

19. John Lewis, *Walking with the Wind* (New York: Simon & Schuster, 1998), 89.

20. Stephen Preskill, *Education in Black and White, Miles Horton and the Highlander Center's Vision for Social Justice* (Oakland, CA: University of California Press, 2021), 1.

21. "Letter from Durr to Director of Highlander Folk School," January 30, 1956, Montgomery, Alabama, https://historicalthinkingmatters.org/rosaparks/0/inquiry/main/resources/20/index.html.

Twenty-Three: Septima Clark, Charleston, South Carolina, 1898

1. Katherine Mellen Charron, *Freedom's Teacher* (Durham: University of North Carolina Press, 2009), 21.

2. Maria Peña, "Poinsettia: How a U.S. Diplomat Made a Mexican Flower an International Favorite," Library of Congress, December 22, 2021.

3. Septima Poinsette Clark, *Ready from Within: Septima Clark and the Civil Rights Movement* (Navarro, CA: Wild Trees Press, 1986), 98.

4. Charron, *Freedom's Teacher*, 51.

5. Lewis K. McMillan, *The Founding of South Carolina's State College for Negroes* (Orangeburg: South Carolina State A&M College), 9.

6. The Gullah Geechee, Gullah Geechee Cultural Heritage Corridor Commission, https://gullahgeecheecorridor.org.

7. Charron, *Freedom's Teacher*, 67.

8. Vicki L. Crawford, *Women in the Civil Rights Movement: Trailblazers and Torchbearers* (Brooklyn, NY: Carlson Publishing, 1993), 86.

9. Septima Poinsette Clark with LeGette Blythe, *Echo in My Soul* (New York: Dutton, 1962), 67.

10. Clark, *Ready from Within*, 113.

11. Charron, *Freedom's Teacher*, 266.

12. Charron, *Freedom's Teacher*, 322.

13. Charron, *Freedom's Teacher*, 72.

14. Clark, *Freedom's Teacher*, 117.

15. Neal Devins, "The Academic Expert before Congress: Observations and Lessons from Bill Van Alstyne's Testimony," *Duke Law Journal* 54, no. 6, Special Symposium Issue: The Fifth Annual Public Law Conference: Honoring the Scholarship and Contributions of William Van Alstyne (April 2005): 1525–54.

16. Erich Goode and Ben-Yehuda Nachman, "Moral Panics: Culture, Politics, and Social Construction," *Annual Review of Sociology* (1994).

17. Dorothy Cotton, *If Your Back's Not Bent* (New York: Atria Books, 2012), 107.

18. Cotton, *If Your Back's Not Bent*, 107.

19. Clark, *Ready from Within*, 103.

20. Charron, *Freedom's Teacher*, 5.

21. David P. Levine, "The Birth of the Citizenship Schools: Entwining the Struggles for Literacy and Freedom," *History of Education Quarterly* 44, no. 3 (Autumn 2004): 391.

22. Eliot Wigginton, *Refuse to Stand Silently By: An Oral History of Grass Roots Social Activism in America, 1921–64* (New York: Doubleday, 1991), 250.

23. Levine, "The Birth of the Citizenship Schools," 401.

24. Charron, *Freedom's Teacher*, 252.

25. Charron, *Freedom's Teacher*, 258.

26. Charron, *Freedom's Teacher*, 269.

Twenty-Four: America, 1950s

1. James Q. Whitman, *Hitler's American Model: The United States and the Making of Nazi Race Law* (Princeton, NJ: Princeton University Press, 2017), 4.

2. DeNeen L. Brown, "The Determined Father Who Took Linda Brown by the Hand and Made History," *Washington Post*, March 27, 2018.

3. Earl Warren, *The Memoirs of Earl Warren* (Garden City, NY: Doubleday, 1977), 86.

4. "Five Hundred Take Klan Oath in Hills," *San Francisco Chronicle*, May 7, 1922, 10.
5. Alden Whitman, "For 16 Years, Warren Saw the Constitution as Protector of Rights and Equality," *New York Times*, July 10, 1974, 24–25.
6. Whitman, "For 16 Years, Warren Saw the Constitution as Protector of Rights and Equality," 24–25.
7. *Mendez v. Westminster*: "Paving the Way to School Desegregation," Constitutional Rights Foundation, Bill of Rights in Action 23, no. 2 (Summer 2007).
8. Ed Cray, *Chief Justice: A Biography of Earl Warren* (New York: Simon & Schuster, 1997), 287.
9. Linda Brown Thompson, Speech at University of Michigan for the *Brown v. Board of Education* Anniversary, January 12, 2004, C-SPAN.

Twenty-Five: Teenagers in the American South, 1950s

1. Allison Keyes, "The Youngest of the Little Rock Nine Speaks Out About Holding onto History," *Smithsonian*, September 5, 2017.
2. Elizabeth Eckford, "Little Rock, 1957: The First Day," *Facing South: The Online Magazine of the Institute for Southern Studies*, August 1, 1979.
3. Telegram from President Dwight D. Eisenhower to Governor Orval E. Faubus, September 5, 1957, https://www.eisenhowerlibrary.gov/sites/default/files/research /online-documents/civil-rights-little-rock/press-release-dde-telegram-to -faubus.pdf.
4. Statements by President Eisenhower and Governor Faubus from Newport, Rhode Island, September 14, 1957, Kevin McCann Collection of Press and Radio Conferences and Press Releases, Box 20, September 1957; NAID #17366732, https:// www.eisenhowerlibrary.gov/sites/default/files/research/online-documents/civil -rights-little-rock/statements-by-dde-and-faubus.pdf.
5. Karen Anderson, *Little Rock: Race and Resistance at Central High School* (Princeton, NJ: Princeton University Press, 2010), 69.
6. Telegram from Little Rock Mayor Woodrow Mann to President Dwight D. Eisenhower, September 23, 1957, DDE's Records as President, Official File, Box 615, OF 142-A-5-A (2); NAID #12237734, https://www.eisenhowerlibrary.gov /sites/default/files/research/online-documents/civil-rights-little-rock/1957-09 -23-mann-to-dde.pdf.
7. Proclamation 3204, Obstruction of Justice in the State of Arkansas, by the President of the United States of America, September 23, 1957, Kevin McCann Collection; NAID #17366742.
8. Telegram from Little Rock Mayor Woodrow Mann to President Dwight D. Eisenhower, September 24, 1957, DDE's Records as President, Official File, Box 615, OF 142-A-5-A (2); NAID #17366836, https://www.eisenhowerli brary.gov/sites/default/files/research/online-documents/civil-rights-little-rock /1957-09-24-mann-to-dde.pdf.

9. "Guns Force Integration," *Manchester Union-Leader*, September 26, 1957.

10. Speech on radio and television by President Eisenhower, September 24, 1957, Kevin McCann Collection, NAID #17366765, https://www.eisenhowerlibrary .gov/sites/default/files/research/online-documents/civil-rights-little-rock/1957 -09-24-press-release.pdf.

11. Gilder Lehrman Institute of American History, Gilder Lehrman Collection #: GLC09731.07, United Press International, Little Rock, Arkansas, September 30, 1958.

12. "Mothers' League of Central High School Flyer," Encyclopedia of Arkansas, https://encyclopediaofarkansas.net/media/mothers-league-of-central-high -school-flyer-6625/.

13. Anderson, *Little Rock*, 185–88.

14. *The Moton School Story: Children of Courage*, Gallery I: A Call to Action, https:// motonschoolstory.org/gallery-i/.

15. *The Moton School Story: Children of Courage*.

16. "Biography: Barbara Rose Johns Powell, 1935–1991," Moton Museum, https:// motonmuseum.org/learn/biography-barbara-rose-johns-powell/.

17. Katy June-Friesen, "Massive Resistance in a Small Town: Before and After Brown in Prince Edward County, Virginia," *Humanities: The Magazine for the National Endowment for the Humanities* 34, no. 5 (September/October 2013).

18. "White Citizens' Councils," *American Experience*, PBS, https://www.pbs.org /wgbh/americanexperience/features/emmett-citizens-council/.

19. June-Friesen, "Massive Resistance in a Small Town."

20. Jack Bass, *Strom: The Complicated Personal and Political Life of Strom Thurmond* (New York: Public Affairs, 2005), 164.

21. "Virginia Governor Vows to Close Public Schools Rather Than Integrate," Equal Justice Initiative: A History of Racial Injustice, August 24, 1956.

22. June-Friesen, "Massive Resistance in a Small Town."

Twenty-Six: Montgomery, Alabama, 1955

1. Rosa Parks, *Rosa Parks: My Story* (New York: Puffin Books, 1999), 84.

2. Johnson, Bob, "After 67 Years, State Apologizes to Rape Victim," *Montgomery Advertiser*, April 22, 2011, 11.

3. Parks, *Rosa Parks*, 158.

4. Parks, *Rosa Parks*, 116.

5. Martin Luther King Jr., *Stride Toward Freedom; The Montgomery Story* (New York: Harper, 1958), 78.

6. Jo Ann Gibson Robinson, *The Montgomery Bus Boycott and the Women Who Started It: The Memoir of Jo Ann Gibson Robinson* (Knoxville: University of Tennessee Press, 1987), 85–86.

7. "A Letter Sent to Mayor Gayle," in Robinson, *The Montgomery Bus Boycott*, viii.

8. Parks, *Rosa Parks*, 126.

9. Parks, *Rosa Parks*, 126–27.

10. King, *Stride Toward Freedom*, 76.

11. Robinson, *Montgomery Bus Boycott*, 31.

12. King, *Stride Toward Freedom*, 135.

13. Robinson, *Montgomery Bus Boycott*, 140.

14. Phillip Tucker Thomas, *Claudette Colvin: Forgotten Mother of the Civil Rights Movement* (N.p.: PublishNation LLC, 2020), location 1320, Kindle.

15. Phillip M. Hoose, *Claudette Colvin: Twice Toward Justice* (New York: Farrar, Straus & Giroux, 2014), 79.

16. Hoose, *Claudette Colvin*, 88.

17. David Levering Lewis, *King: A Biography* (Chicago: University of Illinois Press, 1970), 76.

18. Hoose, *Claudette Colvin*, 91.

19. "Bus Segregation Is Knocked Out," *Alabama Journal*, November 13, 1956, 1.

20. "Negroes Worship at Montgomery," *Chattanooga Daily Times*, January 13, 1957, 38.

21. Liz Ryan and Willie Edwards Jr., "The Klan Sought to Erase His Memory, His Family Made Sure It Endured," *Alabama Political Reporter*, March 29, 2022.

22. Paul Hendrickson, "Montgomery: The Supporting Actors in the Historic Bus Boycott," *Washington Post*, July 23, 1989.

23. G. Edward White, *Earl Warren: A Public Life* (New York: Oxford University Press, 1982), 77.

24. Septima Poinsette Clark, *Ready from Within: Septima Clark and the Civil Rights Movement* (Navarro, CA: Wild Trees Press, 1986), 346.

25. Marcia Y. Riggs, *Can I Get A Witness?* (London: Orbis Books, 1997), 158.

26. Katherine Mellen Charron, *Freedom's Teacher* (Durham: University of North Carolina Press, 2009), 214.

27. McKenzie Jean-Philippe, "Honoring Civil Rights Heroes Like Claudette Colvin Helps Continue Their Fight," *Oprah Daily*, January 17, 2022.